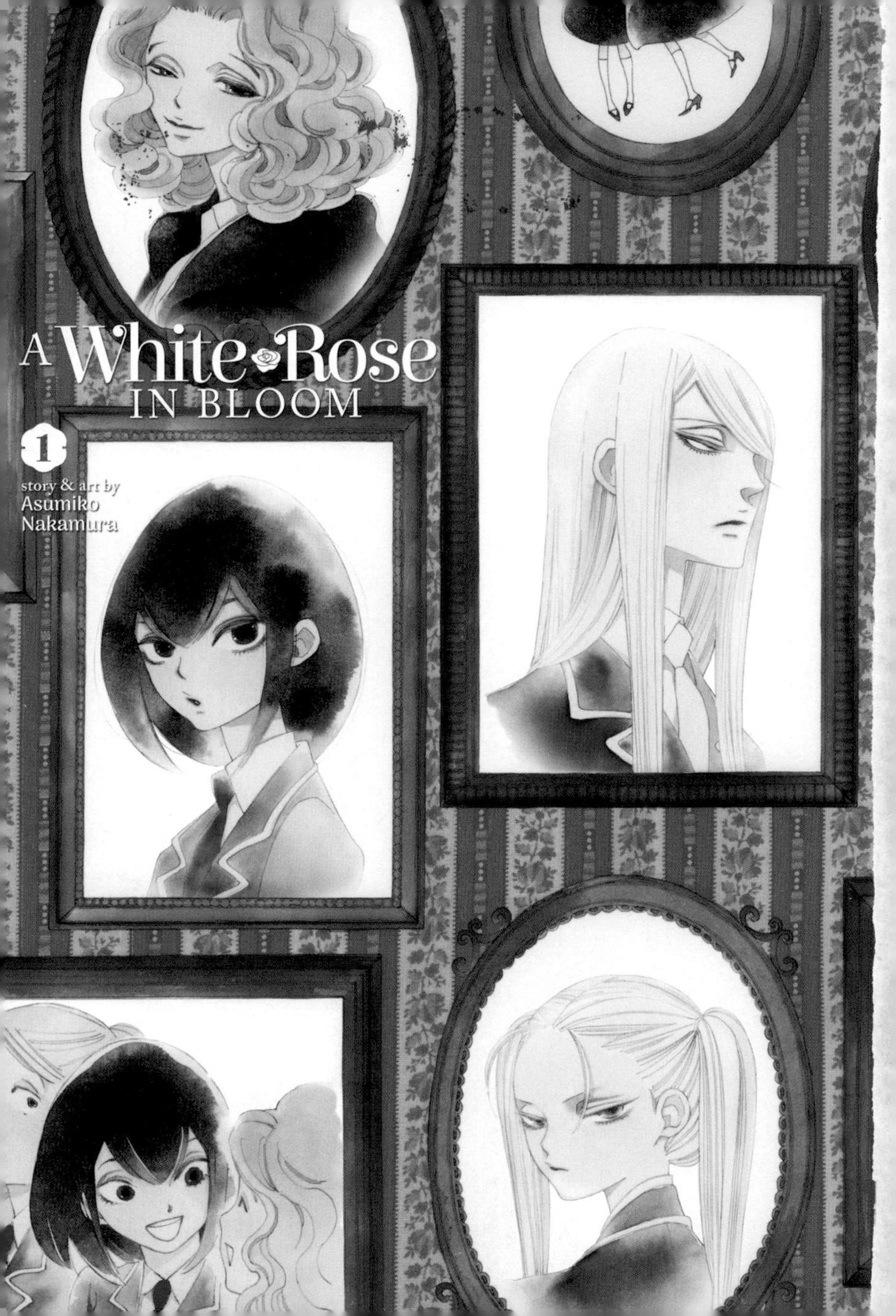
A White Rose
IN BLOOM
1
story & art by
Asumiko
Nakamura

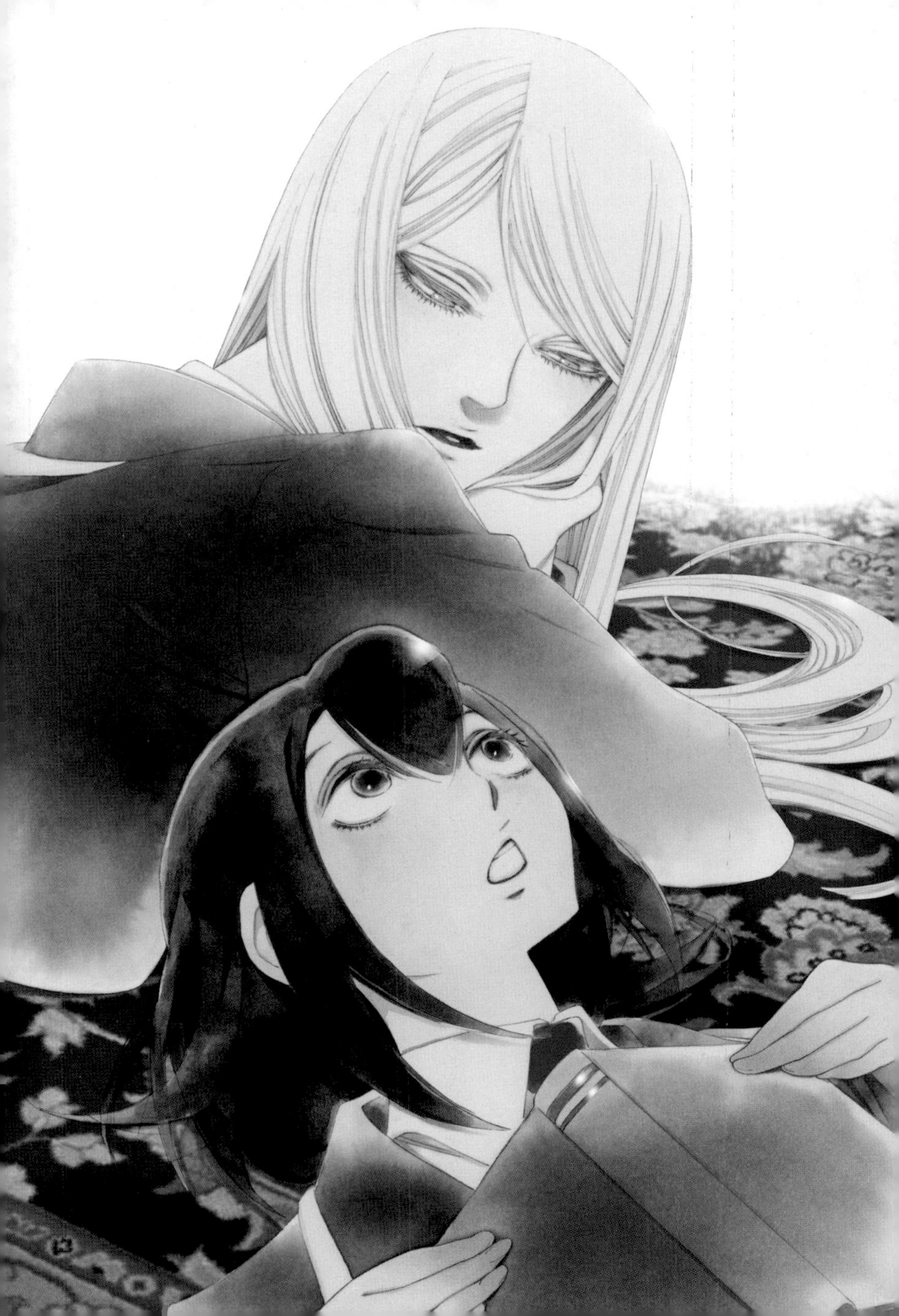

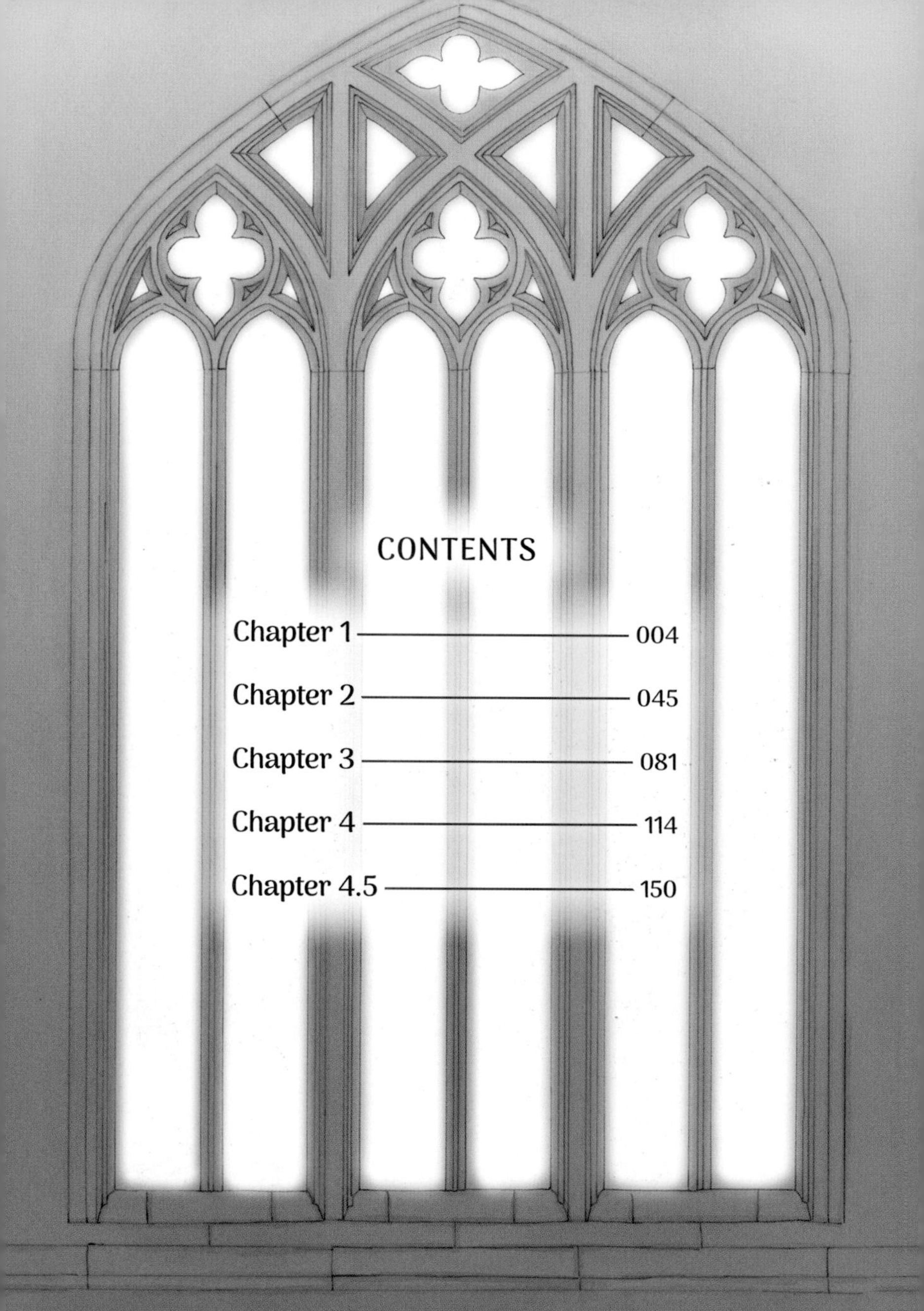

# CONTENTS

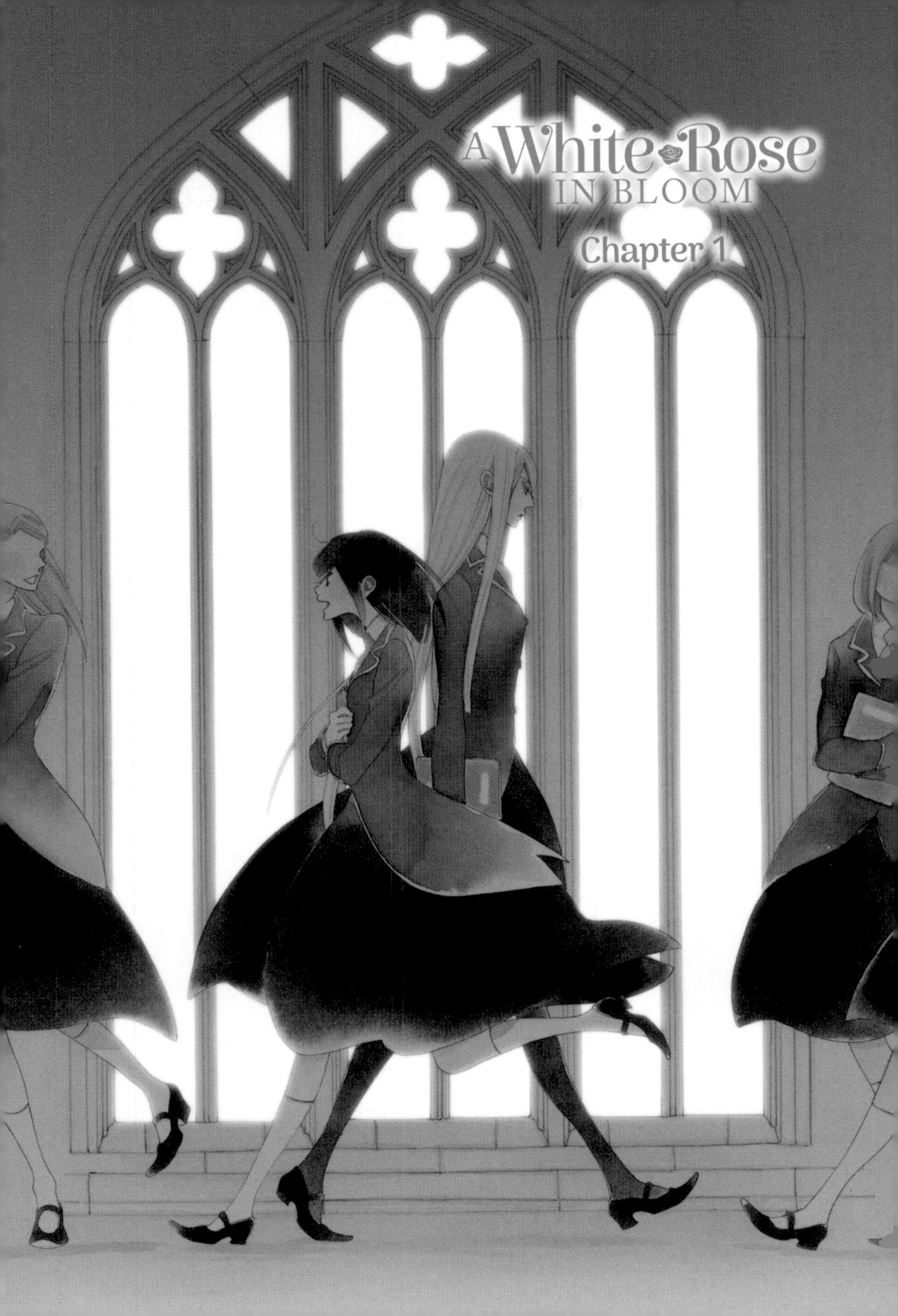
A White Rose
IN BLOOM
Chapter 1

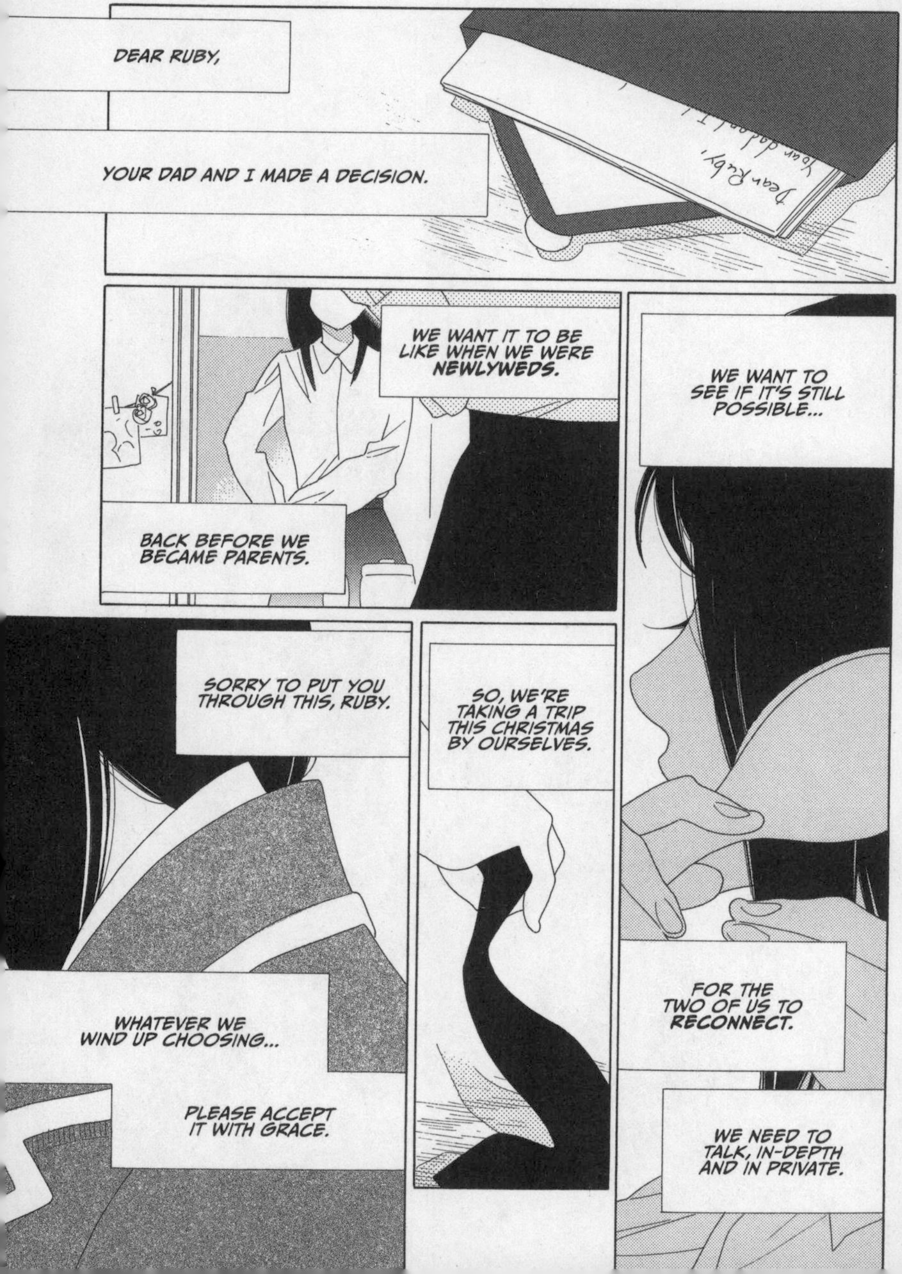

DEAR RUBY,
YOUR DAD AND I MADE A DECISION.
Dear Ruby,
WE WANT TO SEE IF IT'S STILL POSSIBLE...
WE WANT IT TO BE LIKE WHEN WE WERE NEWLYWEDS.
BACK BEFORE WE BECAME PARENTS.
FOR THE TWO OF US TO RECONNECT.
WE NEED TO TALK, IN-DEPTH AND IN PRIVATE.
SO, WE'RE TAKING A TRIP THIS CHRISTMAS BY OURSELVES.
SORRY TO PUT YOU THROUGH THIS, RUBY.
WHATEVER WE WIND UP CHOOSING...
PLEASE ACCEPT IT WITH GRACE.

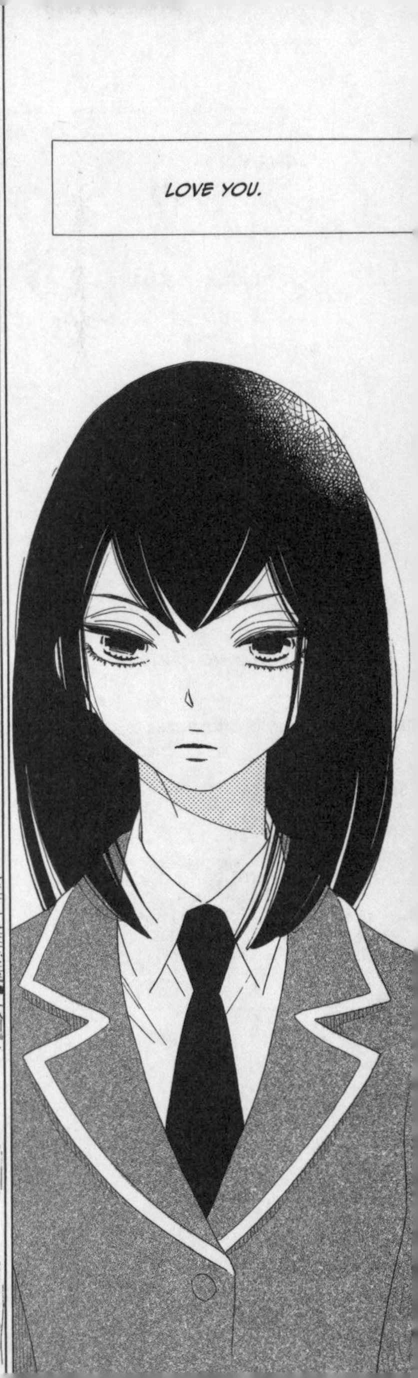
LOVE YOU.

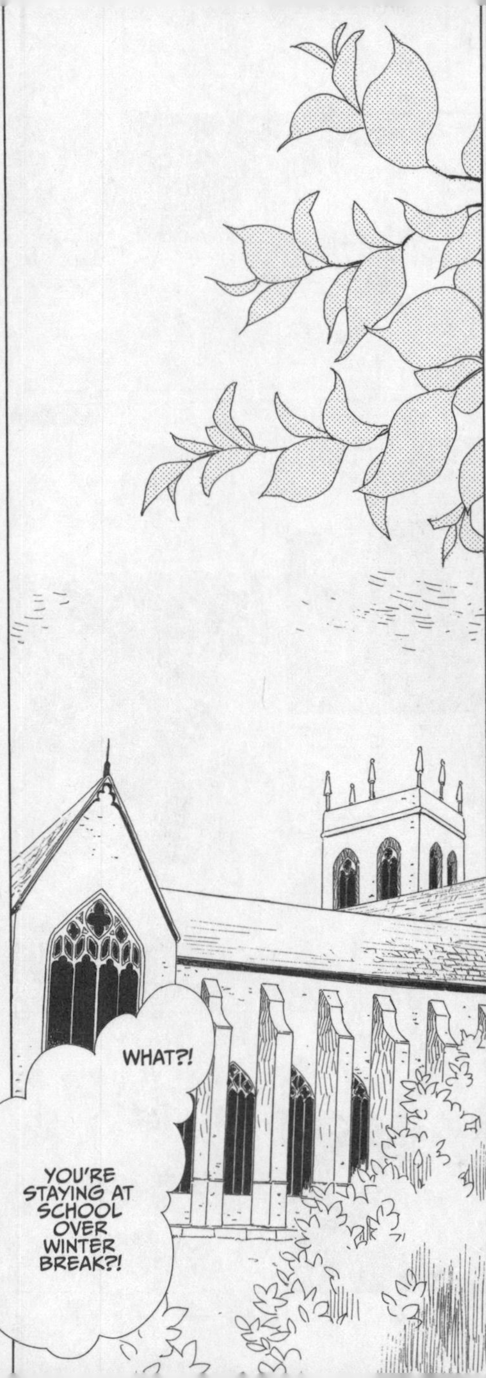
WHAT?!
YOU'RE STAYING AT SCHOOL OVER WINTER BREAK?!

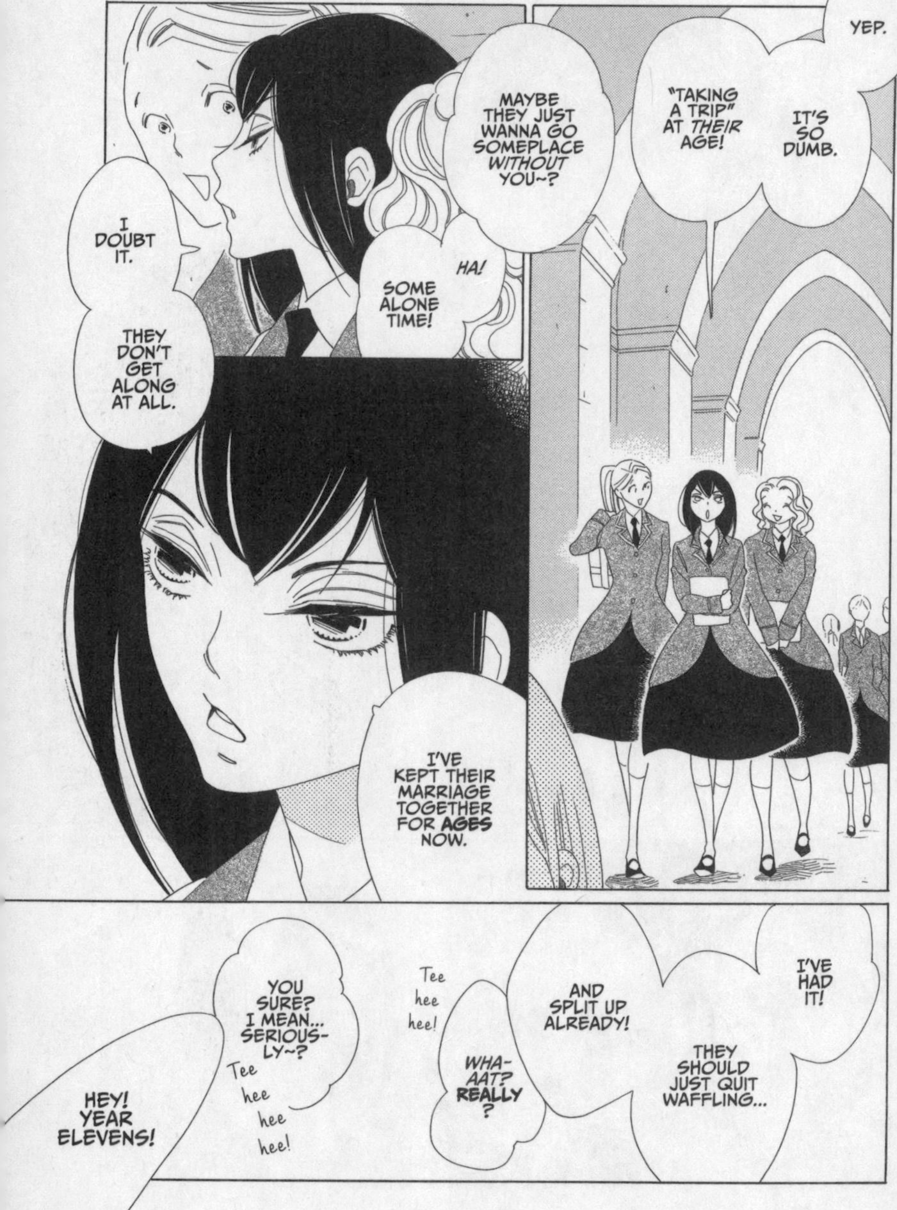
YEP.
IT'S SO DUMB.
"TAKING A TRIP" AT *THEIR* AGE!
MAYBE THEY JUST WANNA GO SOMEPLACE *WITHOUT* YOU~?
*HA!* SOME ALONE TIME!
I DOUBT IT.
THEY DON'T GET ALONG AT ALL.
I'VE KEPT THEIR MARRIAGE TOGETHER FOR **AGES** NOW.
I'VE HAD IT!
THEY SHOULD JUST QUIT WAFFLING...
AND SPLIT UP ALREADY!
*WHA-AAT?* **REALLY**?
Tee hee hee!
YOU SURE? I MEAN... SERIOUSLY~?
Tee hee hee hee!
HEY! YEAR ELEVENS!

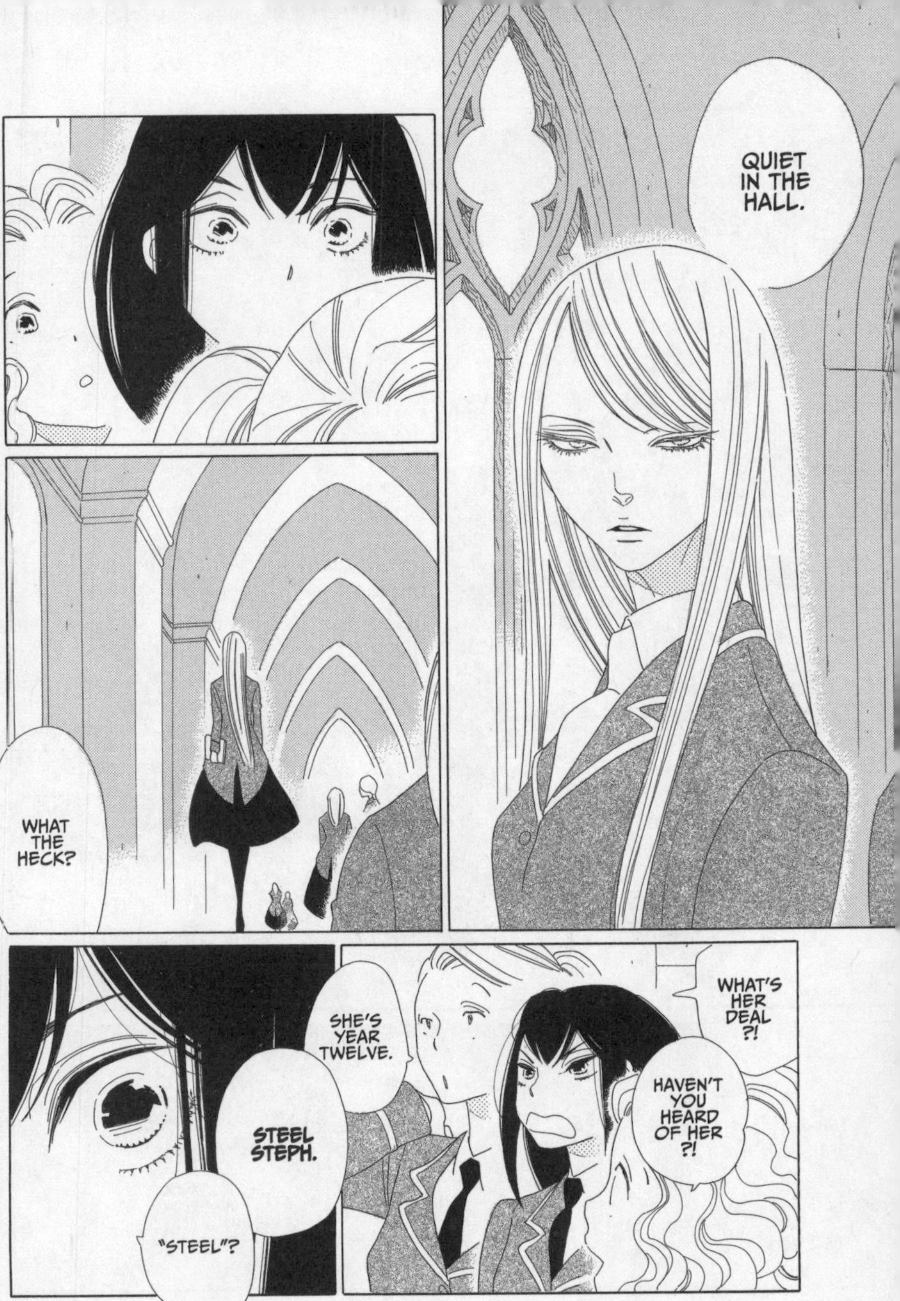
QUIET IN THE HALL.
WHAT THE HECK?
WHAT'S HER DEAL?!
HAVEN'T YOU HEARD OF HER?!
SHE'S YEAR TWELVE.
STEEL STEPH.
"STEEL"?

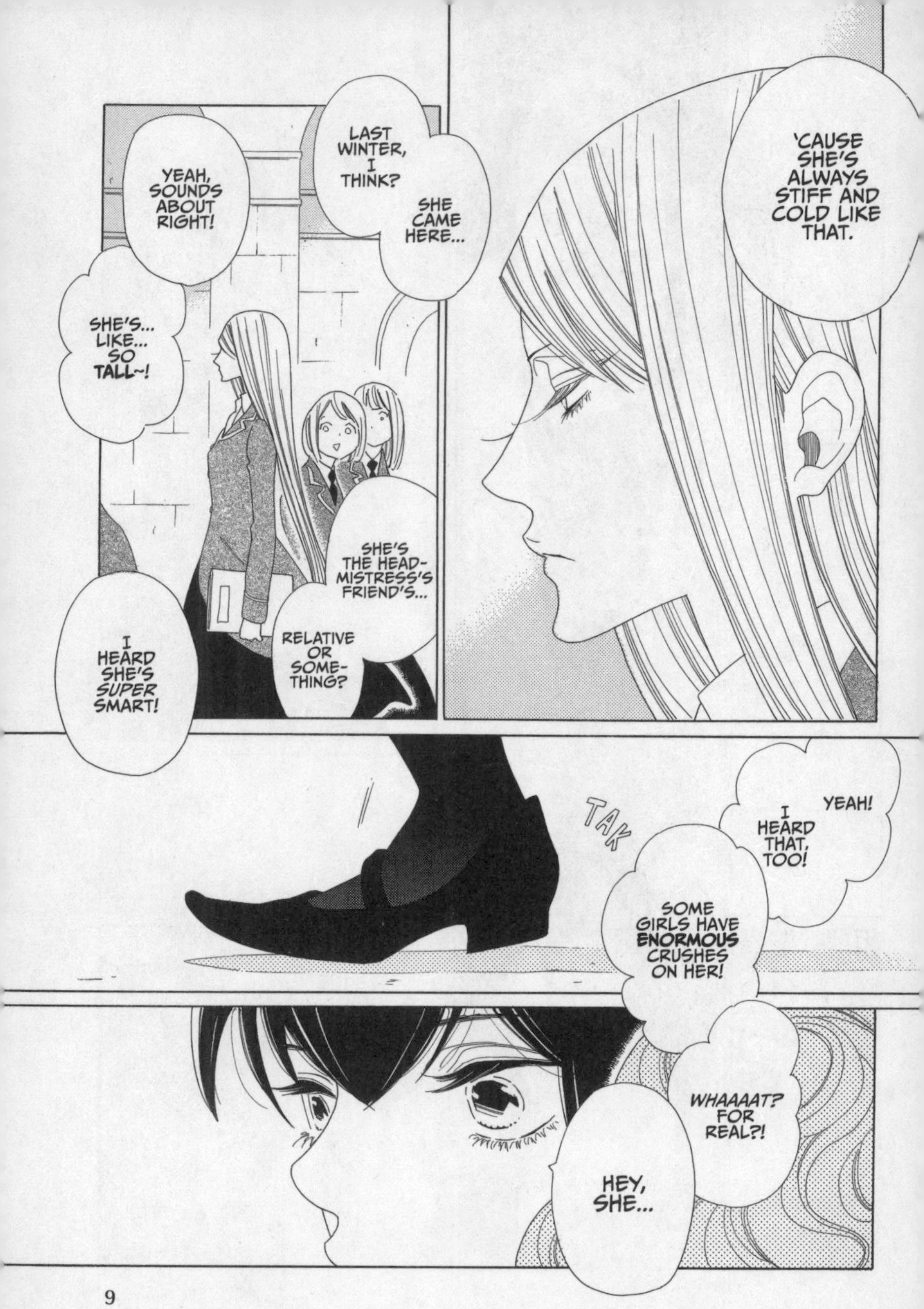
'CAUSE SHE'S ALWAYS STIFF AND COLD LIKE THAT.
LAST WINTER, I THINK?
SHE CAME HERE...
YEAH, SOUNDS ABOUT RIGHT!
SHE'S... LIKE... SO TALL~!
SHE'S THE HEAD-MISTRESS'S FRIEND'S...
RELATIVE OR SOME-THING?
I HEARD SHE'S SUPER SMART!
TAK
YEAH!
I HEARD THAT, TOO!
SOME GIRLS HAVE ENORMOUS CRUSHES ON HER!
WHAAAAT? FOR REAL?!
HEY, SHE...

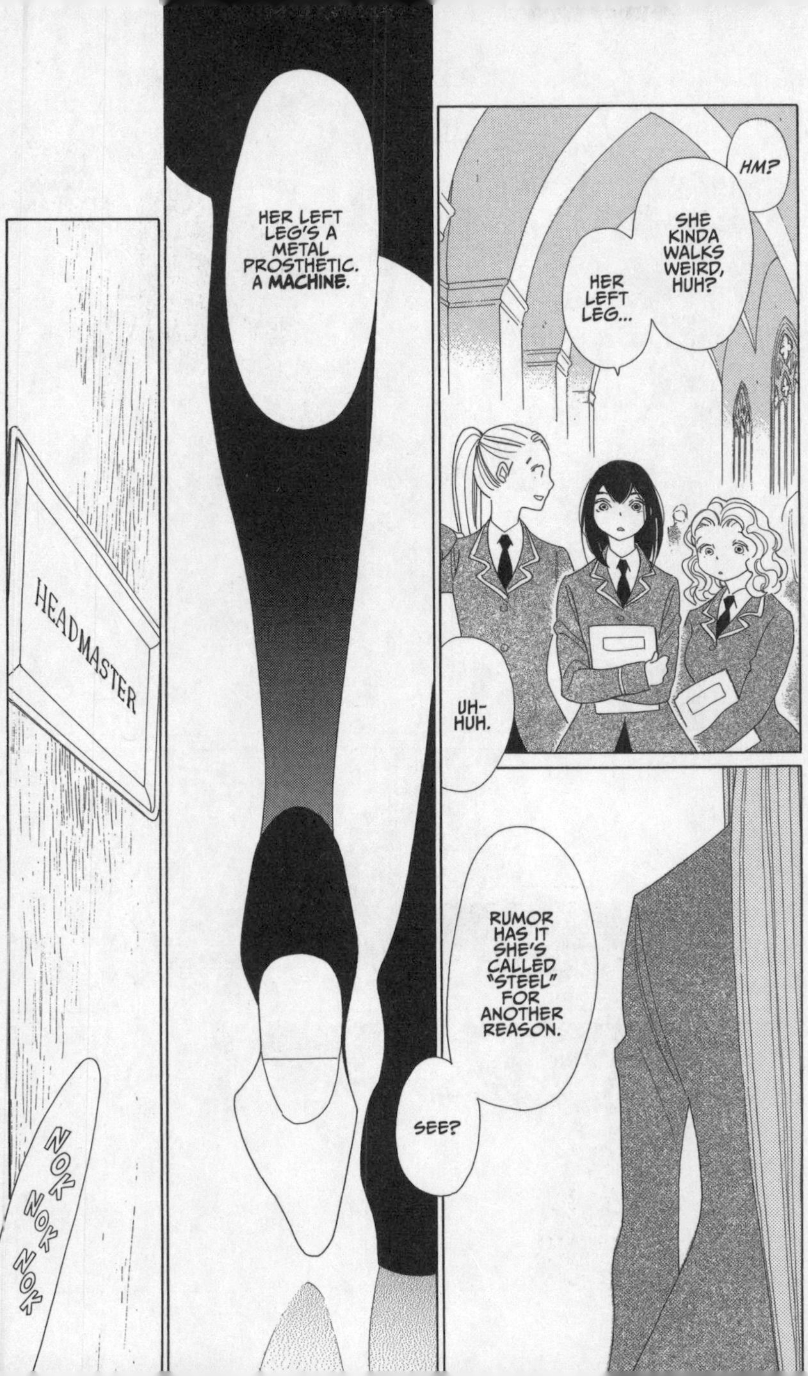
HM?
SHE KINDA WALKS WEIRD, HUH?
HER LEFT LEG...
UH-HUH.
RUMOR HAS IT SHE'S CALLED "STEEL" FOR ANOTHER REASON.
SEE?
HER LEFT LEG'S A METAL PROSTHETIC. A MACHINE.
HEADMASTER
NOK NOK NOK

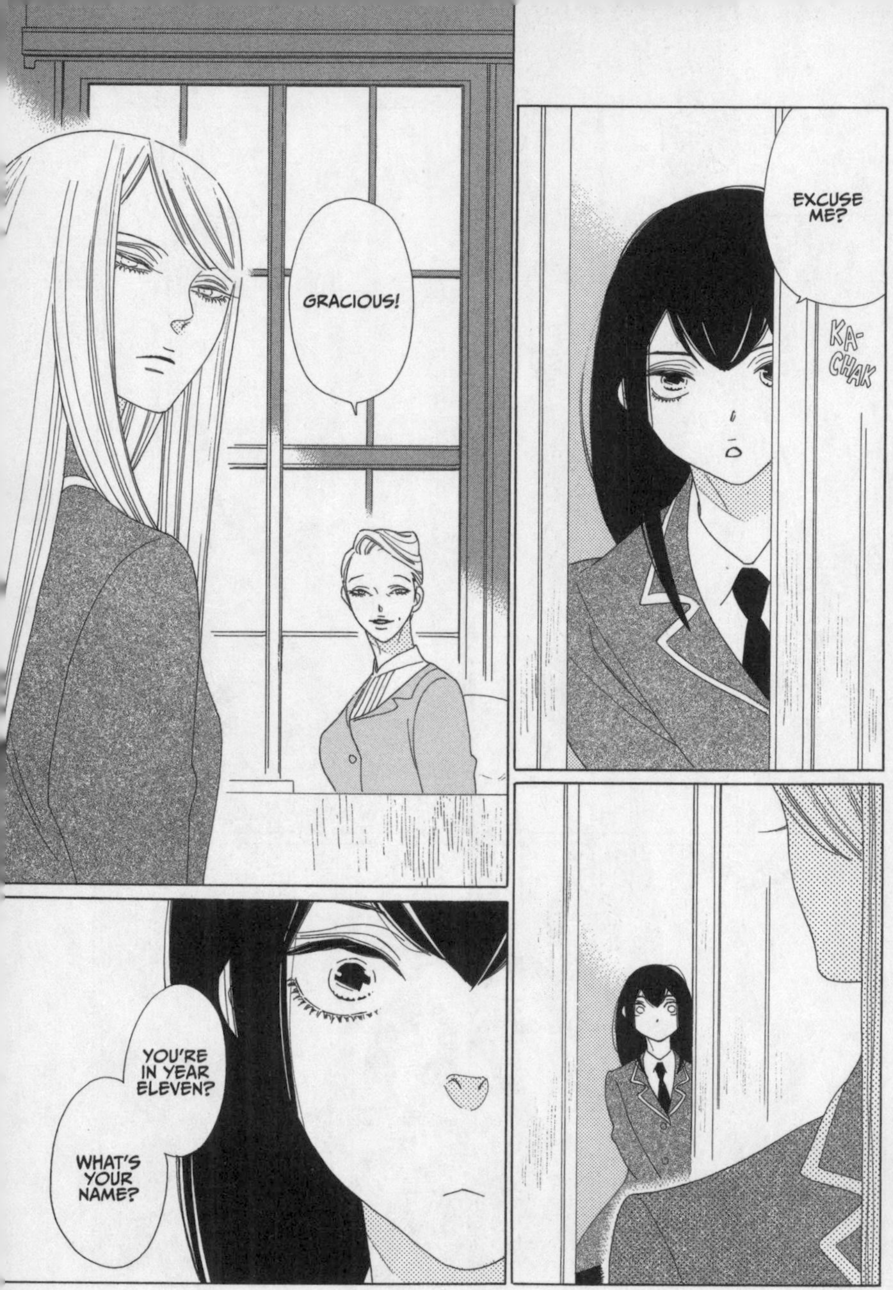
EXCUSE ME?
KA-CHAK
GRACIOUS!
YOU'RE IN YEAR ELEVEN?
WHAT'S YOUR NAME?

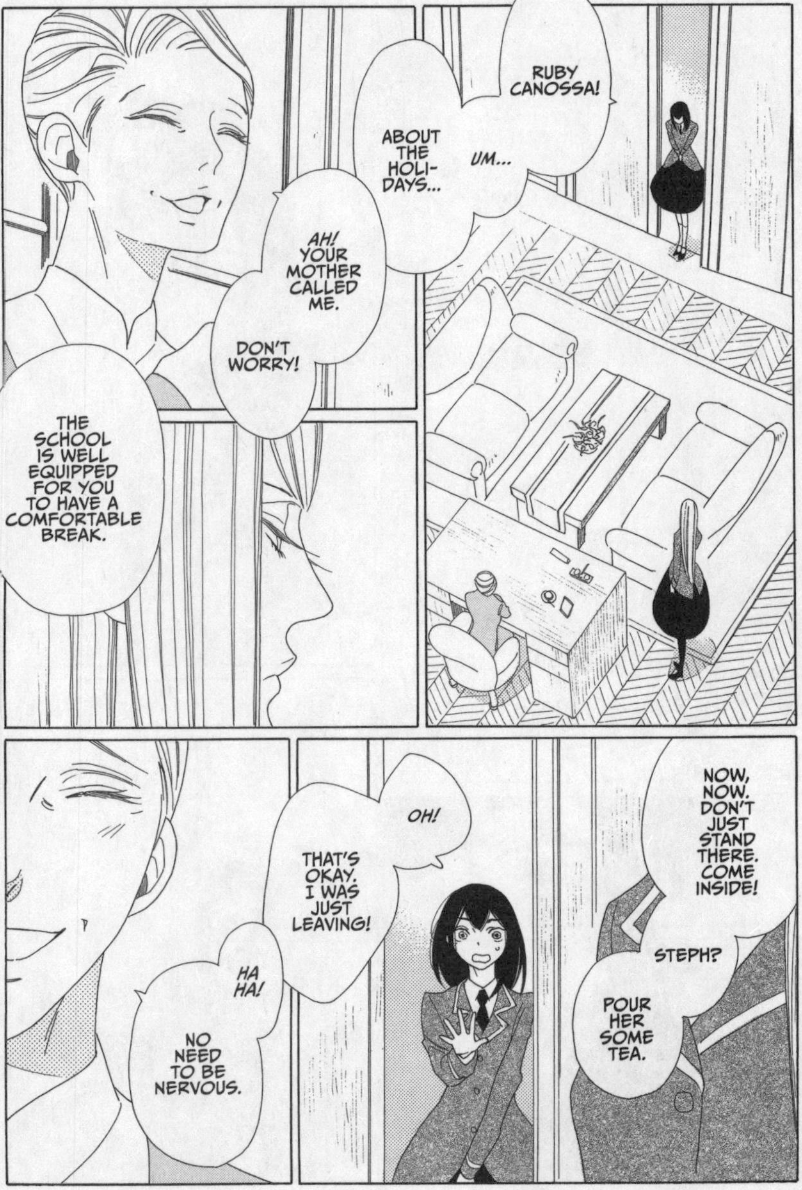

RUBY CANOSSA!
UM...
ABOUT THE HOLI-DAYS...
AH! YOUR MOTHER CALLED ME.
DON'T WORRY!
THE SCHOOL IS WELL EQUIPPED FOR YOU TO HAVE A COMFORTABLE BREAK.
NOW, NOW. DON'T JUST STAND THERE. COME INSIDE!
STEPH?
POUR HER SOME TEA.
OH!
THAT'S OKAY. I WAS JUST LEAVING!
HA HA!
NO NEED TO BE NERVOUS.

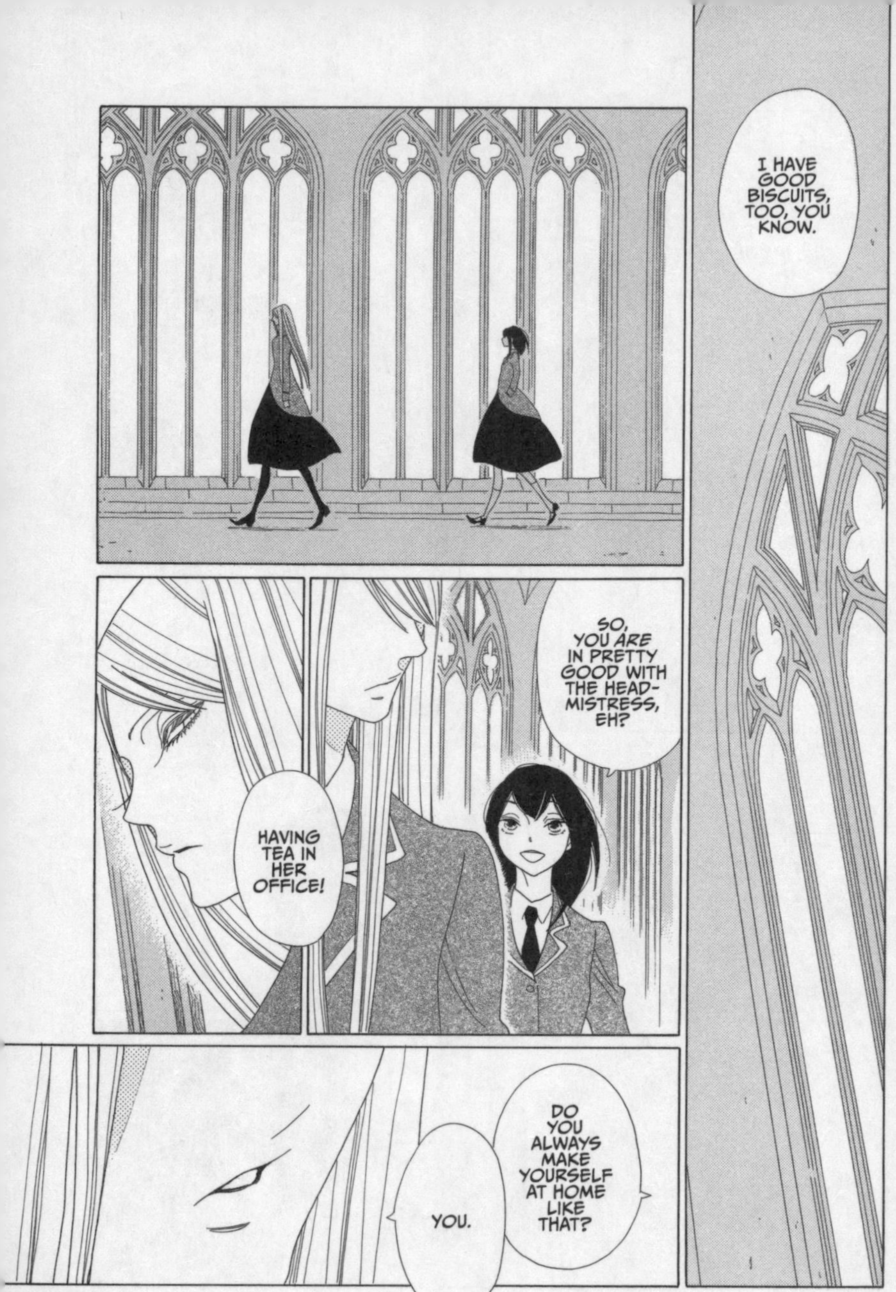
I HAVE GOOD BISCUITS, TOO, YOU KNOW.
SO, YOU ARE IN PRETTY GOOD WITH THE HEAD-MISTRESS, EH?
HAVING TEA IN HER OFFICE!
DO YOU ALWAYS MAKE YOURSELF AT HOME LIKE THAT?
YOU.

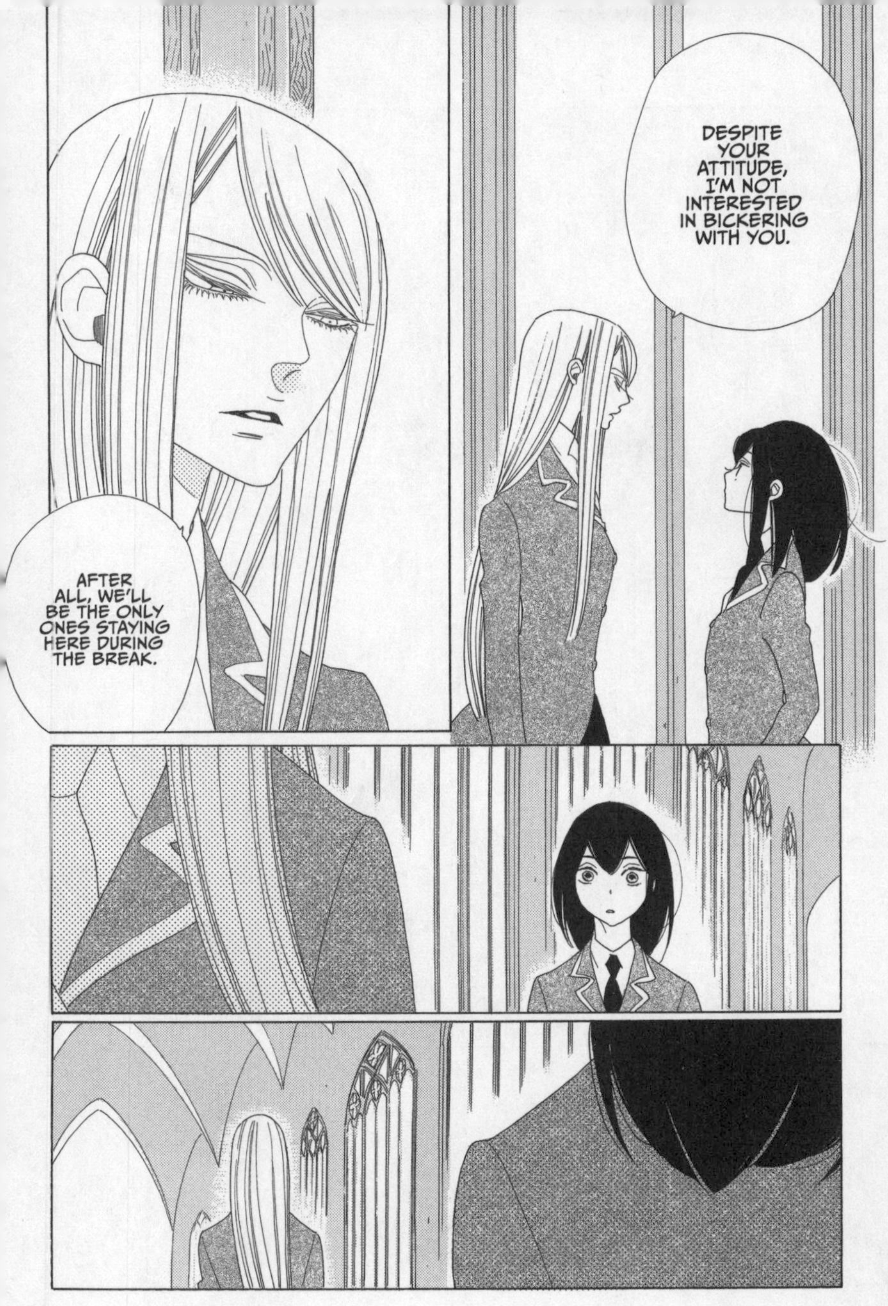
DESPITE YOUR ATTITUDE, I'M NOT INTERESTED IN BICKERING WITH YOU.
AFTER ALL, WE'LL BE THE ONLY ONES STAYING HERE DURING THE BREAK.

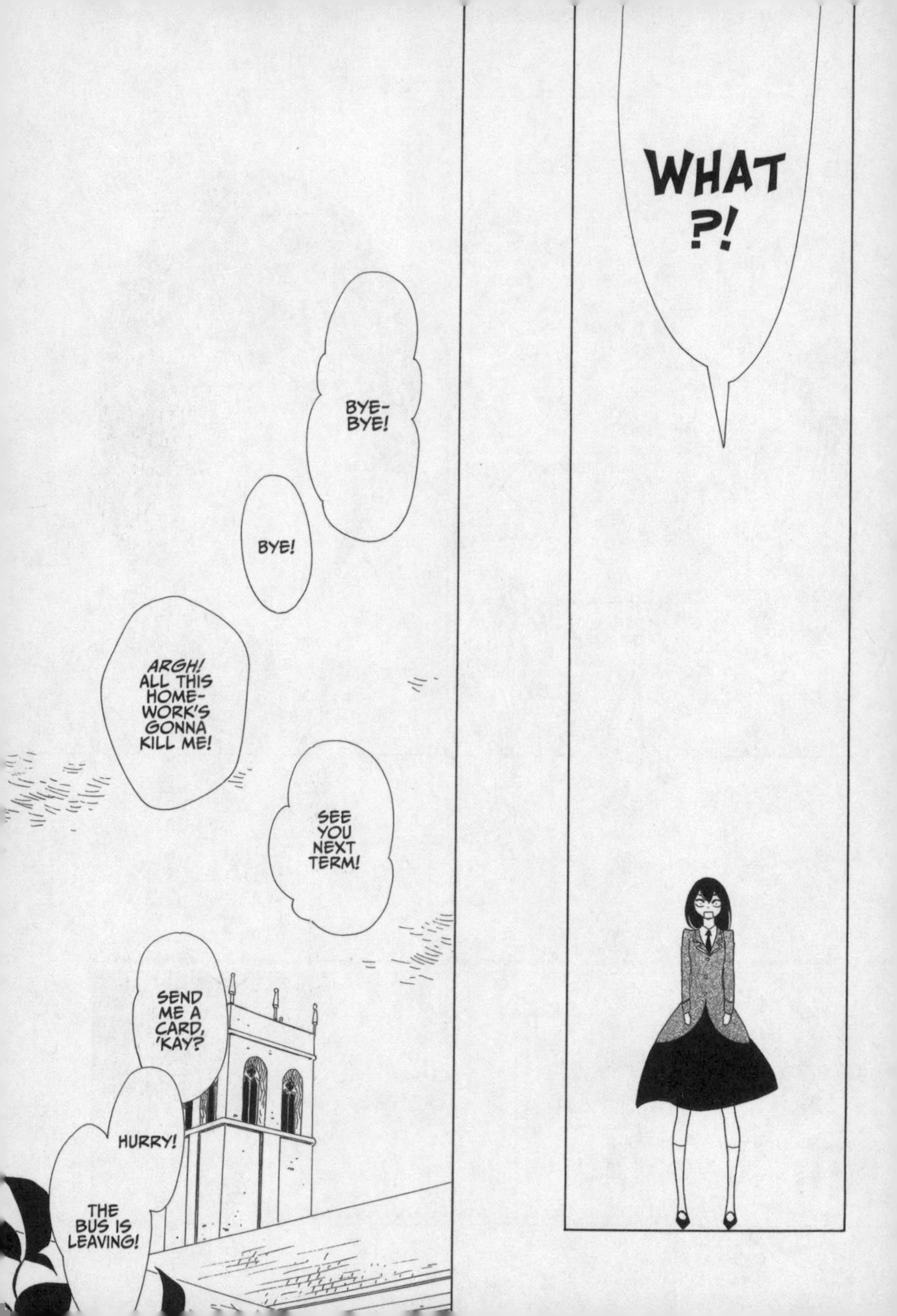
WHAT ?!
BYE-BYE!
BYE!
ARGH! ALL THIS HOMEWORK'S GONNA KILL ME!
SEE YOU NEXT TERM!
SEND ME A CARD, 'KAY?
HURRY!
THE BUS IS LEAVING!

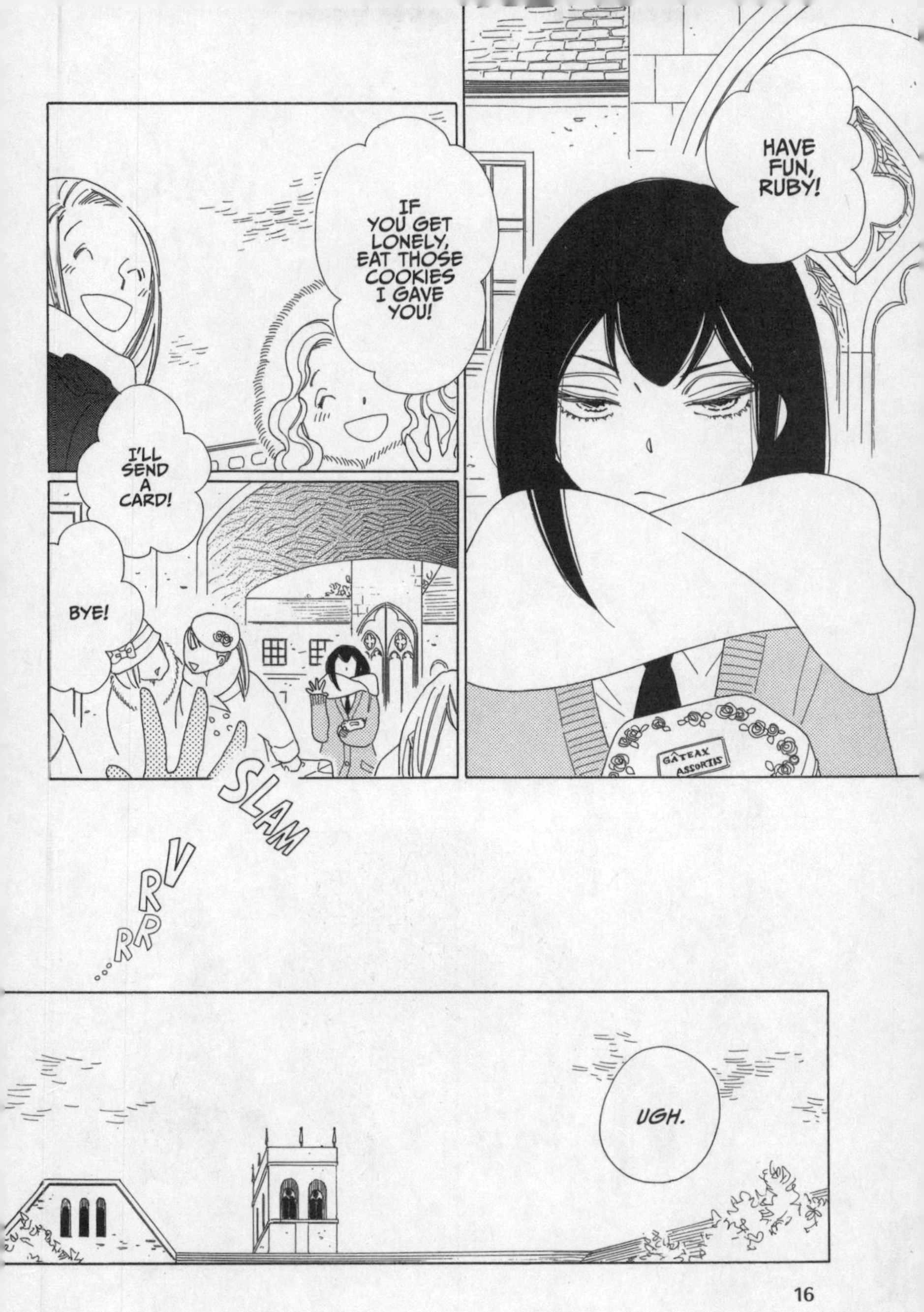
HAVE FUN, RUBY!
IF YOU GET LONELY, EAT THOSE COOKIES I GAVE YOU!
I'LL SEND A CARD!
BYE!
GÂTEAX ASSORTIS
SLAM
RRRV
UGH.

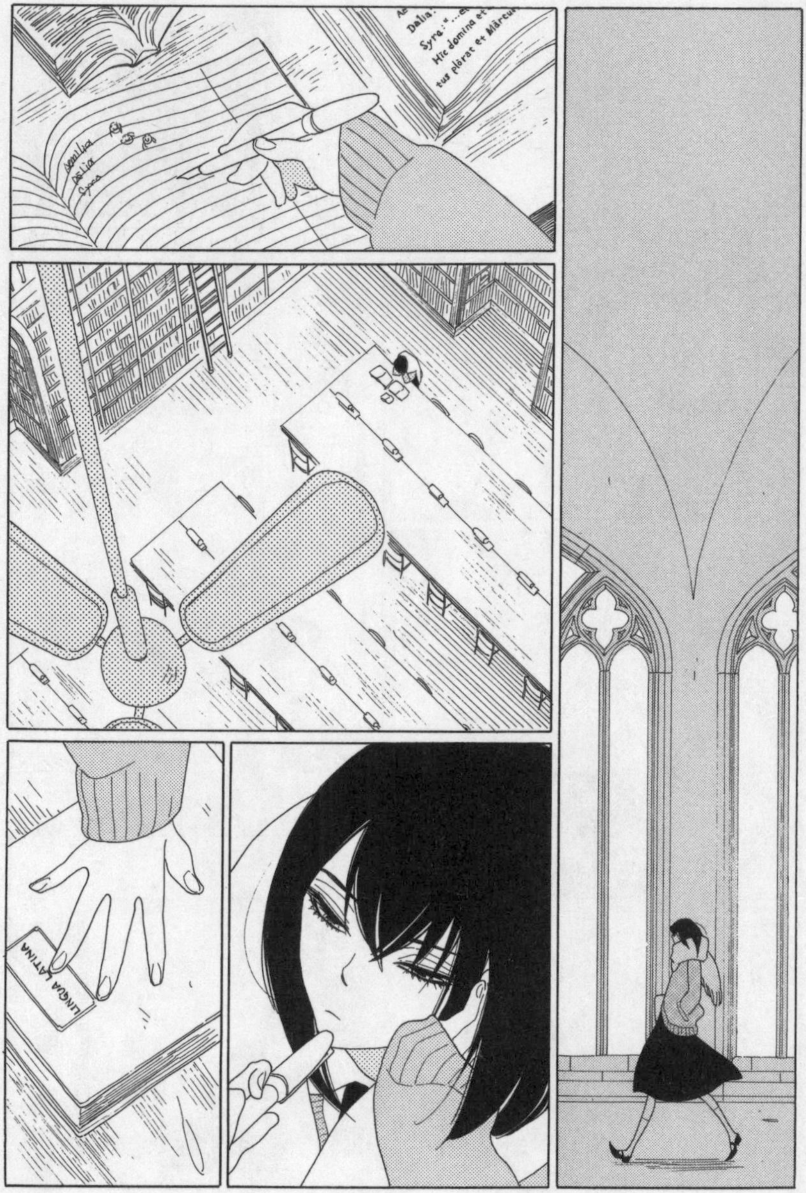
Dalia:
Syra: "...
Hīc domina et
tus plōrat et Mārcu
Aemilia
Dalia
Syra
LINGUA LATINA

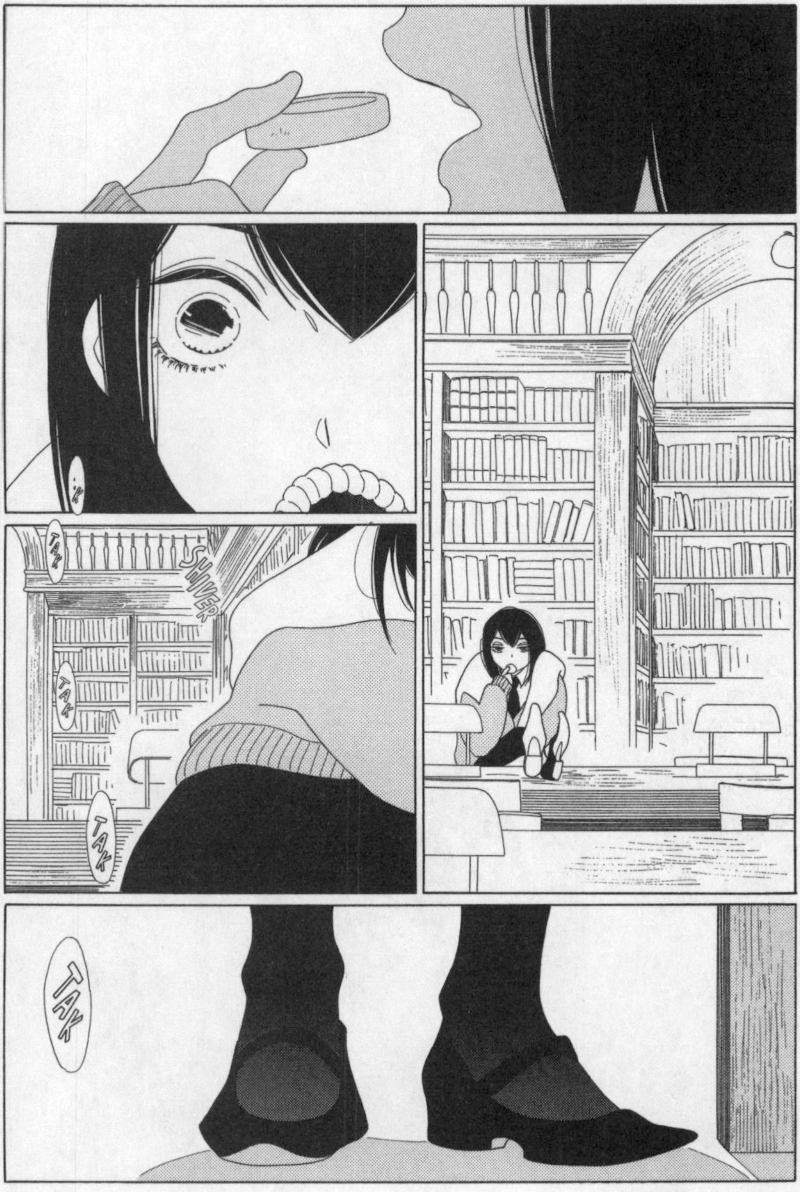

..K
SHIVER
TAK
TAK
TAK
TAK

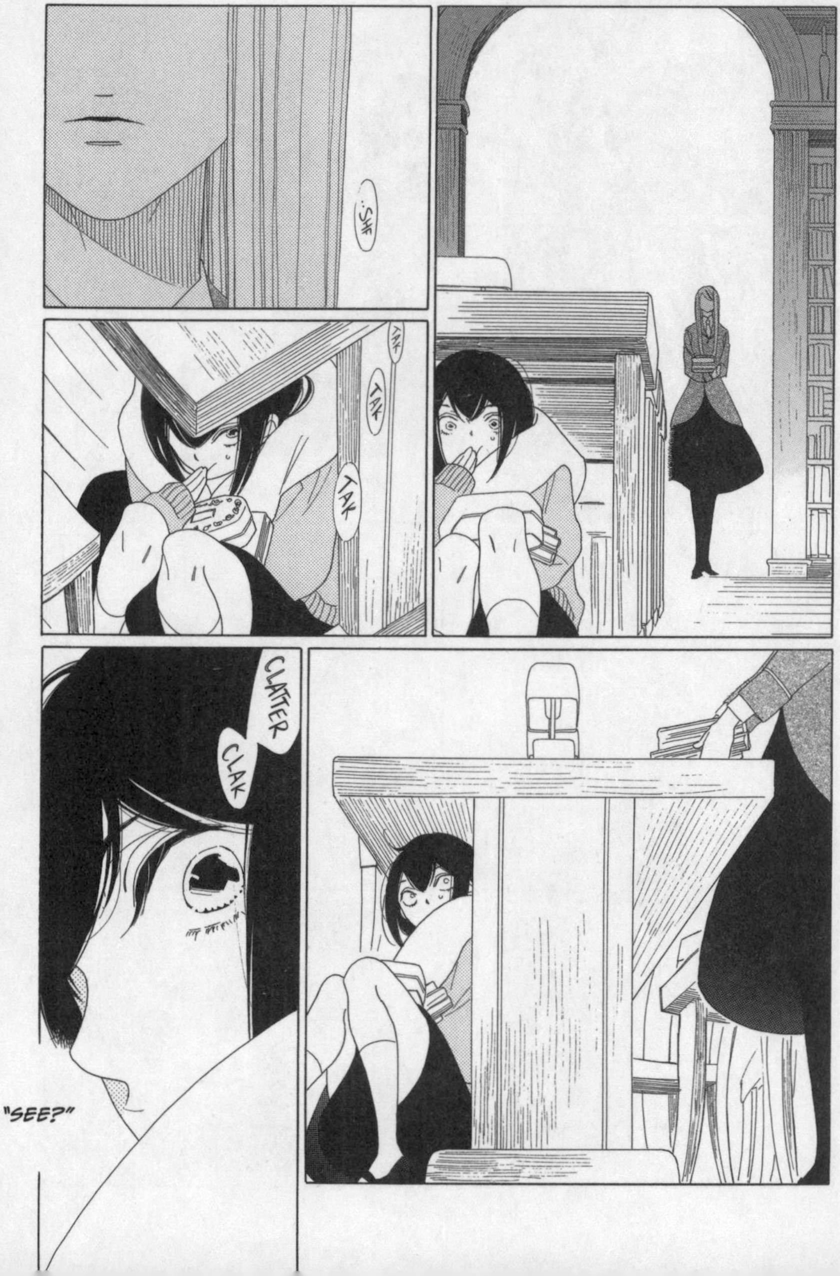
...SHF
TAK
TAK
TAK
CLATTER
CLAK
"SEE?"

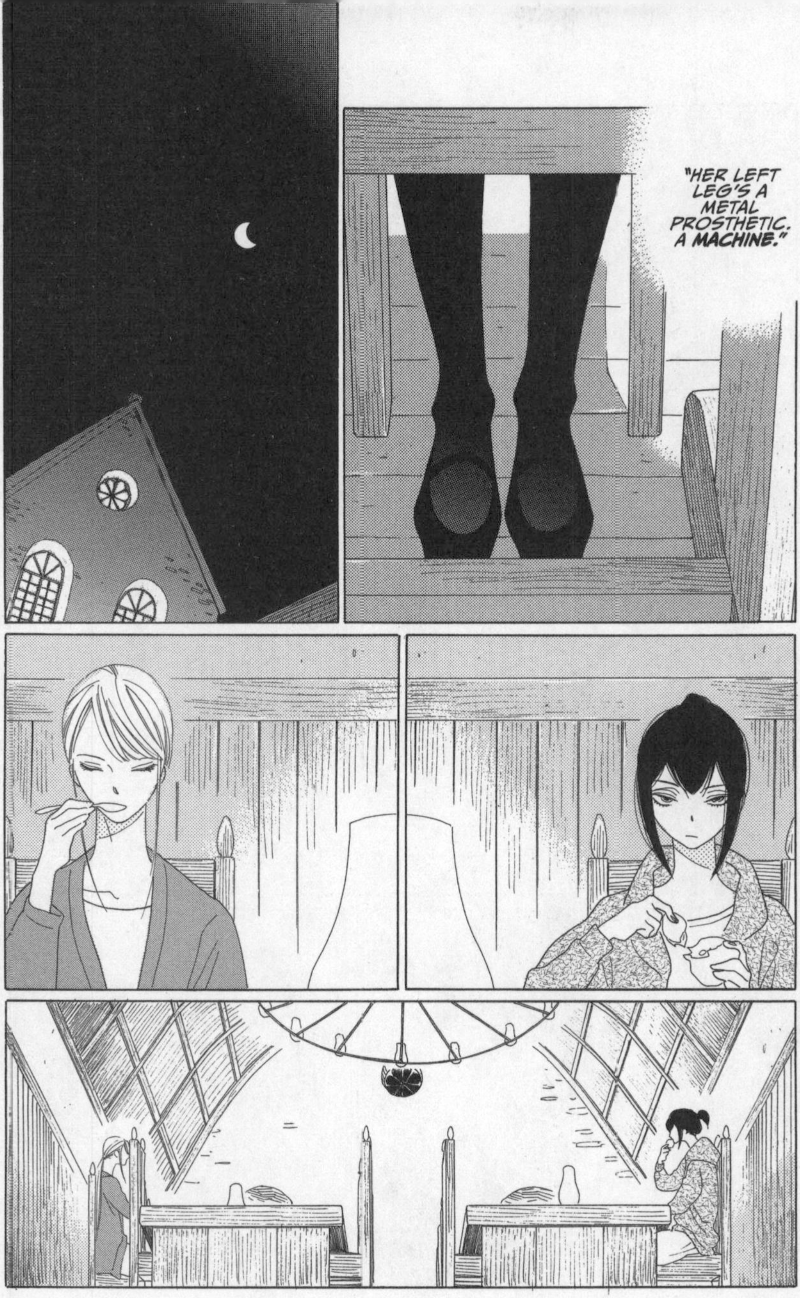
"HER LEFT LEG'S A METAL PROSTHETIC. A MACHINE."

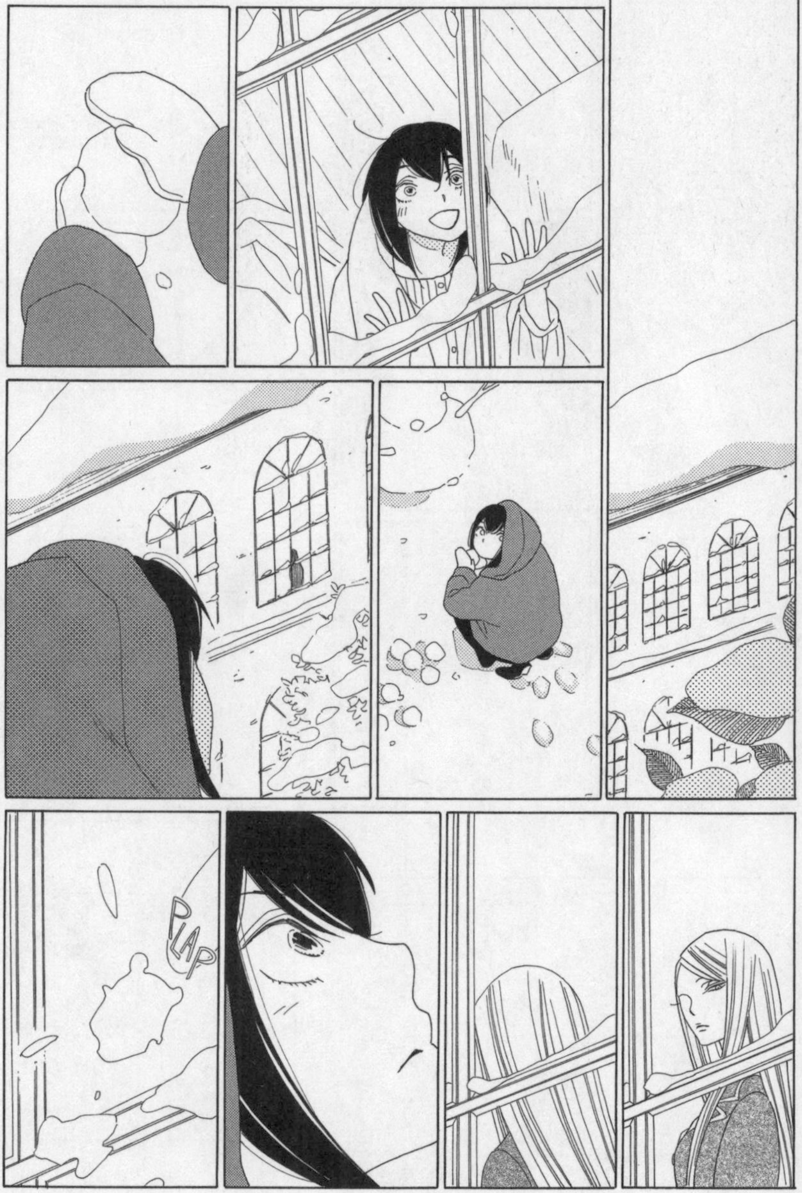
PLAP

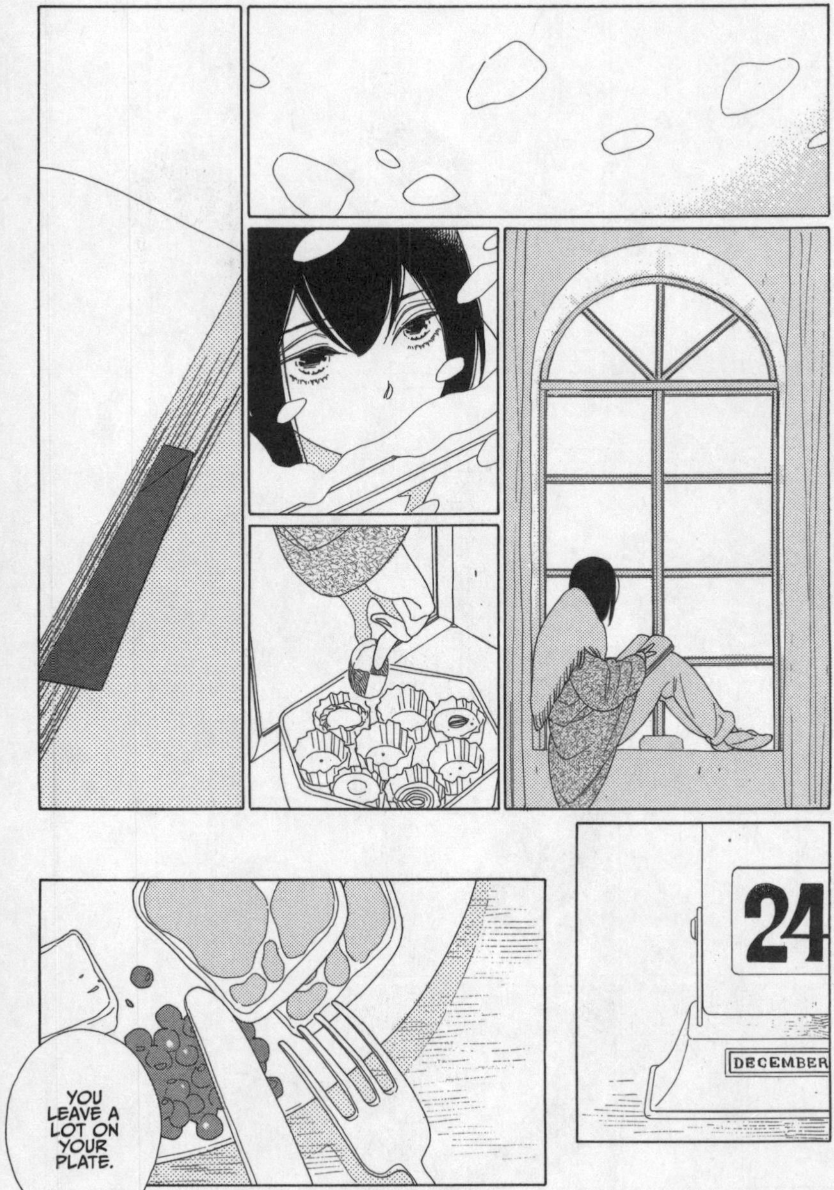
24
DECEMBER
YOU LEAVE A LOT ON YOUR PLATE.

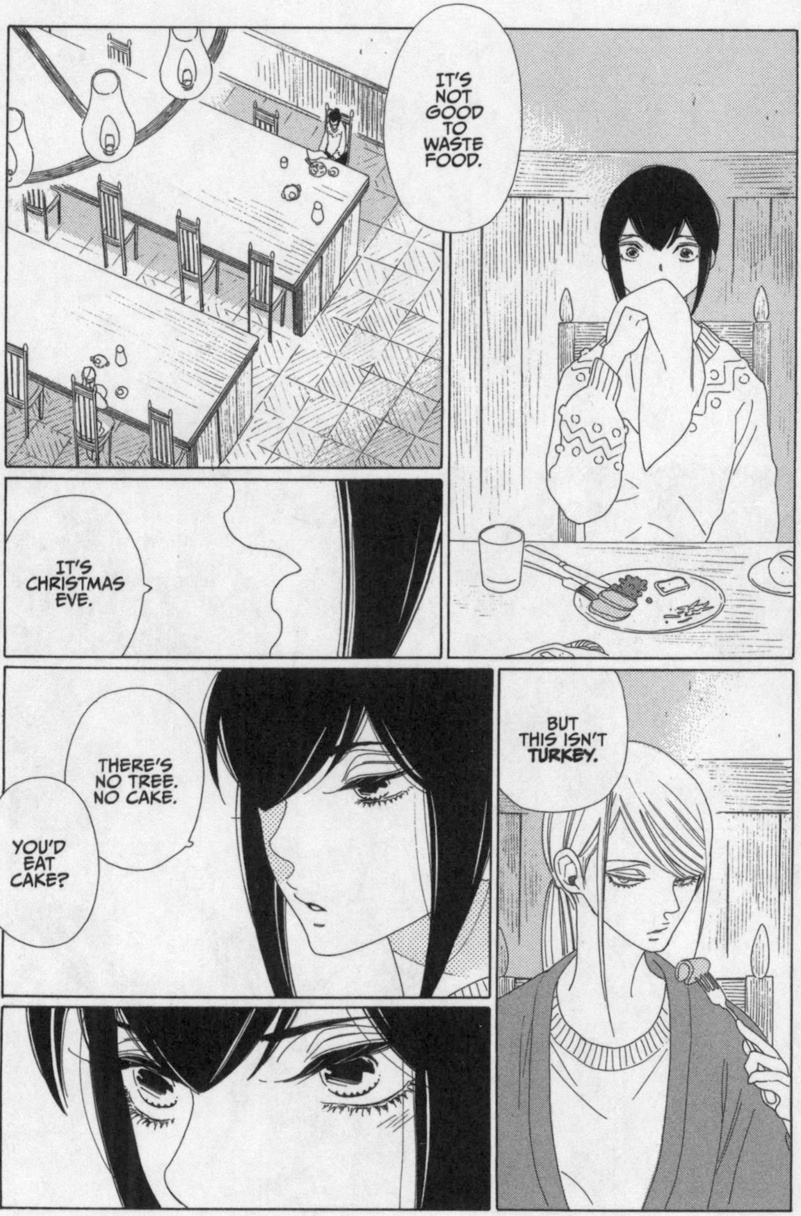
IT'S NOT GOOD TO WASTE FOOD.
IT'S CHRISTMAS EVE.
BUT THIS ISN'T TURKEY.
THERE'S NO TREE. NO CAKE.
YOU'D EAT CAKE?

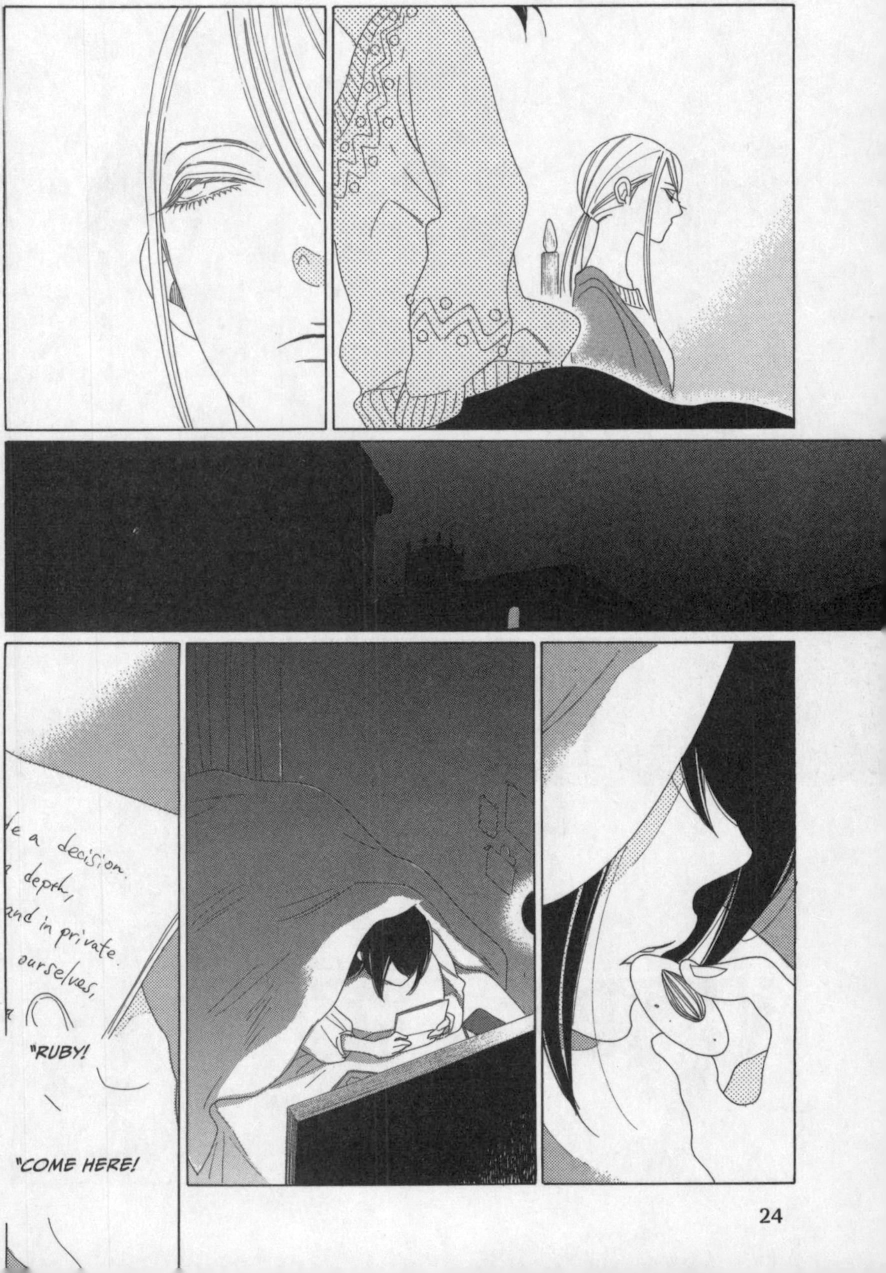
e a decision.
depth,
and in private.
ourselves,
"RUBY!
"COME HERE!

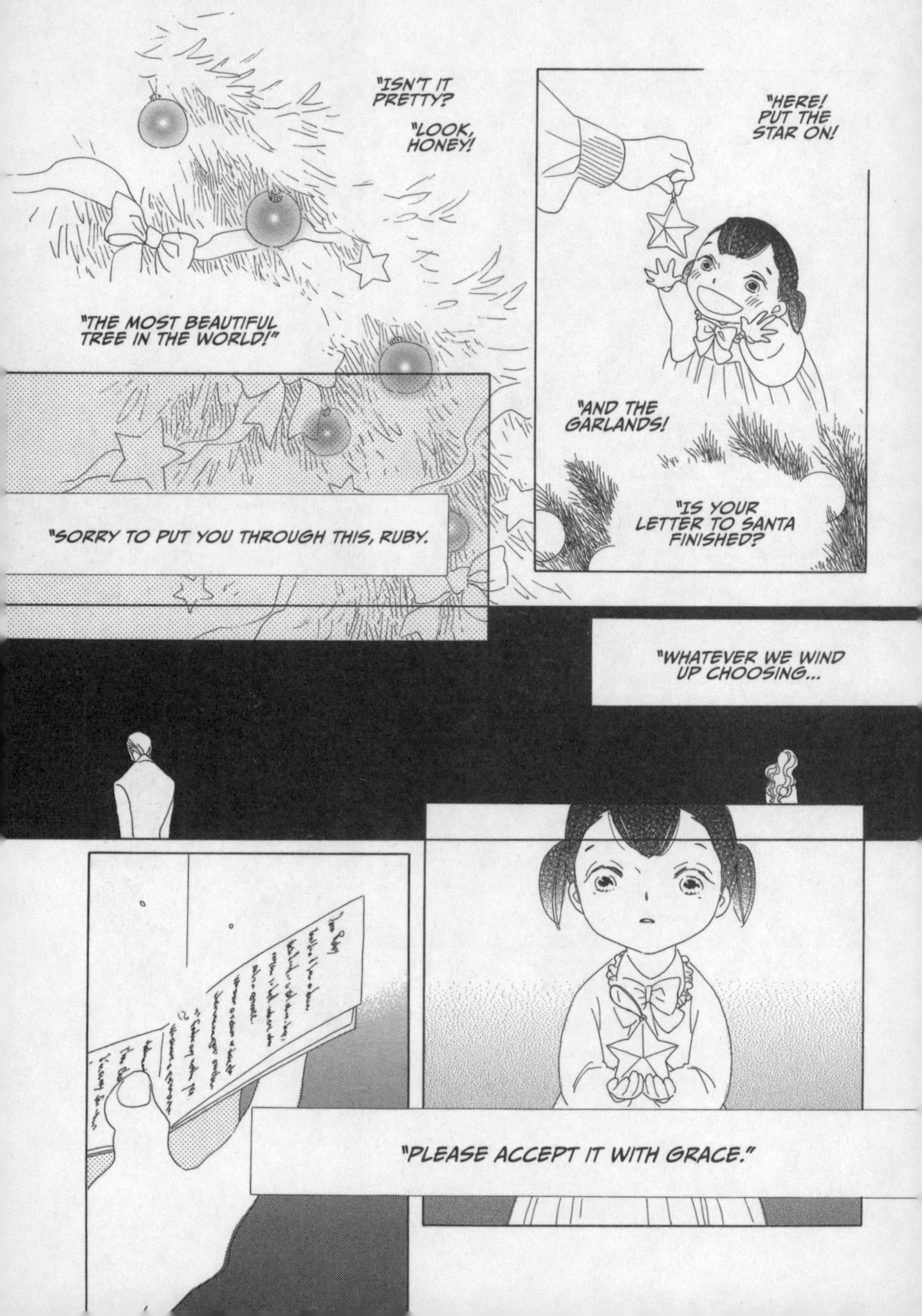
"HERE! PUT THE STAR ON!
"AND THE GARLANDS!
"IS YOUR LETTER TO SANTA FINISHED?
"LOOK, HONEY!
"ISN'T IT PRETTY?
"THE MOST BEAUTIFUL TREE IN THE WORLD!"
"SORRY TO PUT YOU THROUGH THIS, RUBY.
"WHATEVER WE WIND UP CHOOSING...
"PLEASE ACCEPT IT WITH GRACE."

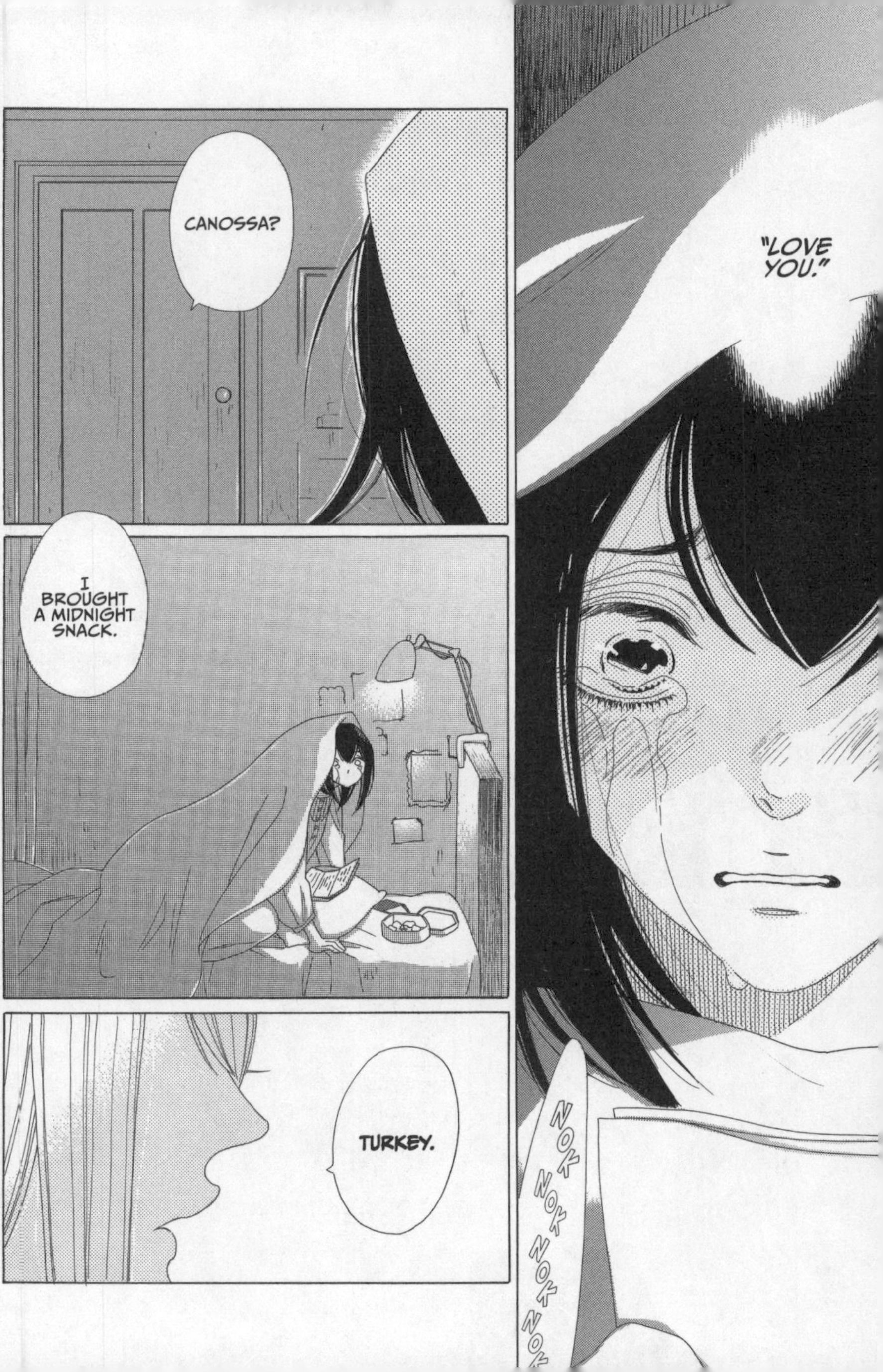
"LOVE YOU."
NOK NOK NOK NOK NOK
CANOSSA?
I BROUGHT A MIDNIGHT SNACK.
TURKEY.

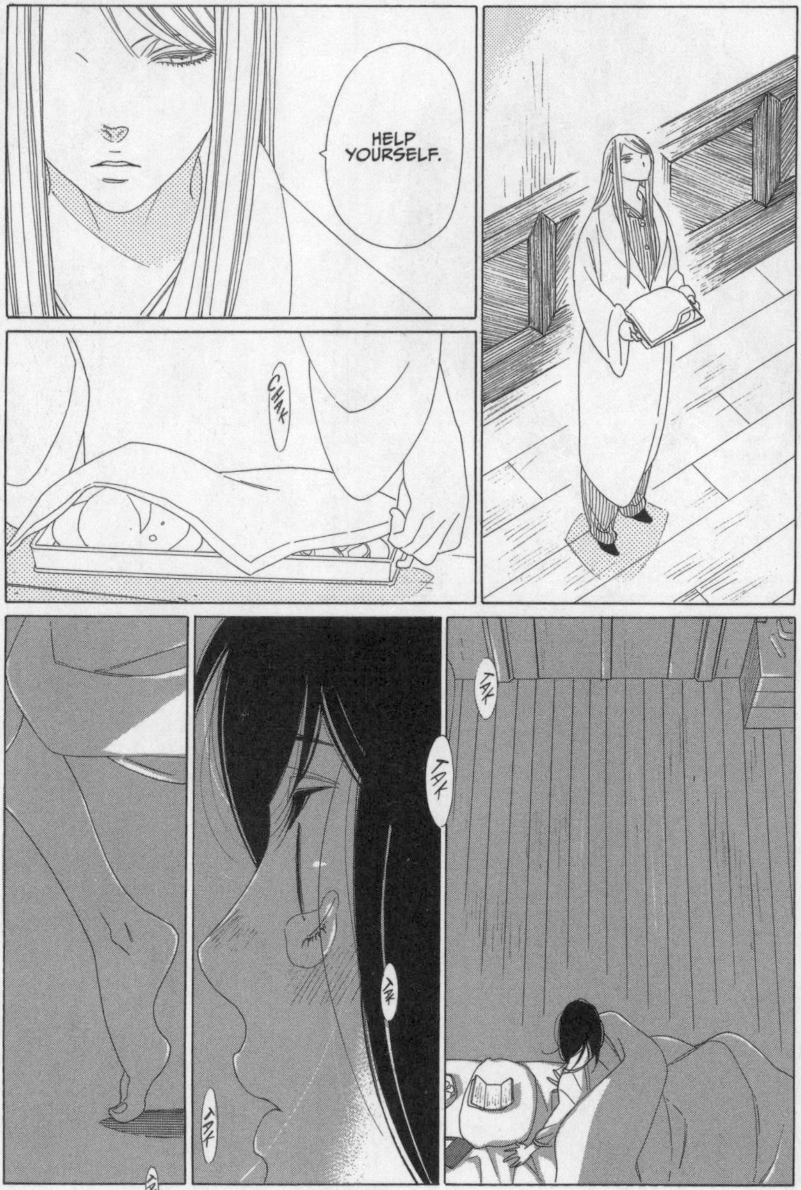
HELP YOURSELF.
CHAK
TAK
TAK
TAK
TAK
TAK

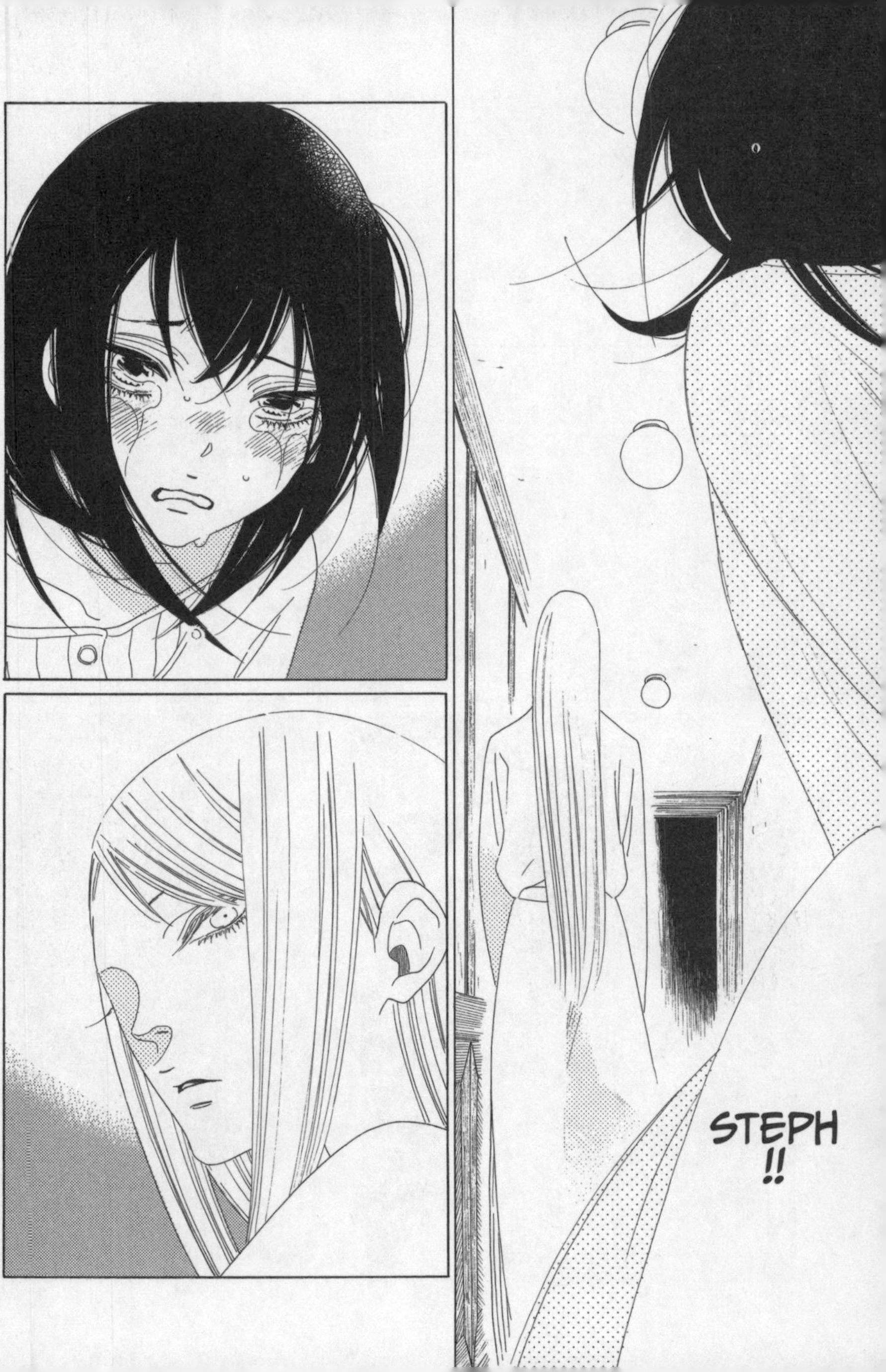
STEPH
!!

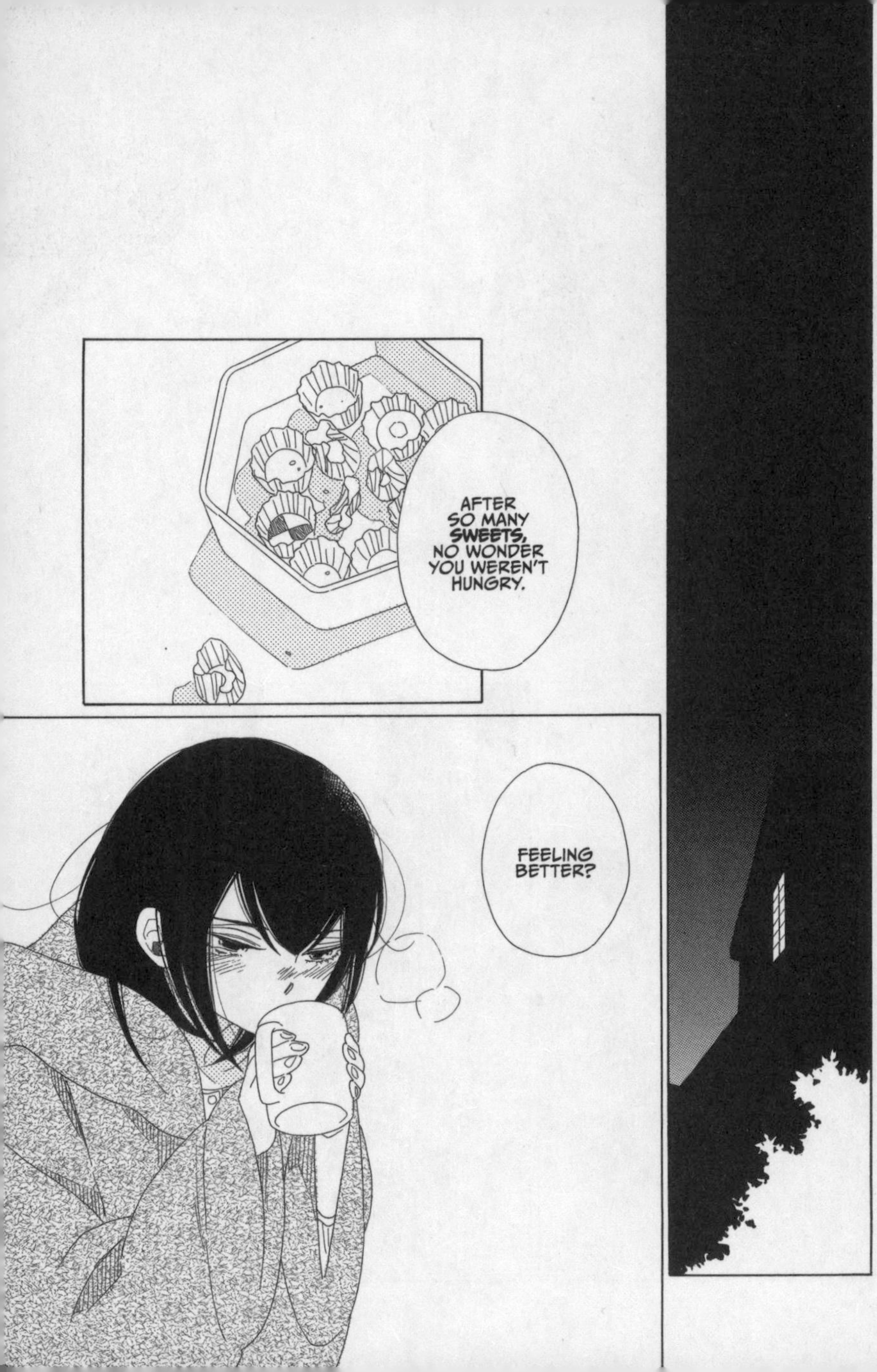
AFTER SO MANY SWEETS, NO WONDER YOU WEREN'T HUNGRY.
FEELING BETTER?

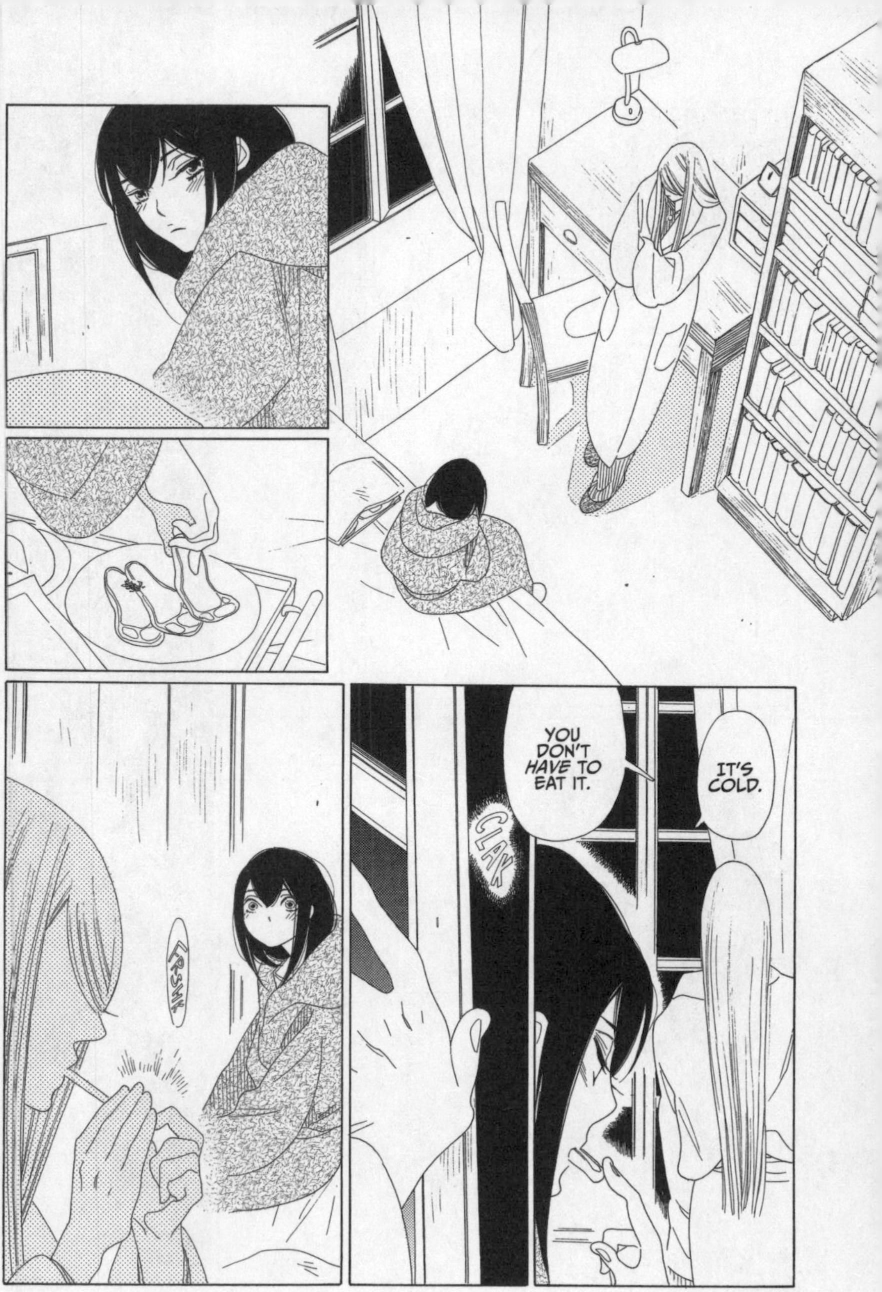
IT'S COLD.
YOU DON'T HAVE TO EAT IT.
CLAK
FRSHK

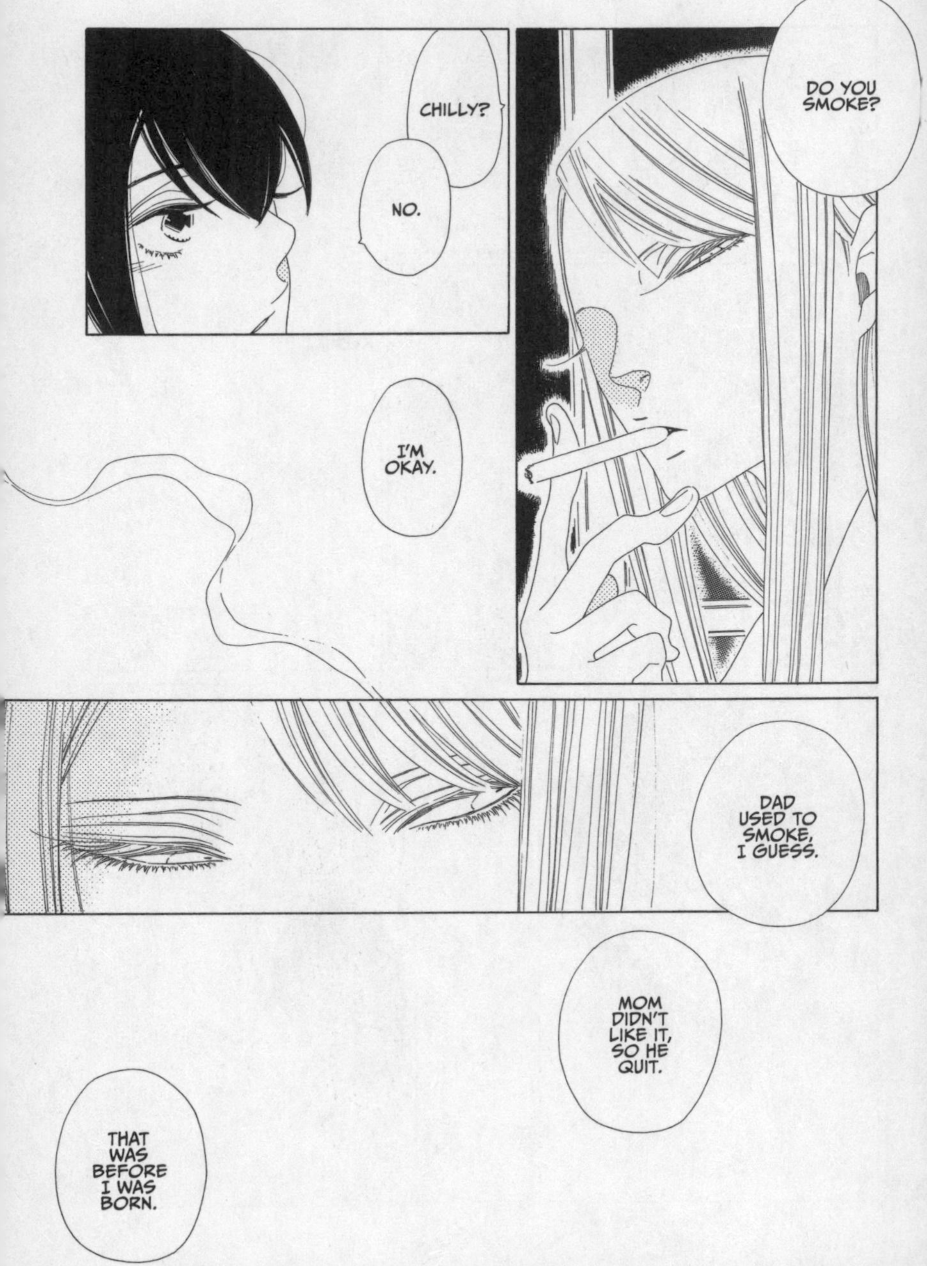
DO YOU SMOKE?
CHILLY?
NO.
I'M OKAY.
DAD USED TO SMOKE, I GUESS.
MOM DIDN'T LIKE IT, SO HE QUIT.
THAT WAS BEFORE I WAS BORN.

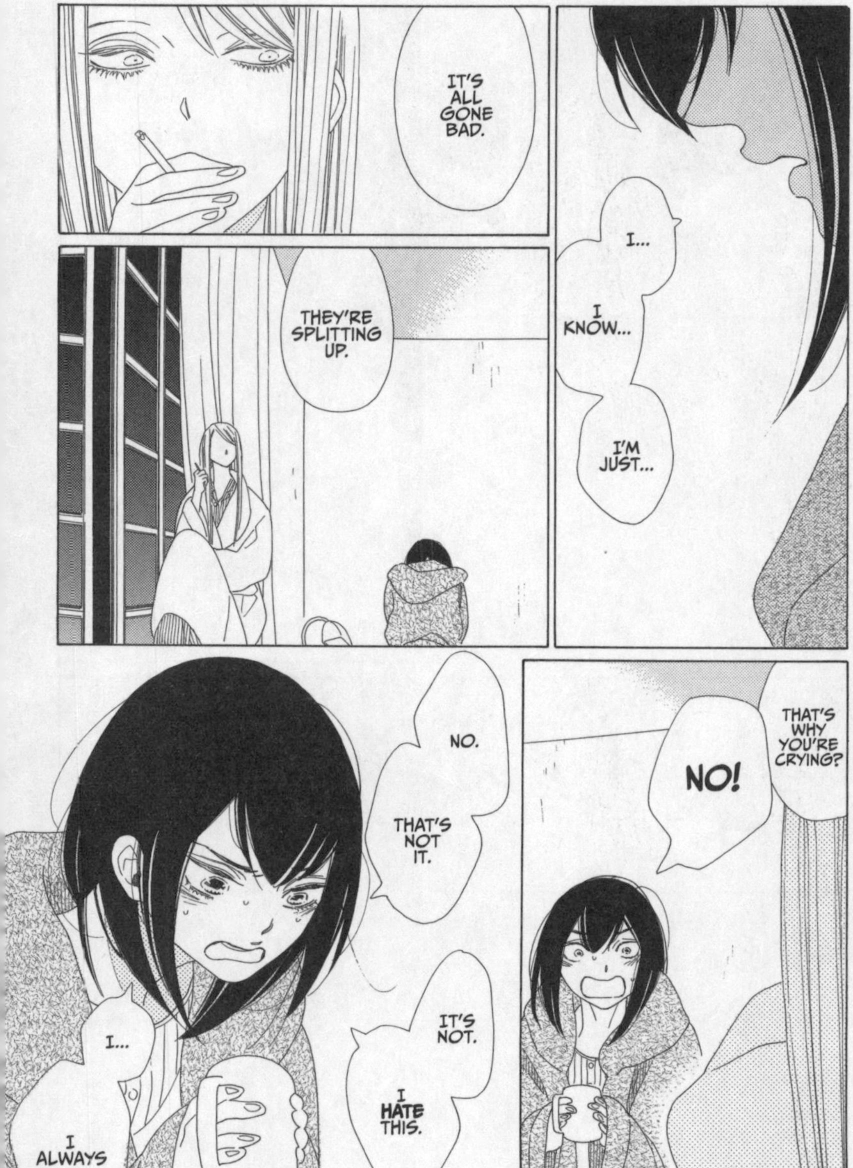
I...
I KNOW...
I'M JUST...
IT'S ALL GONE BAD.
THEY'RE SPLITTING UP.
THAT'S WHY YOU'RE CRYING?
NO!
NO.
THAT'S NOT IT.
IT'S NOT.
I HATE THIS.
I...
I ALWAYS ...

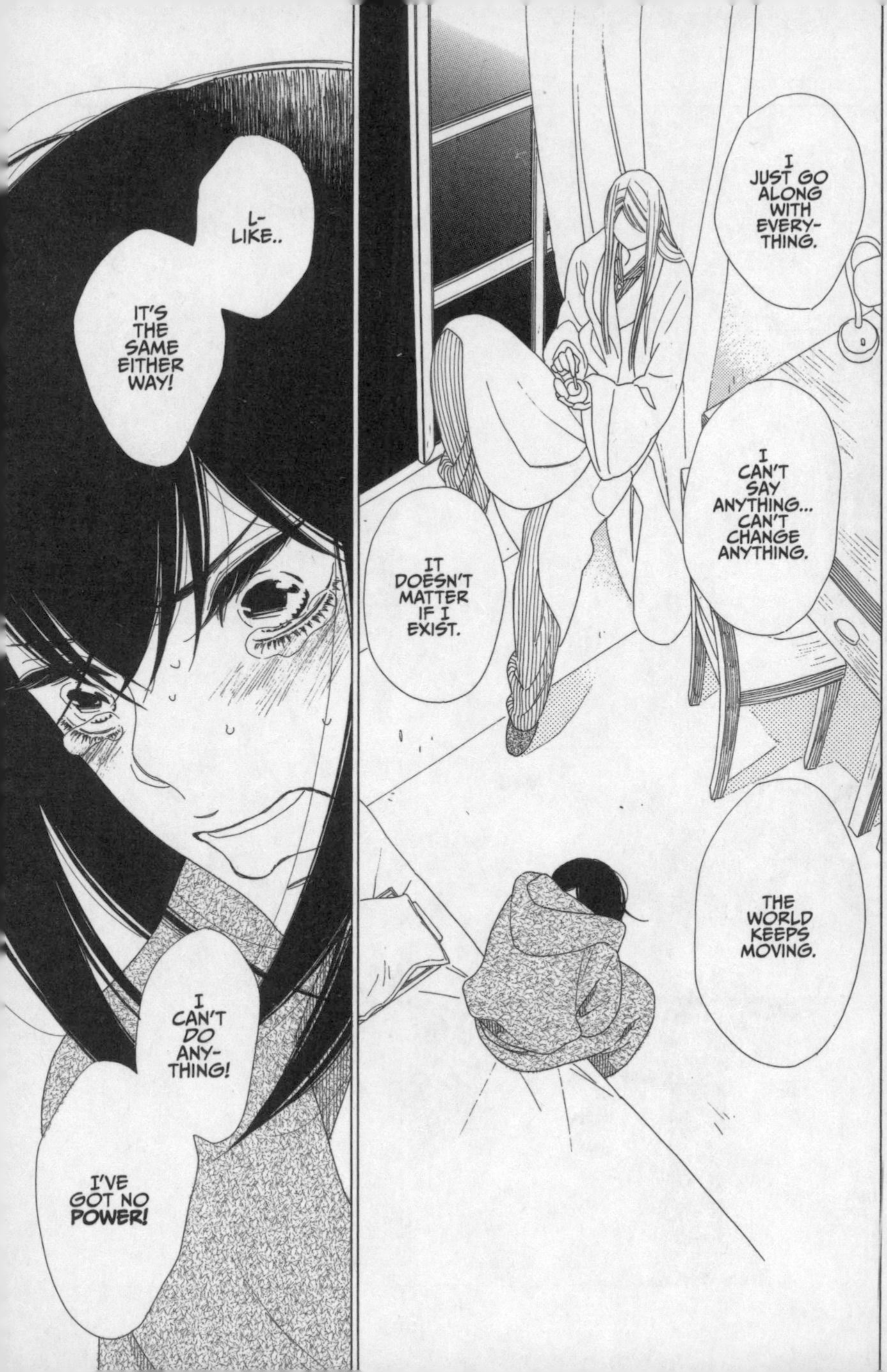
I JUST GO ALONG WITH EVERY-THING.
I CAN'T SAY ANYTHING... CAN'T CHANGE ANYTHING.
IT DOESN'T MATTER IF I EXIST.
THE WORLD KEEPS MOVING.
L-LIKE..
IT'S THE SAME EITHER WAY!
I CAN'T DO ANY-THING!
I'VE GOT NO POWER!

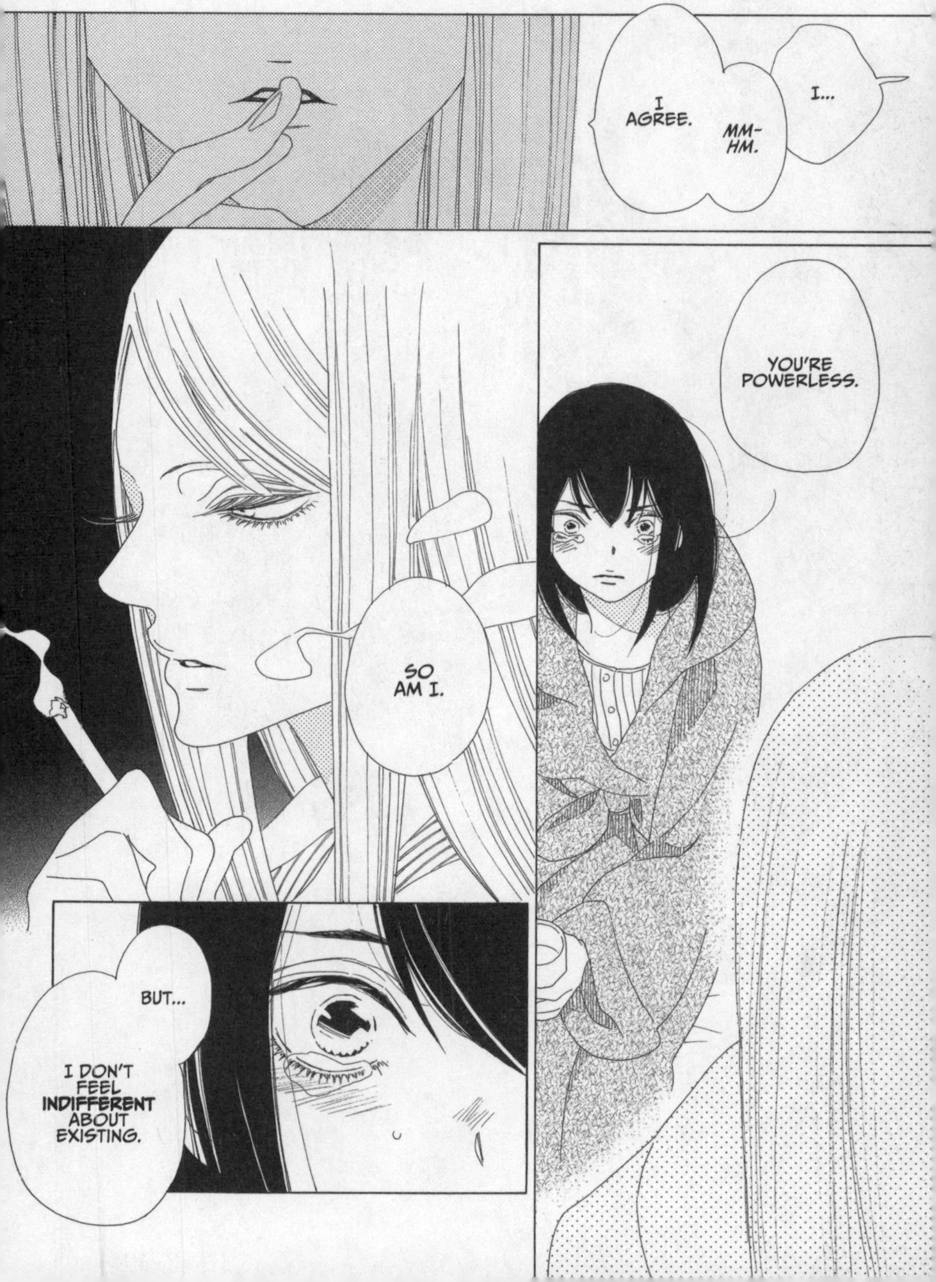
I...
MM-HM.
I AGREE.
YOU'RE POWERLESS.
SO AM I.
BUT...
I DON'T FEEL **INDIFFERENT** ABOUT EXISTING.

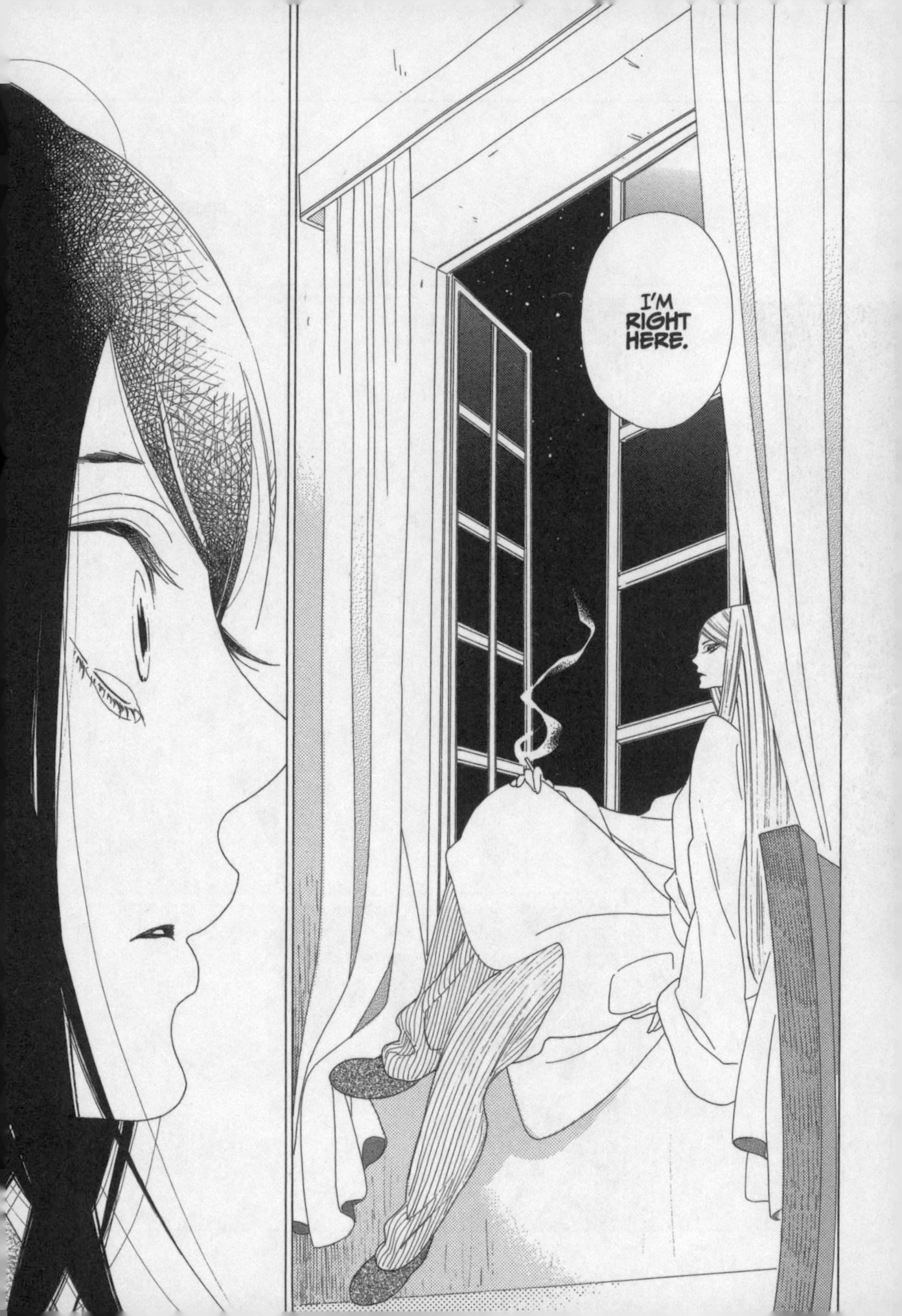
I'M RIGHT HERE.

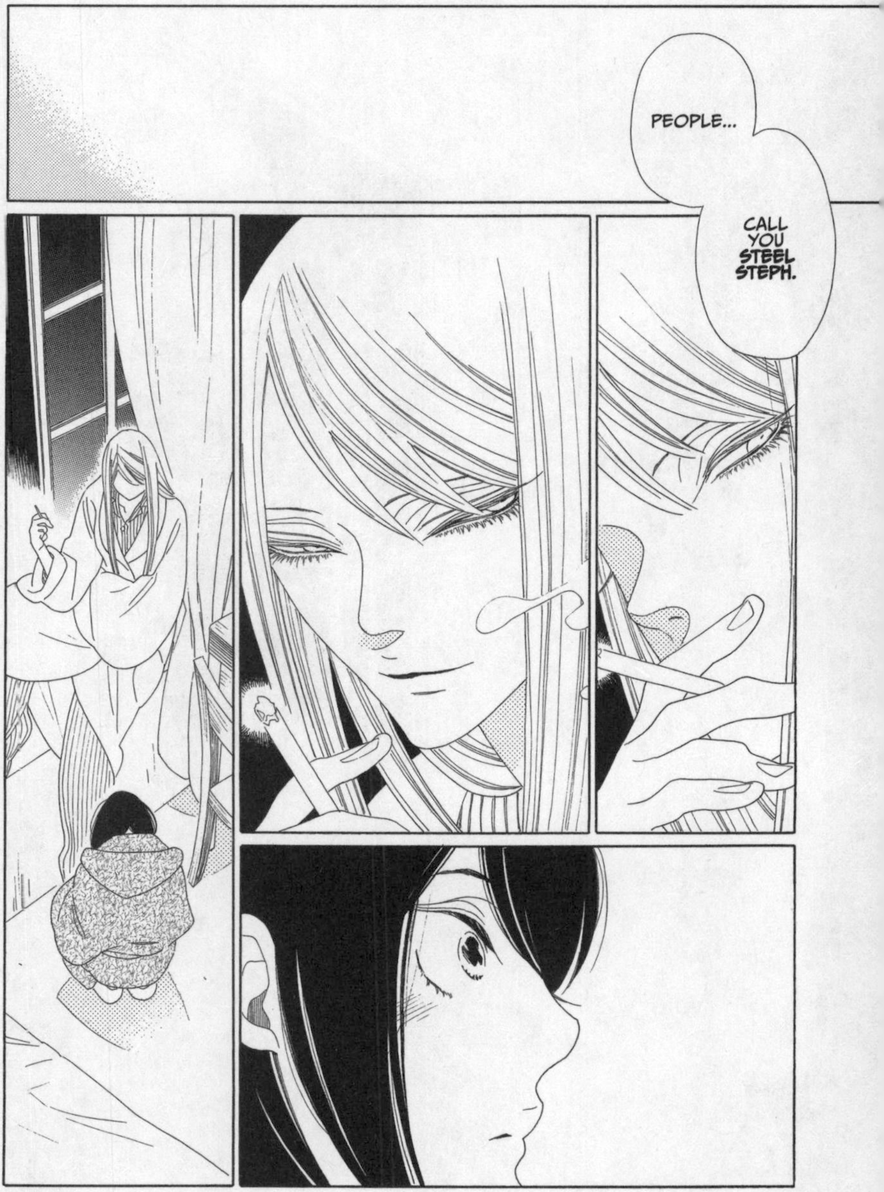
PEOPLE...
CALL YOU STEEL STEPH.

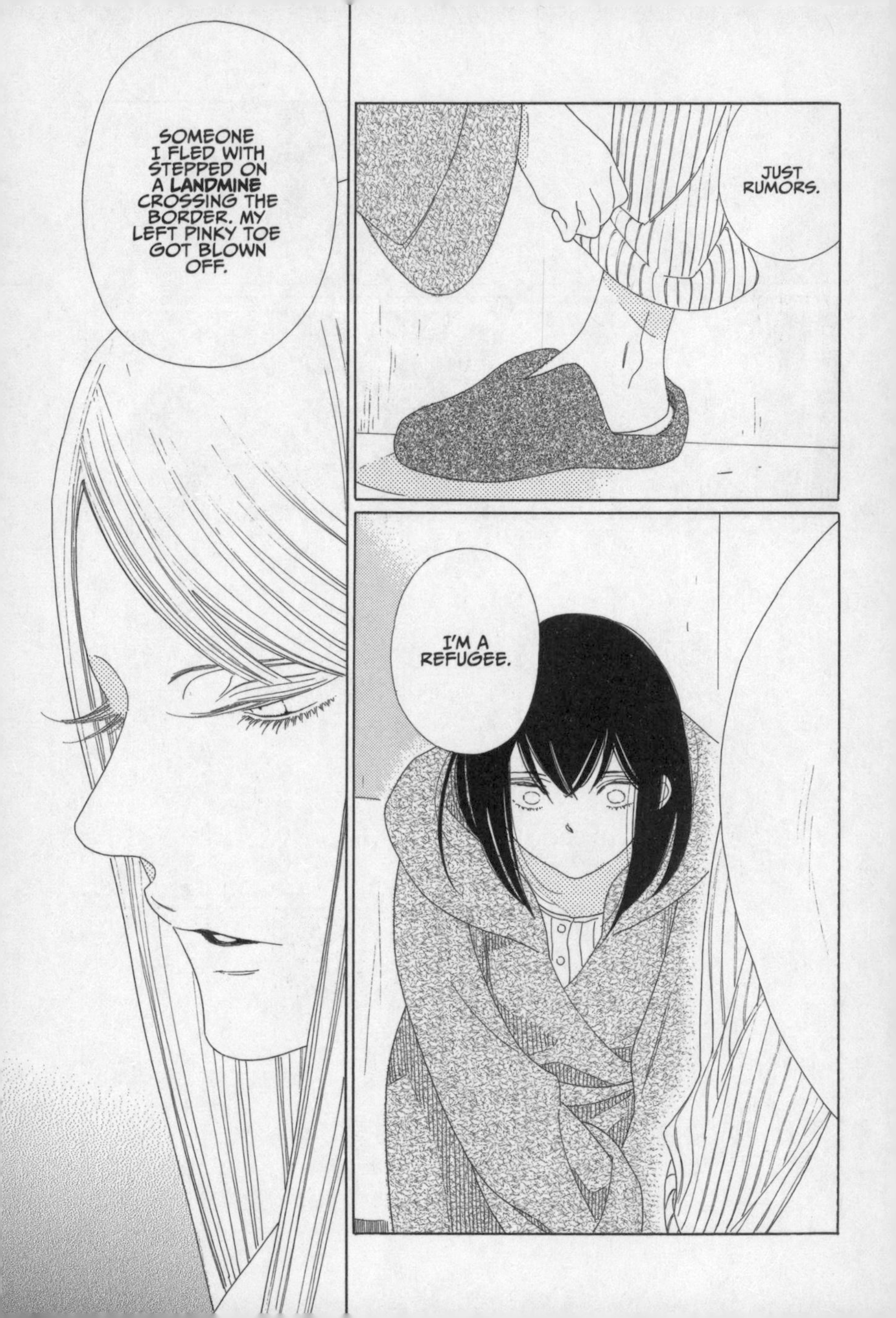
JUST RUMORS.
I'M A REFUGEE.
SOMEONE I FLED WITH STEPPED ON A **LANDMINE** CROSSING THE BORDER. MY LEFT PINKY TOE GOT BLOWN OFF.

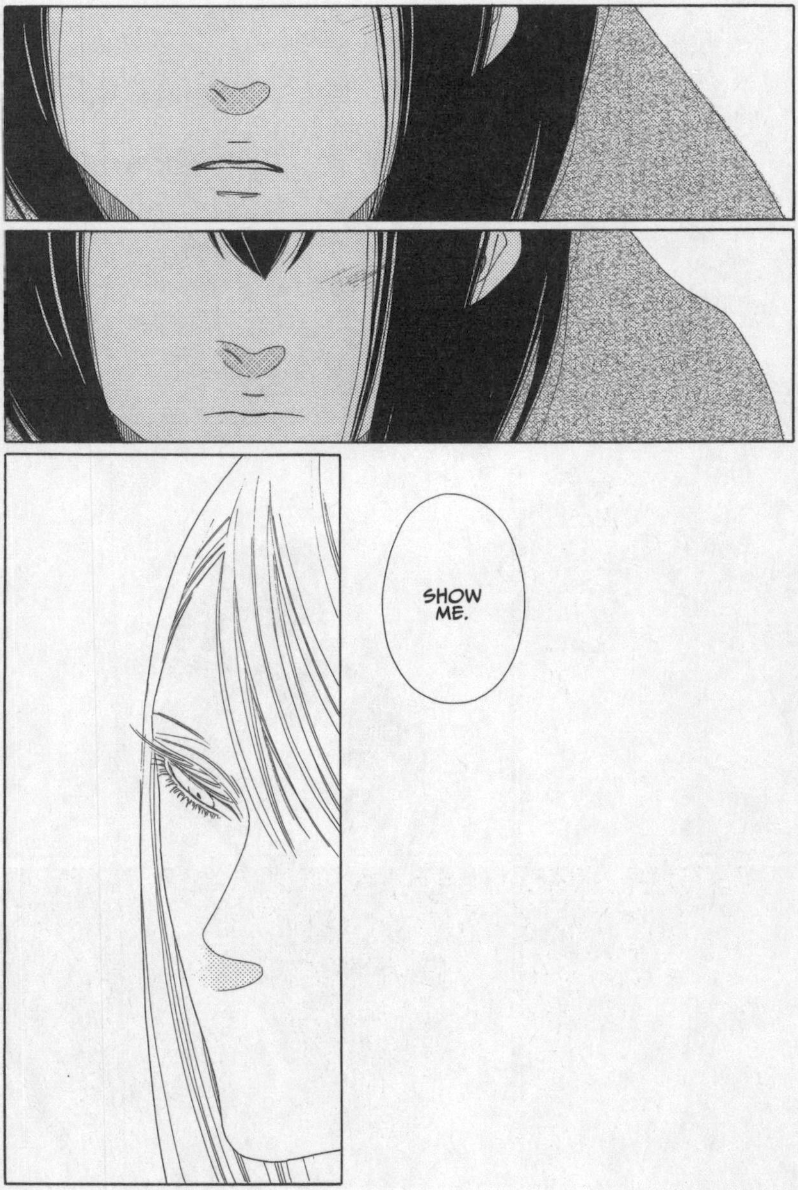
SHOW ME.

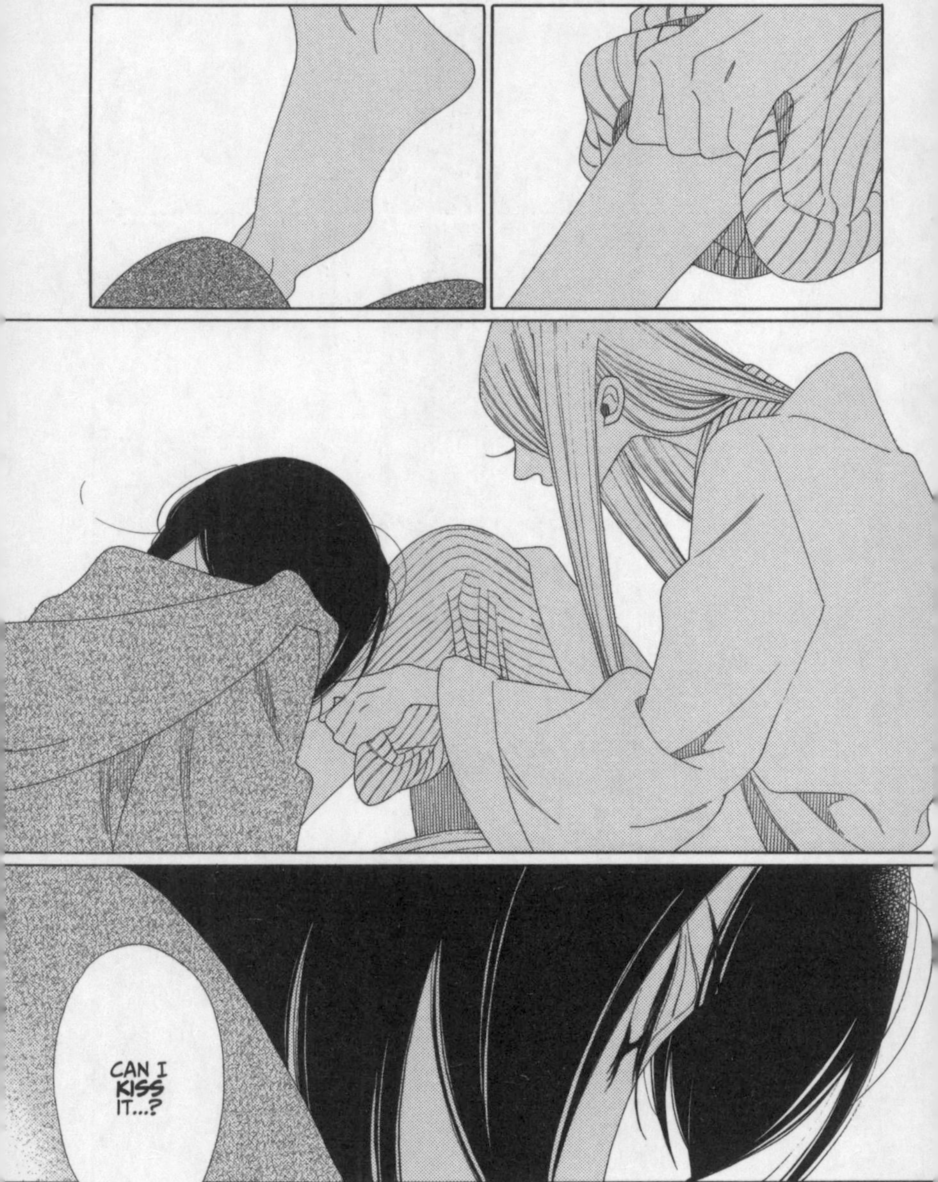
CAN I KISS IT...?

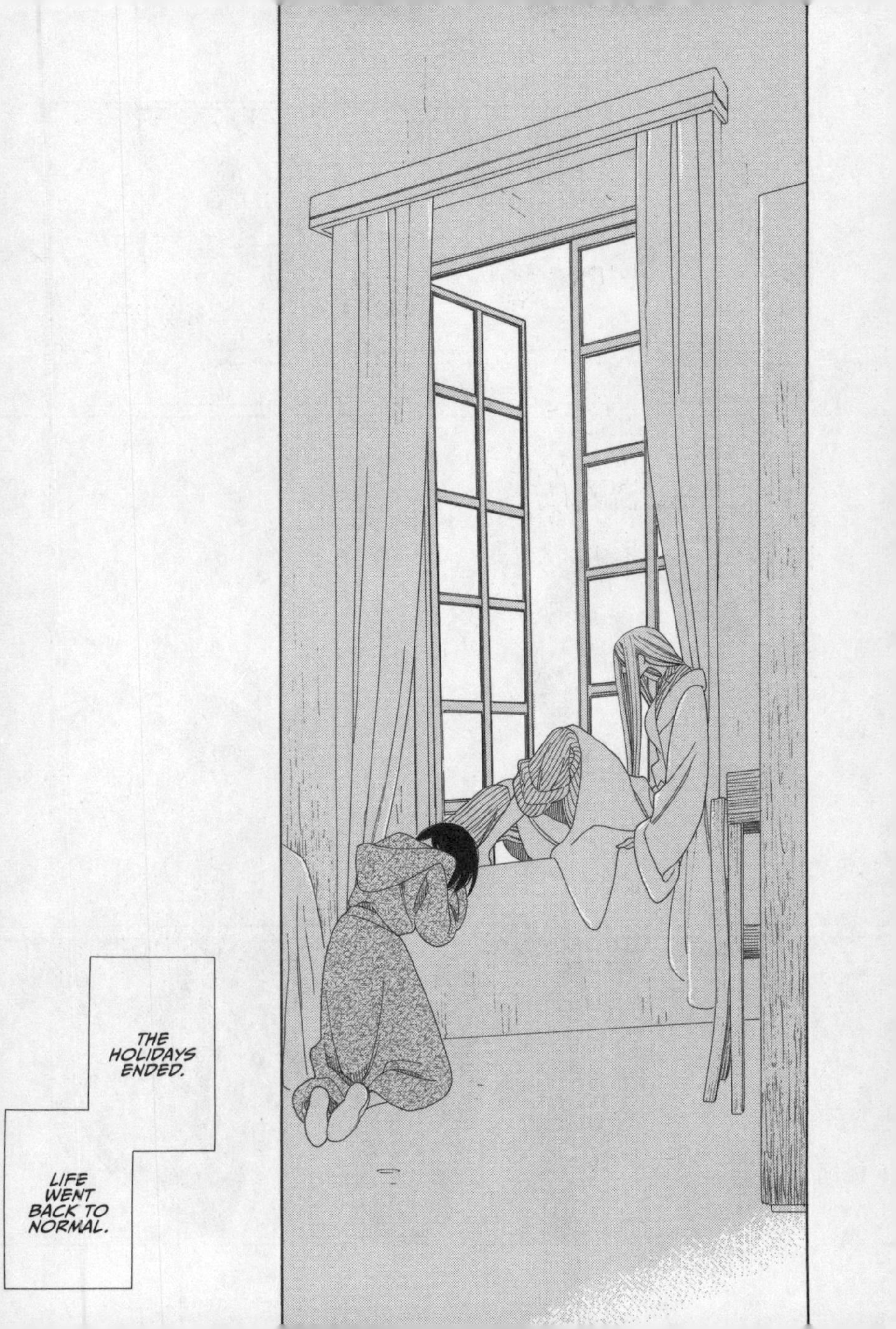
THE HOLIDAYS ENDED.
LIFE WENT BACK TO NORMAL.

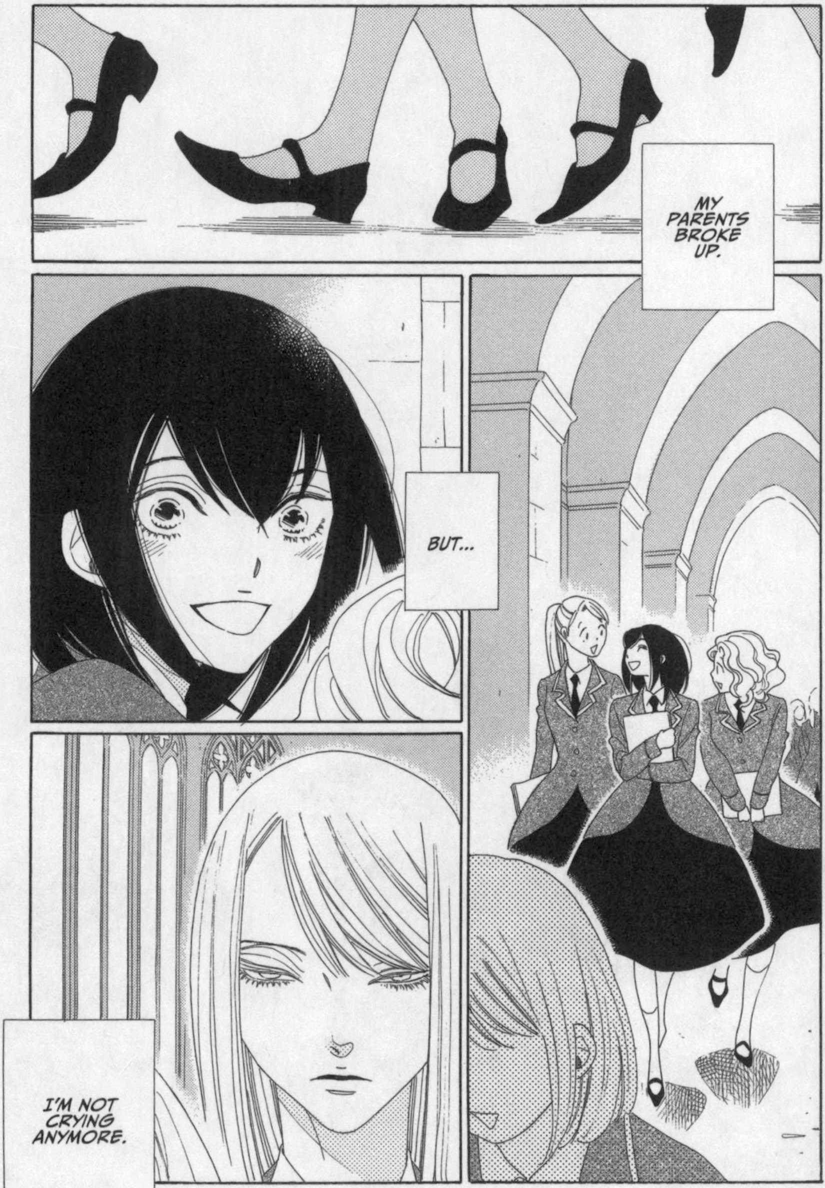
MY PARENTS BROKE UP.
BUT...
I'M NOT CRYING ANYMORE.

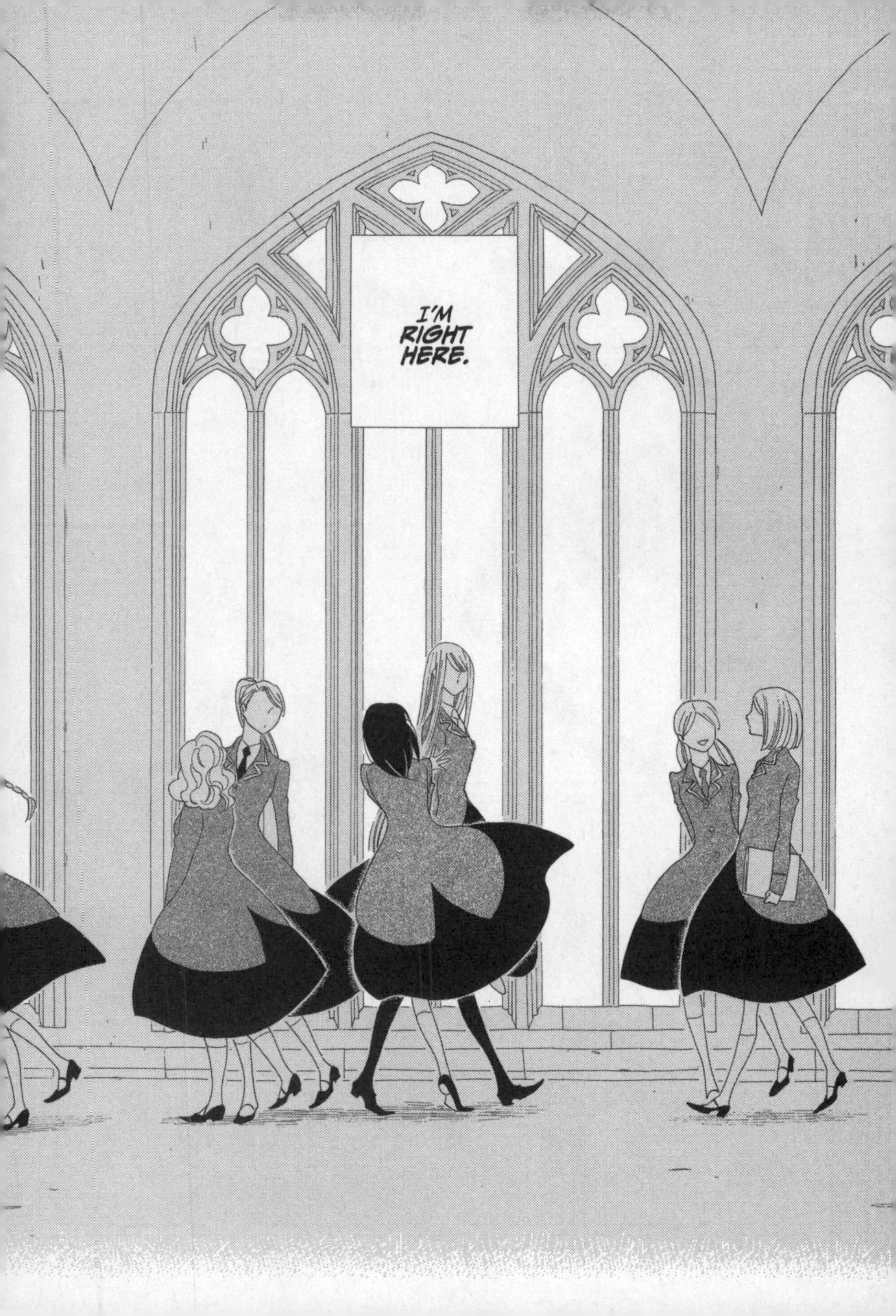
I'M RIGHT HERE.

メ
ジ
ロ
バ
ナ
の
咲
く

メジロバナの咲く

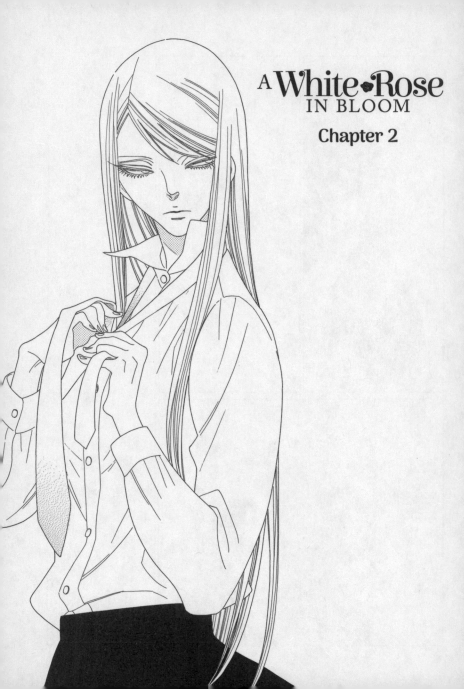

# A White Rose IN BLOOM

## Chapter 2

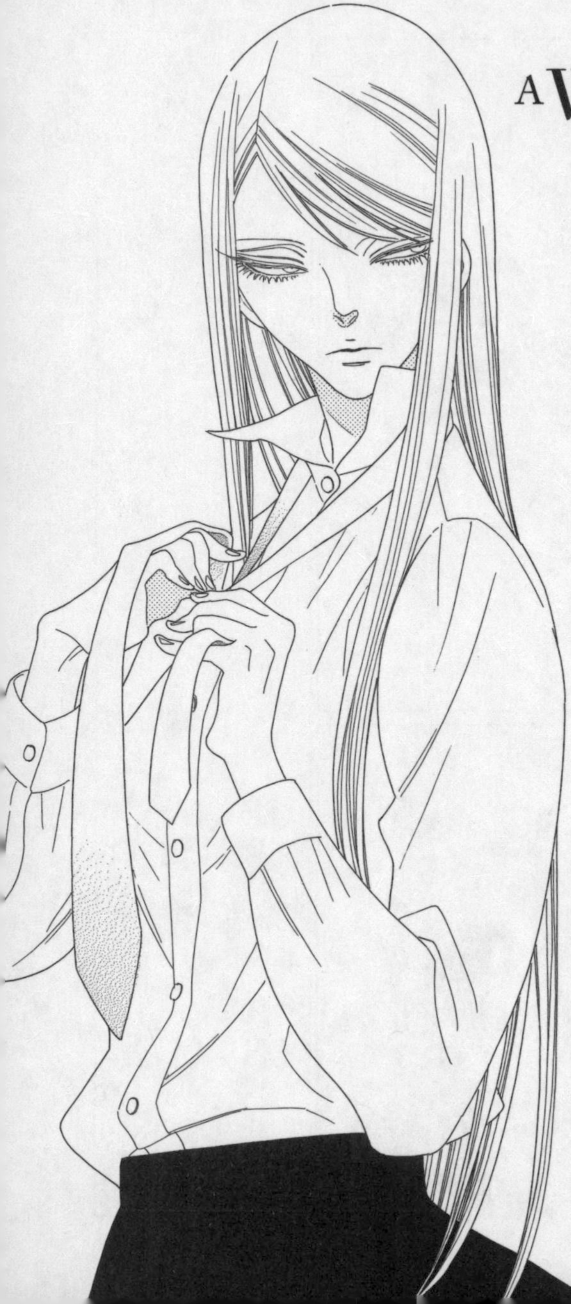

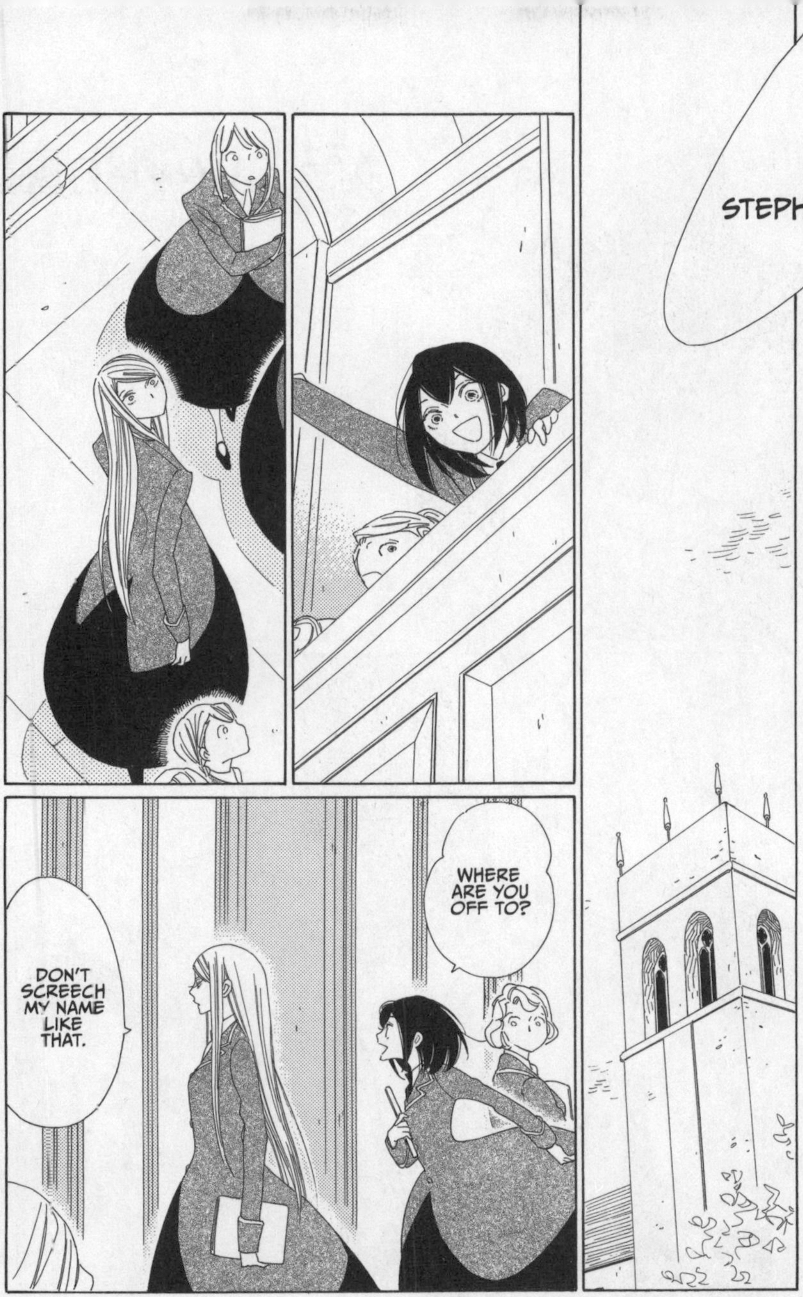
STEPH!
WHERE ARE YOU OFF TO?
DON'T SCREECH MY NAME LIKE THAT.

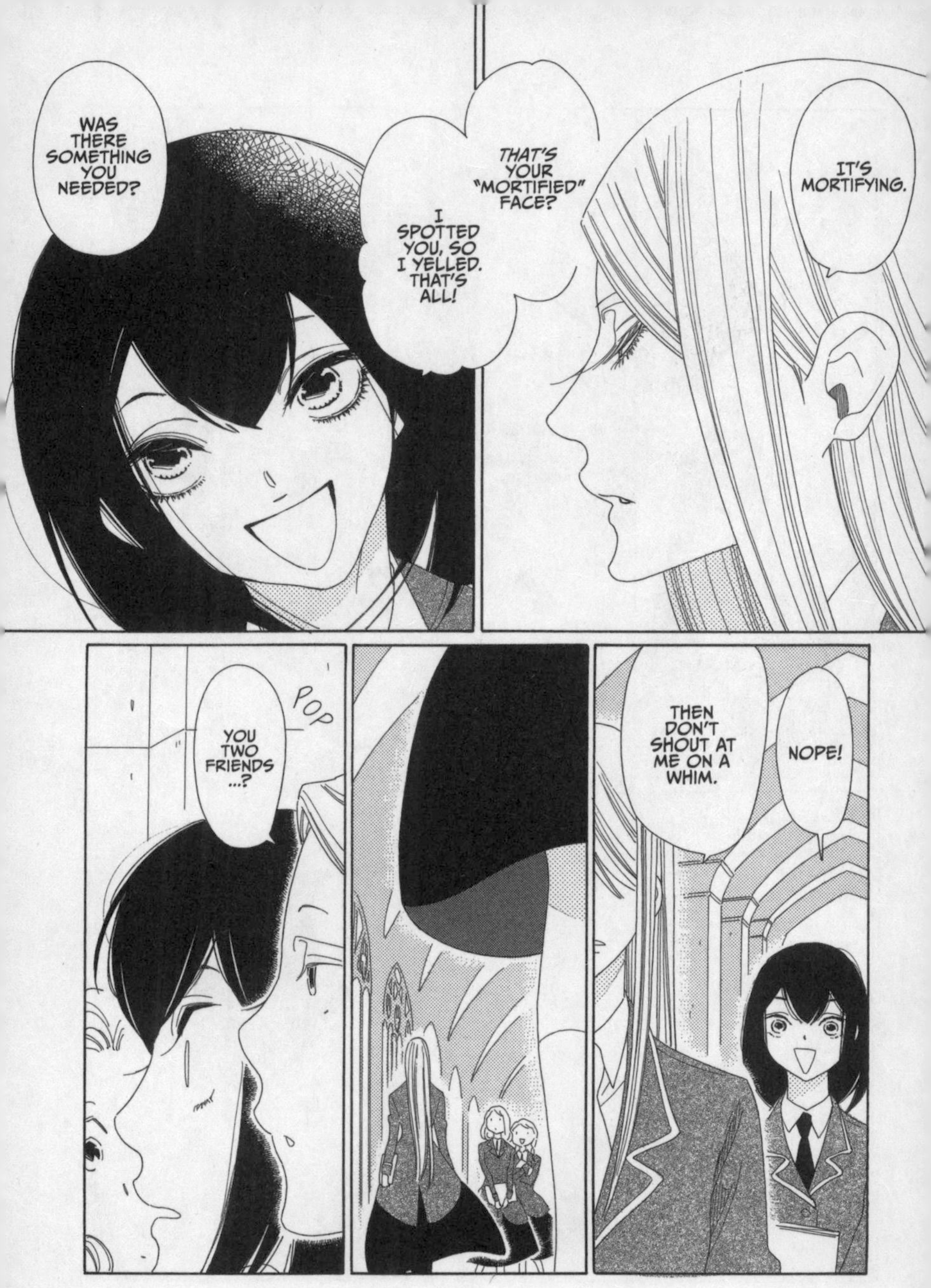
IT'S MORTIFYING.
THAT'S YOUR "MORTIFIED" FACE?
I SPOTTED YOU, SO I YELLED. THAT'S ALL!
WAS THERE SOMETHING YOU NEEDED?
THEN DON'T SHOUT AT ME ON A WHIM.
NOPE!
POP
YOU TWO FRIENDS ...?

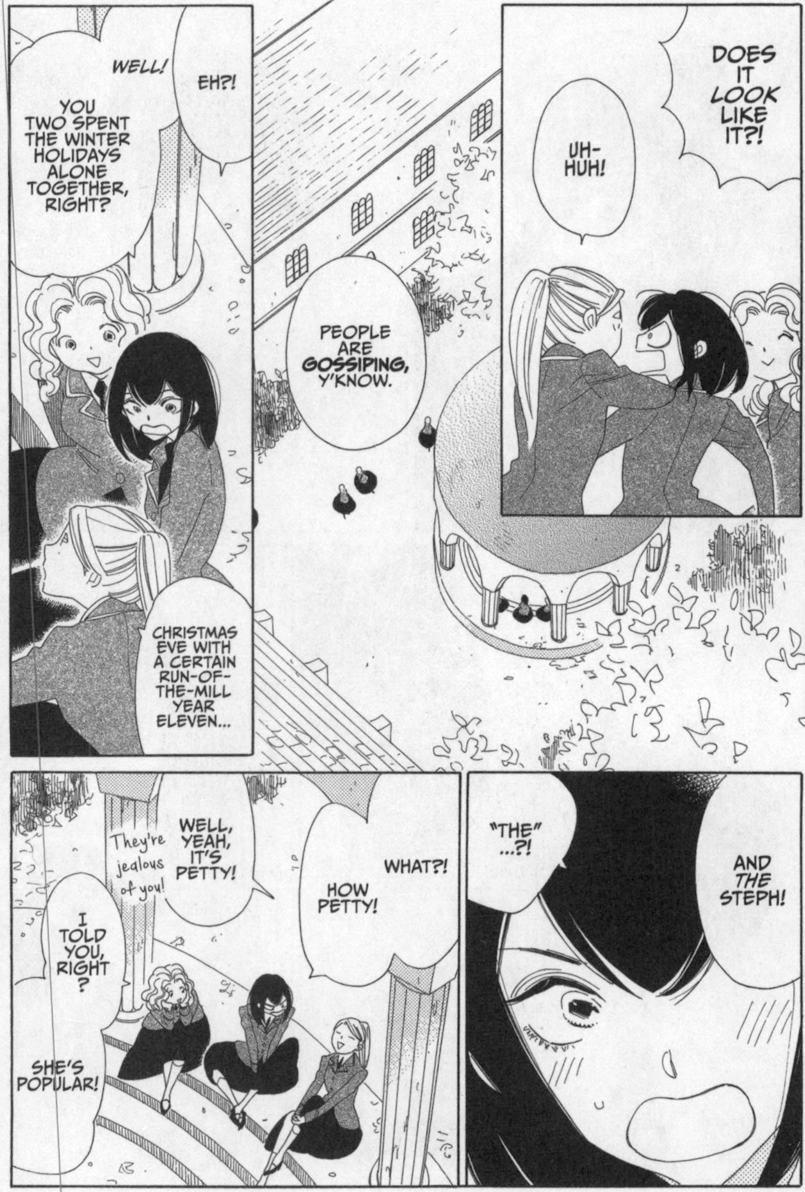
DOES IT *LOOK* LIKE IT?!
UH-HUH!
PEOPLE ARE **GOSSIPING**, Y'KNOW.
EH?!
*WELL!*
YOU TWO SPENT THE WINTER HOLIDAYS ALONE TOGETHER, RIGHT?
CHRISTMAS EVE WITH A CERTAIN RUN-OF-THE-MILL YEAR ELEVEN...
AND *THE* STEPH!
"THE" ...?!
WHAT?!
HOW PETTY!
WELL, YEAH, IT'S PETTY!
They're jealous of you!
I TOLD YOU, RIGHT?
SHE'S POPULAR!

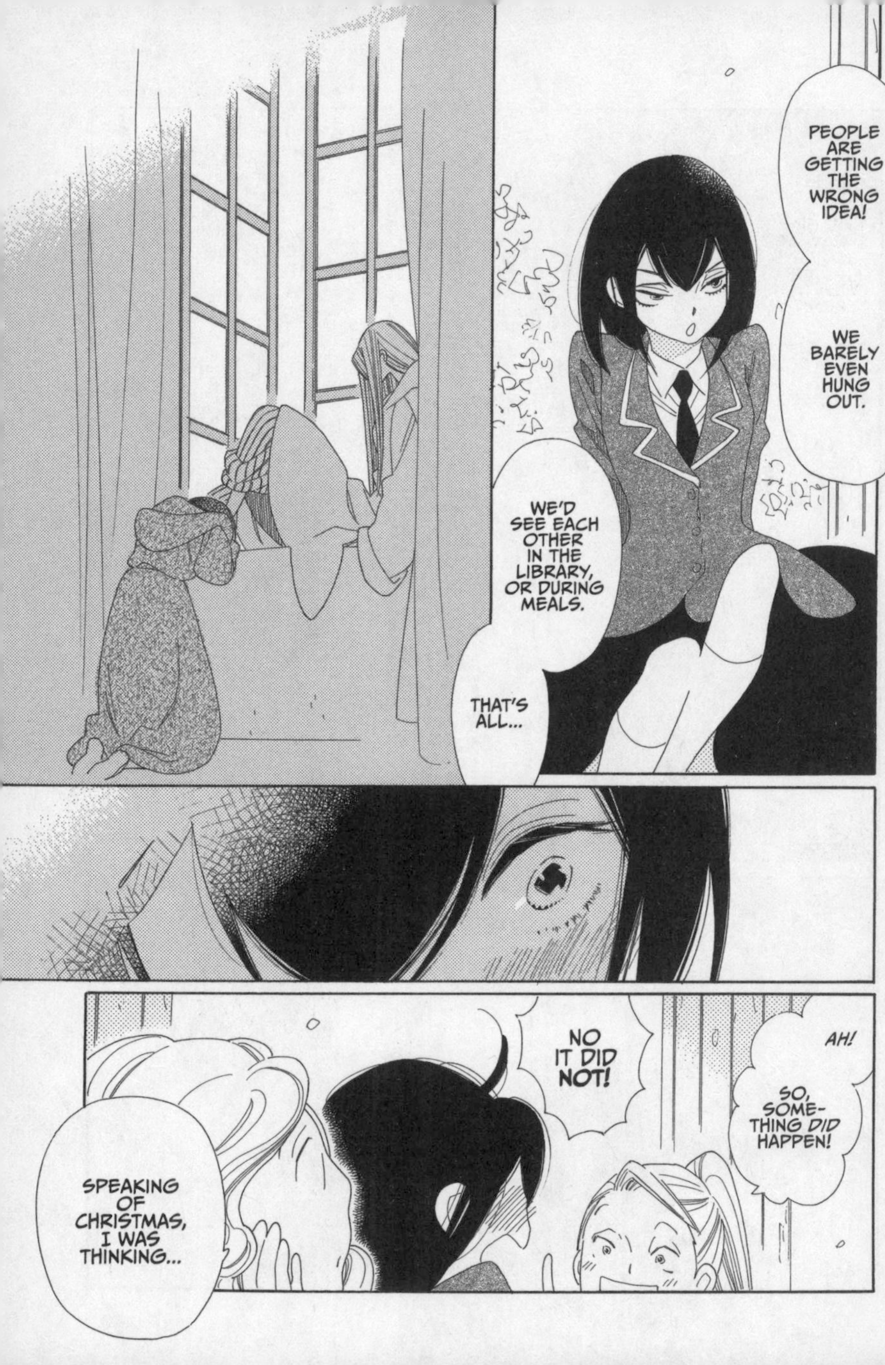
PEOPLE ARE GETTING THE WRONG IDEA!
WE BARELY EVEN HUNG OUT.
WE'D SEE EACH OTHER IN THE LIBRARY, OR DURING MEALS.
THAT'S ALL...
AH!
SO, SOME-THING *DID* HAPPEN!
NO IT DID **NOT!**
SPEAKING OF CHRISTMAS, I WAS THINKING...

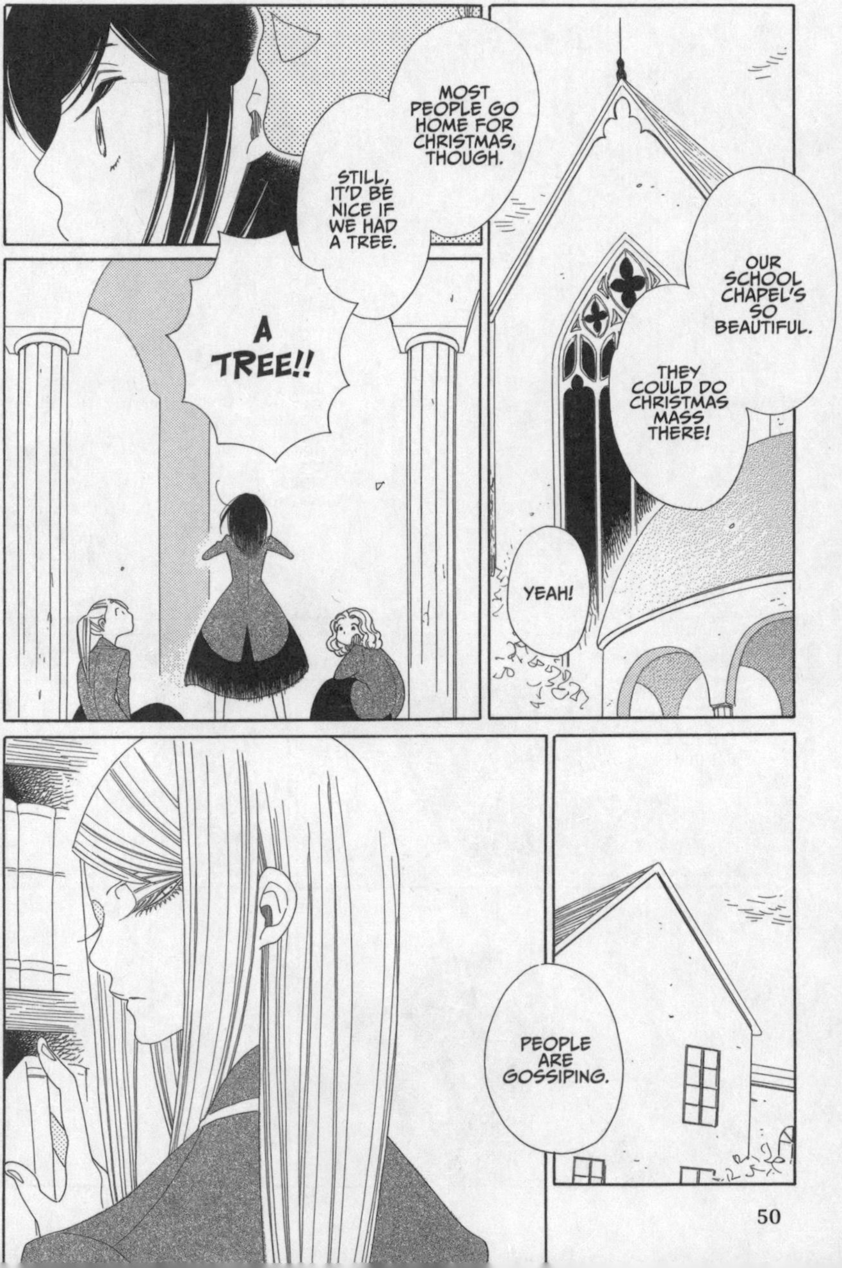
OUR SCHOOL CHAPEL'S SO BEAUTIFUL.
THEY COULD DO CHRISTMAS MASS THERE!
YEAH!
MOST PEOPLE GO HOME FOR CHRISTMAS, THOUGH.
STILL, IT'D BE NICE IF WE HAD A TREE.
A TREE!!
PEOPLE ARE GOSSIPING.

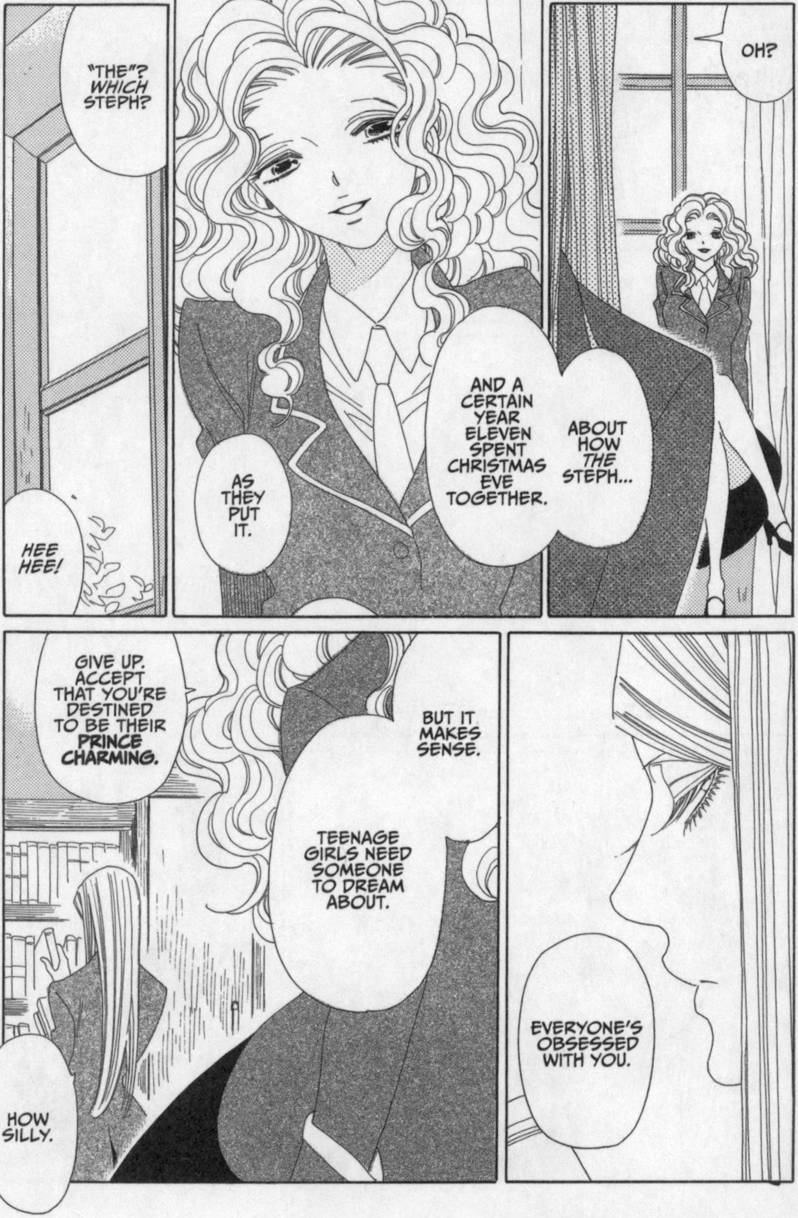
OH?
ABOUT HOW *THE* STEPH...
AND A CERTAIN YEAR ELEVEN SPENT CHRISTMAS EVE TOGETHER.
AS THEY PUT IT.
"THE"? *WHICH* STEPH?
*HEE HEE!*
EVERYONE'S OBSESSED WITH YOU.
BUT IT MAKES SENSE.
TEENAGE GIRLS NEED SOMEONE TO DREAM ABOUT.
GIVE UP. ACCEPT THAT YOU'RE DESTINED TO BE THEIR **PRINCE CHARMING.**
HOW SILLY.

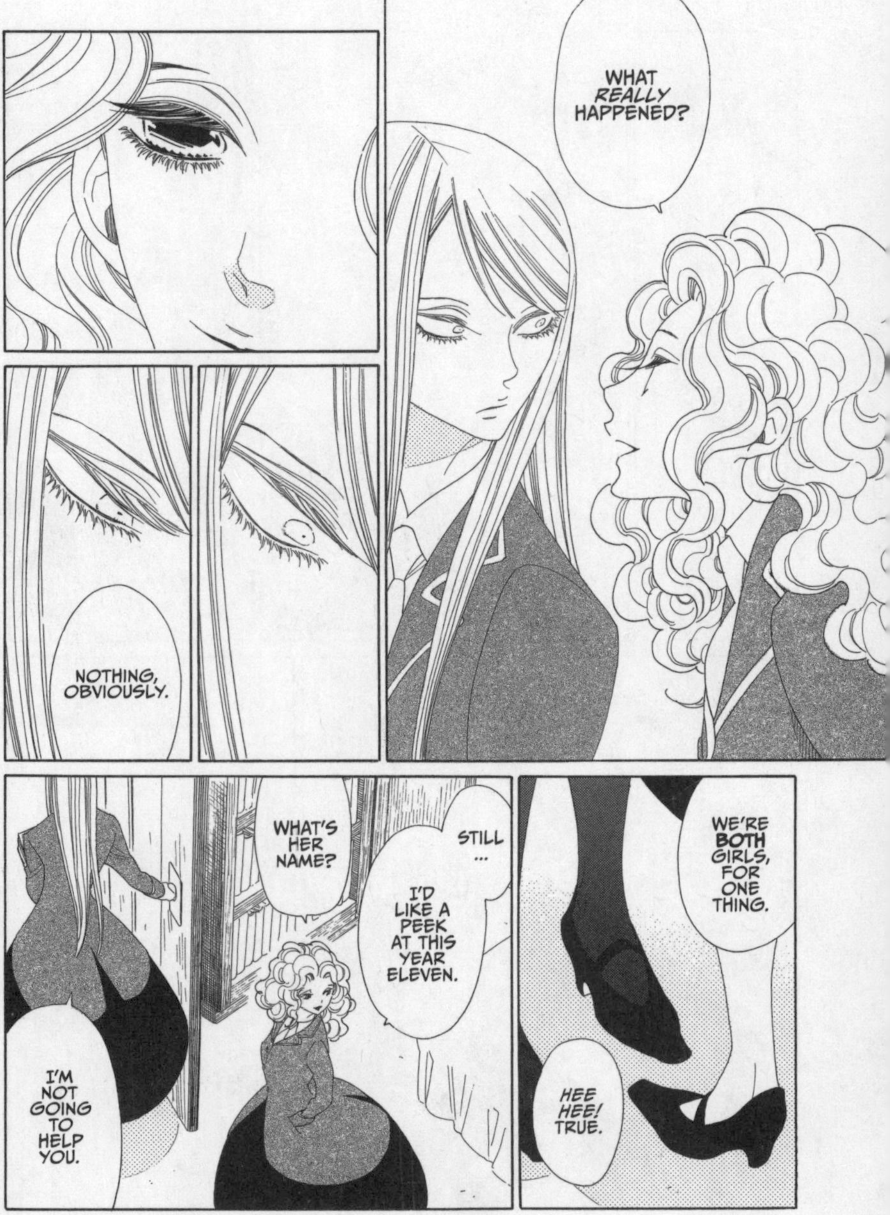
WHAT *REALLY* HAPPENED?
NOTHING, OBVIOUSLY.
WE'RE **BOTH** GIRLS, FOR ONE THING.
*HEE HEE!* TRUE.
STILL ...
I'D LIKE A PEEK AT THIS YEAR ELEVEN.
WHAT'S HER NAME?
I'M NOT GOING TO HELP YOU.

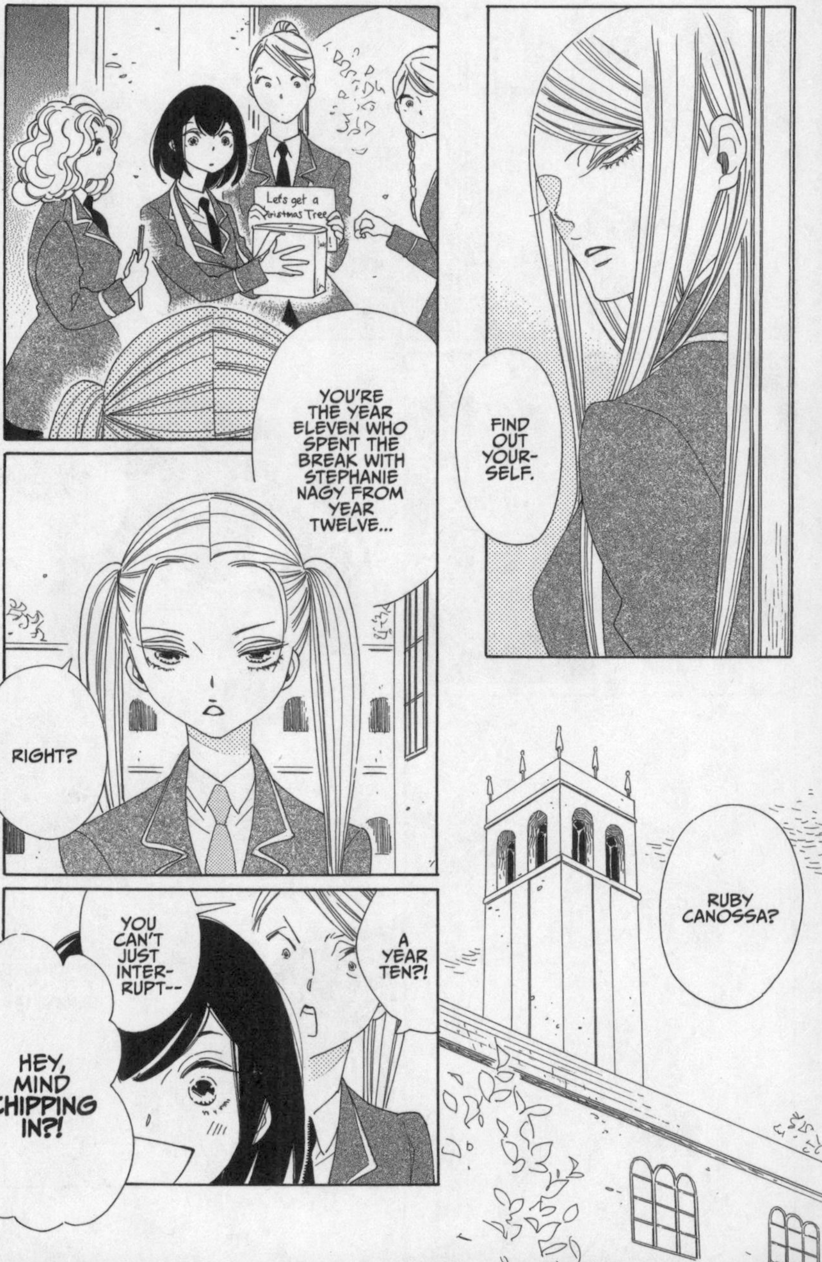

FIND OUT YOUR-SELF.
Let's get a Christmas Tree
YOU'RE THE YEAR ELEVEN WHO SPENT THE BREAK WITH STEPHANIE NAGY FROM YEAR TWELVE...
RIGHT?
RUBY CANOSSA?
A YEAR TEN?!
YOU CAN'T JUST INTER-RUPT--
HEY, MIND CHIPPING IN?!

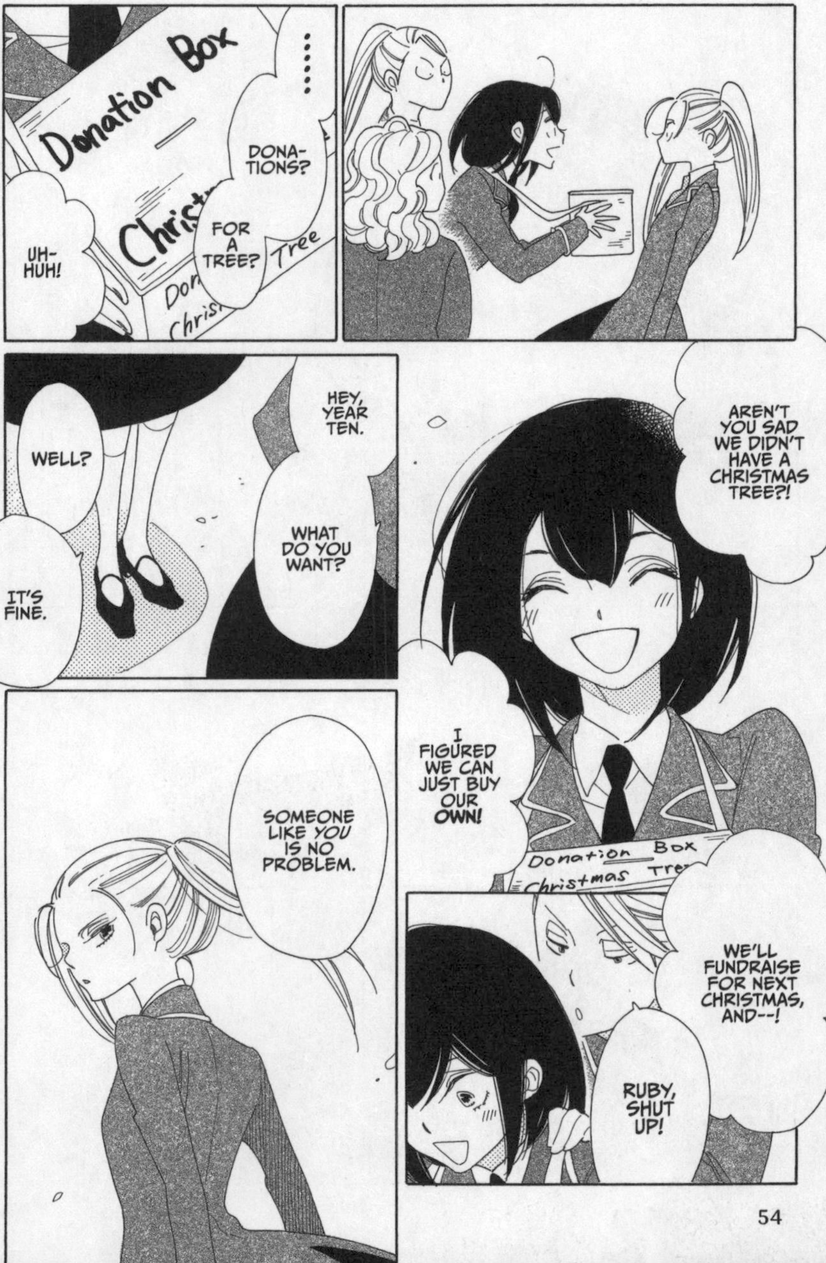
Donation Box
......
DONA-TIONS?
FOR A TREE?
Tree
UH-HUH!
AREN'T YOU SAD WE DIDN'T HAVE A CHRISTMAS TREE?!
I FIGURED WE CAN JUST BUY OUR OWN!
Donation Box
Christmas
WE'LL FUNDRAISE FOR NEXT CHRISTMAS, AND--!
RUBY, SHUT UP!
HEY, YEAR TEN.
WHAT DO YOU WANT?
WELL?
IT'S FINE.
SOMEONE LIKE YOU IS NO PROBLEM.

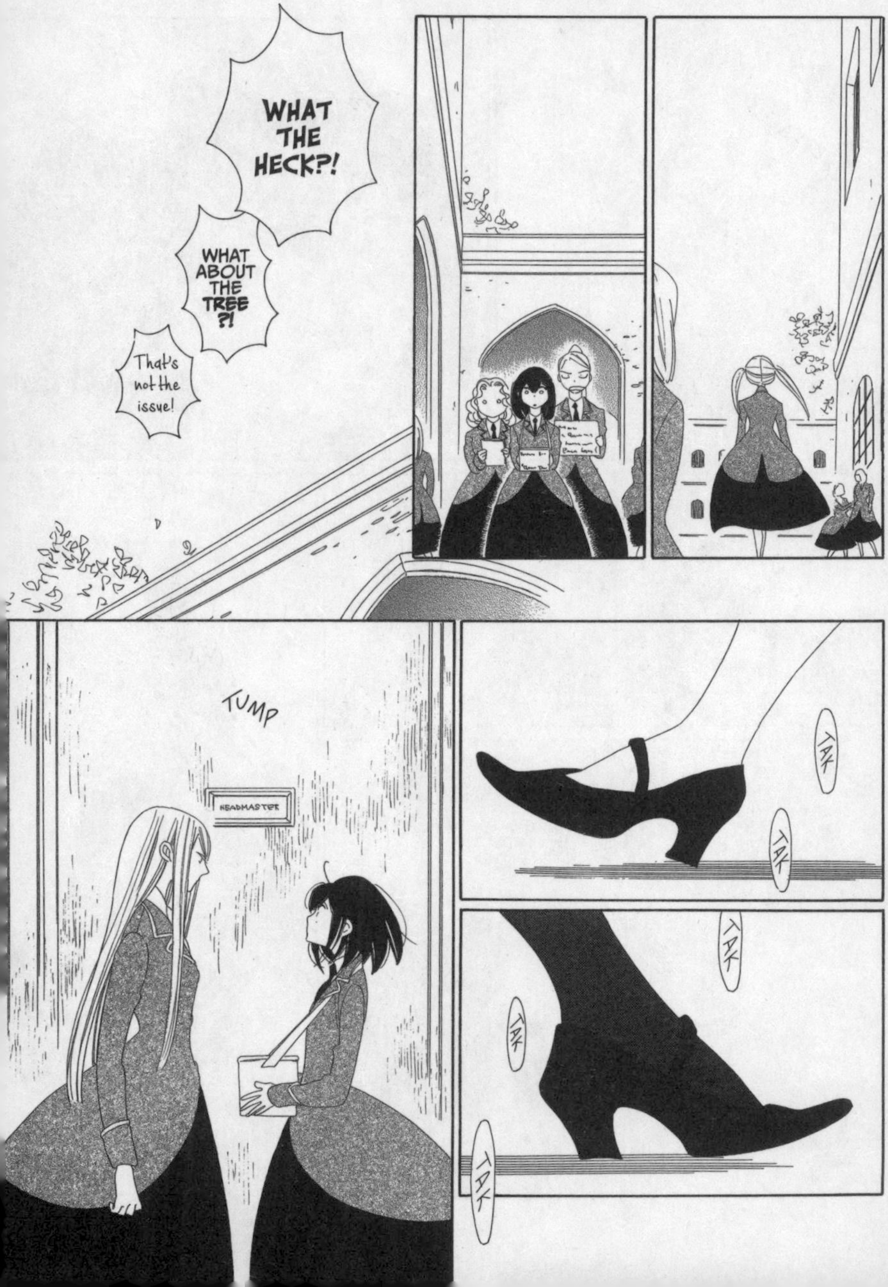
WHAT THE HECK?!
WHAT ABOUT THE TREE ?!
That's not the issue!
TAK
TAK
TAK
TAK
TUMP
HEADMASTER

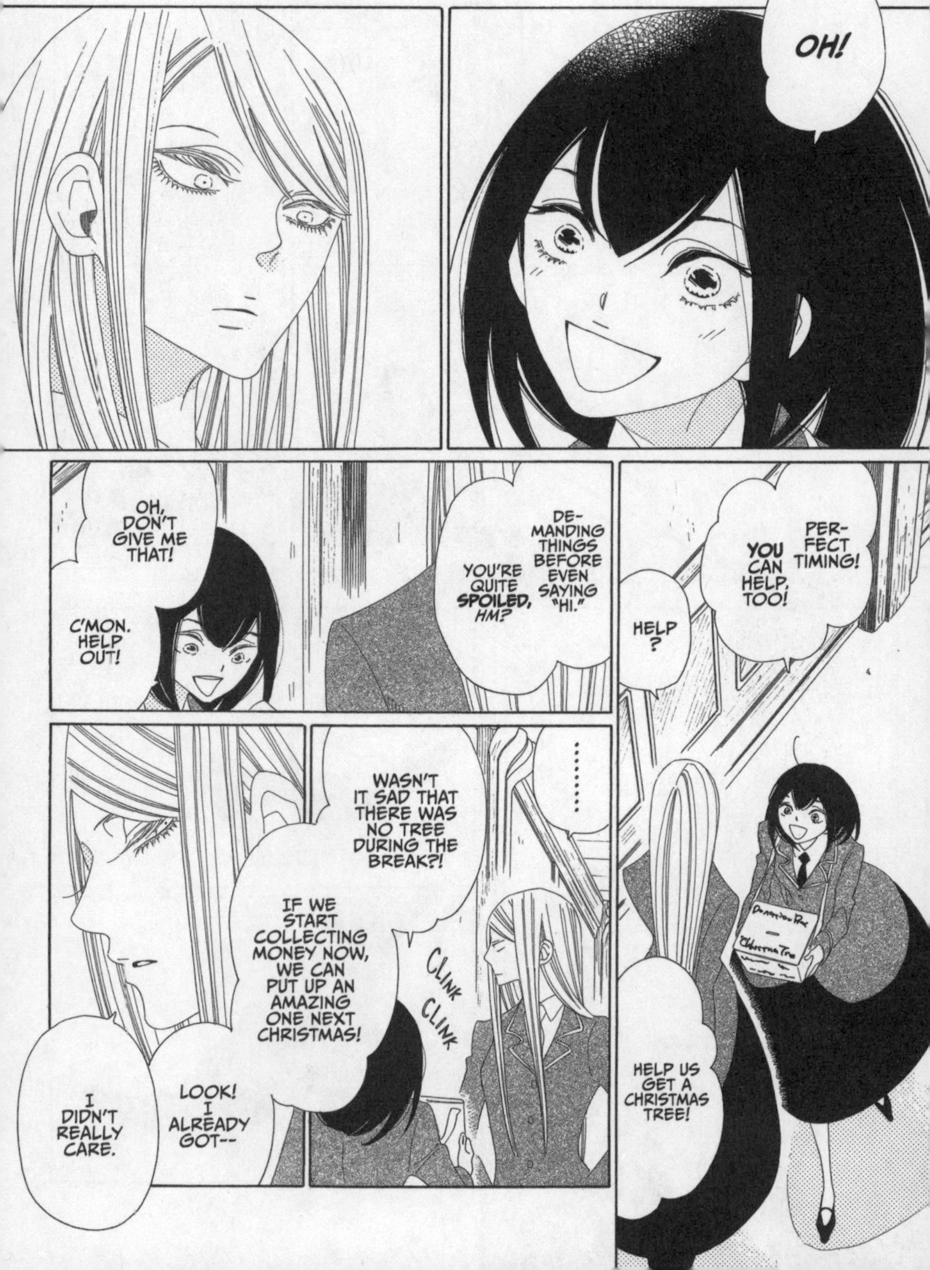
OH!
PER-FECT TIMING!
YOU CAN HELP, TOO!
HELP?
HELP US GET A CHRISTMAS TREE!
DE-MANDING THINGS BEFORE EVEN SAYING "HI."
YOU'RE QUITE **SPOILED,** *HM?*
OH, DON'T GIVE ME THAT!
C'MON. HELP OUT!
......
WASN'T IT SAD THAT THERE WAS NO TREE DURING THE BREAK?!
IF WE START COLLECTING MONEY NOW, WE CAN PUT UP AN AMAZING ONE NEXT CHRISTMAS!
CLINK
CLINK
LOOK! I ALREADY GOT--
I DIDN'T REALLY CARE.

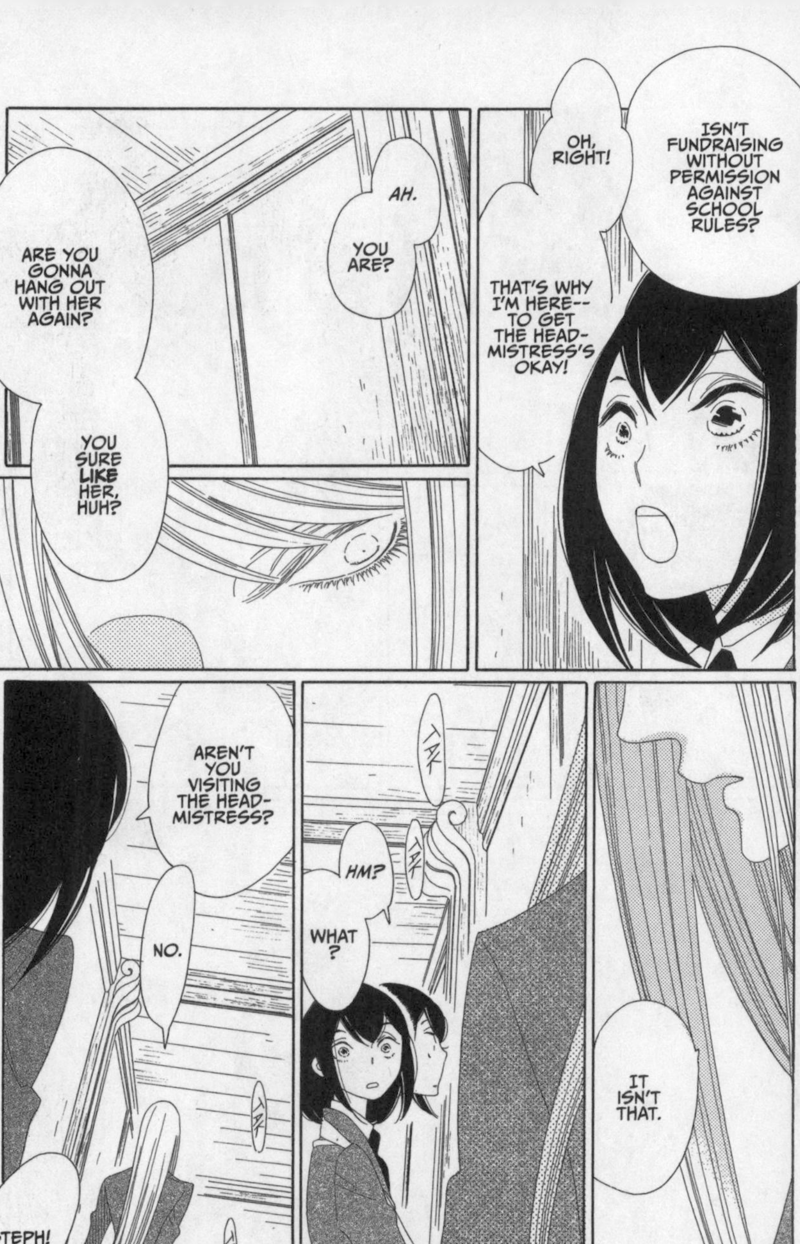
ISN'T FUNDRAISING WITHOUT PERMISSION AGAINST SCHOOL RULES?
OH, RIGHT!
THAT'S WHY I'M HERE-- TO GET THE HEAD-MISTRESS'S OKAY!
AH.
YOU ARE?
ARE YOU GONNA HANG OUT WITH HER AGAIN?
YOU SURE LIKE HER, HUH?
IT ISN'T THAT.
TAK
TAK
HM?
WHAT?
AREN'T YOU VISITING THE HEAD-MISTRESS?
NO.
TAK
TAK
STEPH!

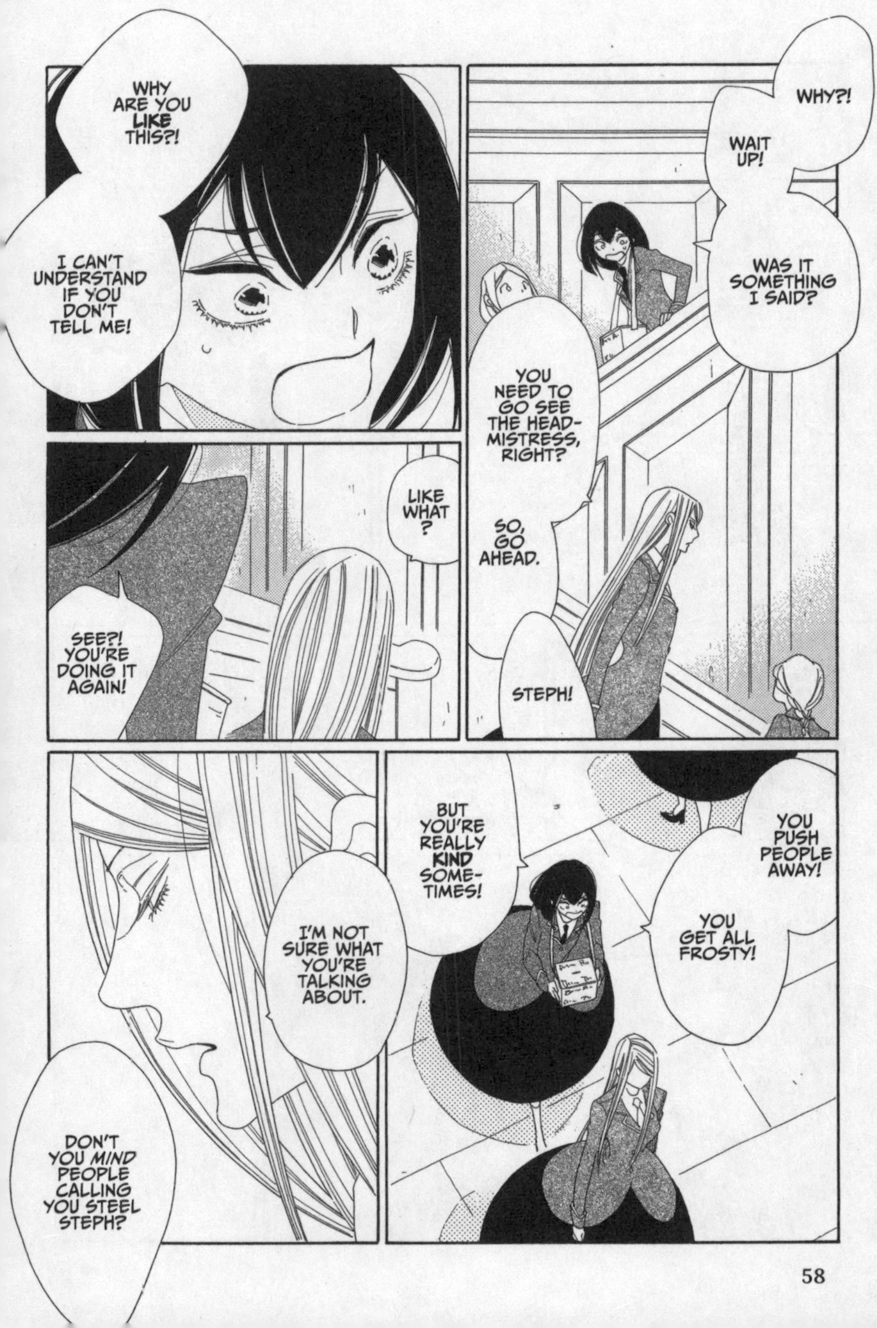
WHY?!
WAIT UP!
WAS IT SOMETHING I SAID?
YOU NEED TO GO SEE THE HEAD-MISTRESS, RIGHT?
SO, GO AHEAD.
STEPH!
WHY ARE YOU **LIKE** THIS?!
I CAN'T UNDERSTAND IF YOU DON'T TELL ME!
LIKE WHAT?
SEE?! YOU'RE DOING IT AGAIN!
YOU PUSH PEOPLE AWAY!
YOU GET ALL FROSTY!
BUT YOU'RE REALLY **KIND** SOME-TIMES!
I'M NOT SURE WHAT YOU'RE TALKING ABOUT.
DON'T YOU *MIND* PEOPLE CALLING YOU STEEL STEPH?

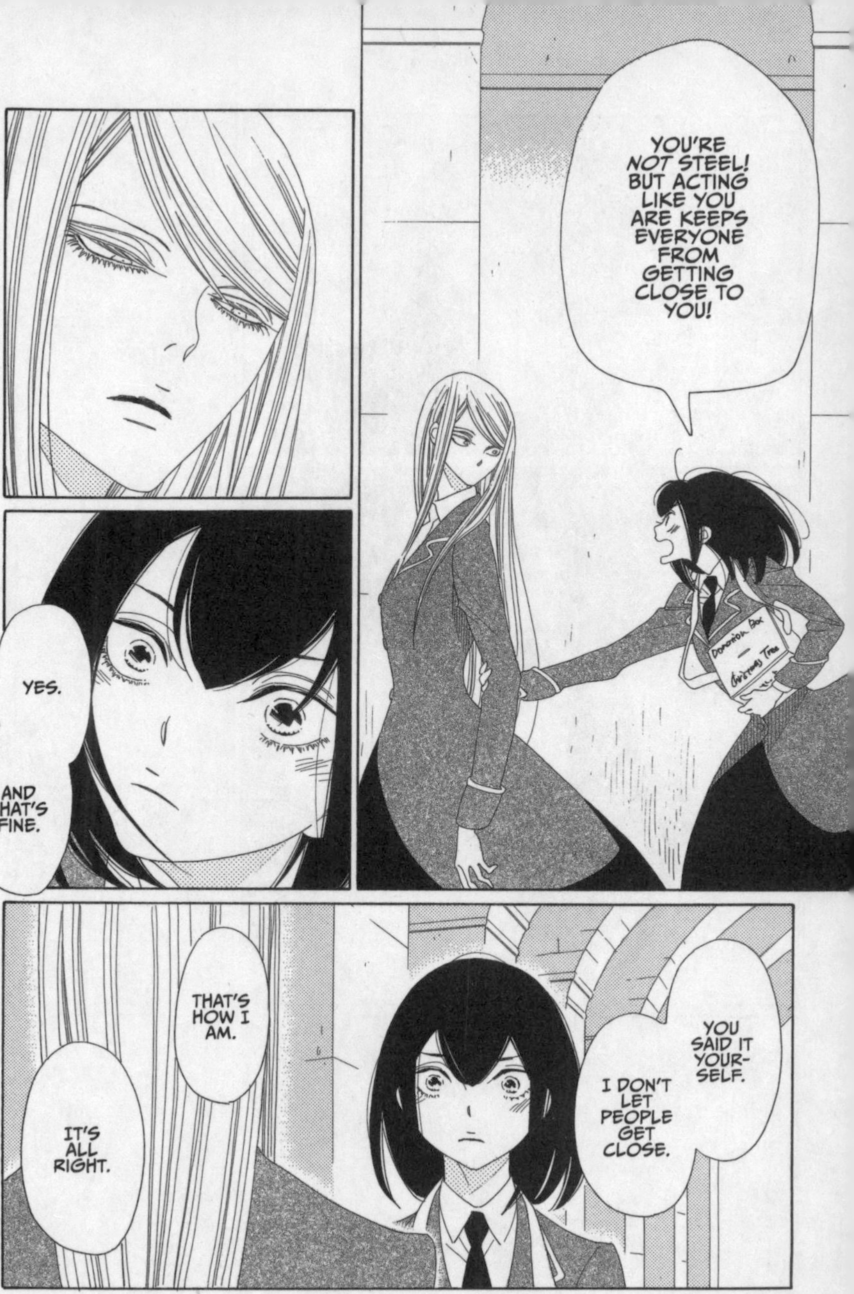
YOU'RE *NOT* STEEL! BUT ACTING LIKE YOU ARE KEEPS EVERYONE FROM GETTING CLOSE TO YOU!
YES.
AND THAT'S FINE.
YOU SAID IT YOUR-SELF.
I DON'T LET PEOPLE GET CLOSE.
THAT'S HOW I AM.
IT'S ALL RIGHT.

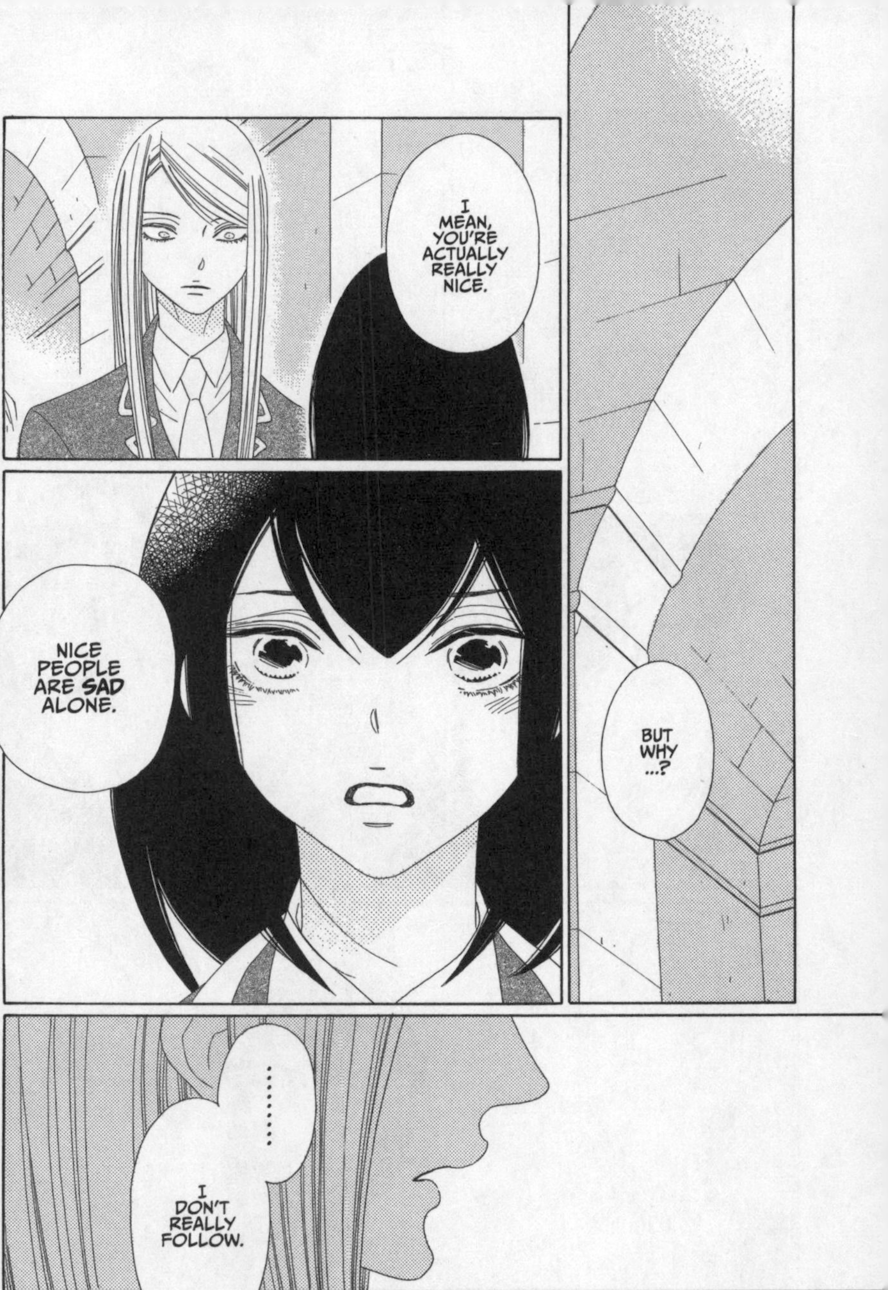
BUT WHY ...?
I MEAN, YOU'RE ACTUALLY REALLY NICE.
NICE PEOPLE ARE SAD ALONE.
......
I DON'T REALLY FOLLOW.

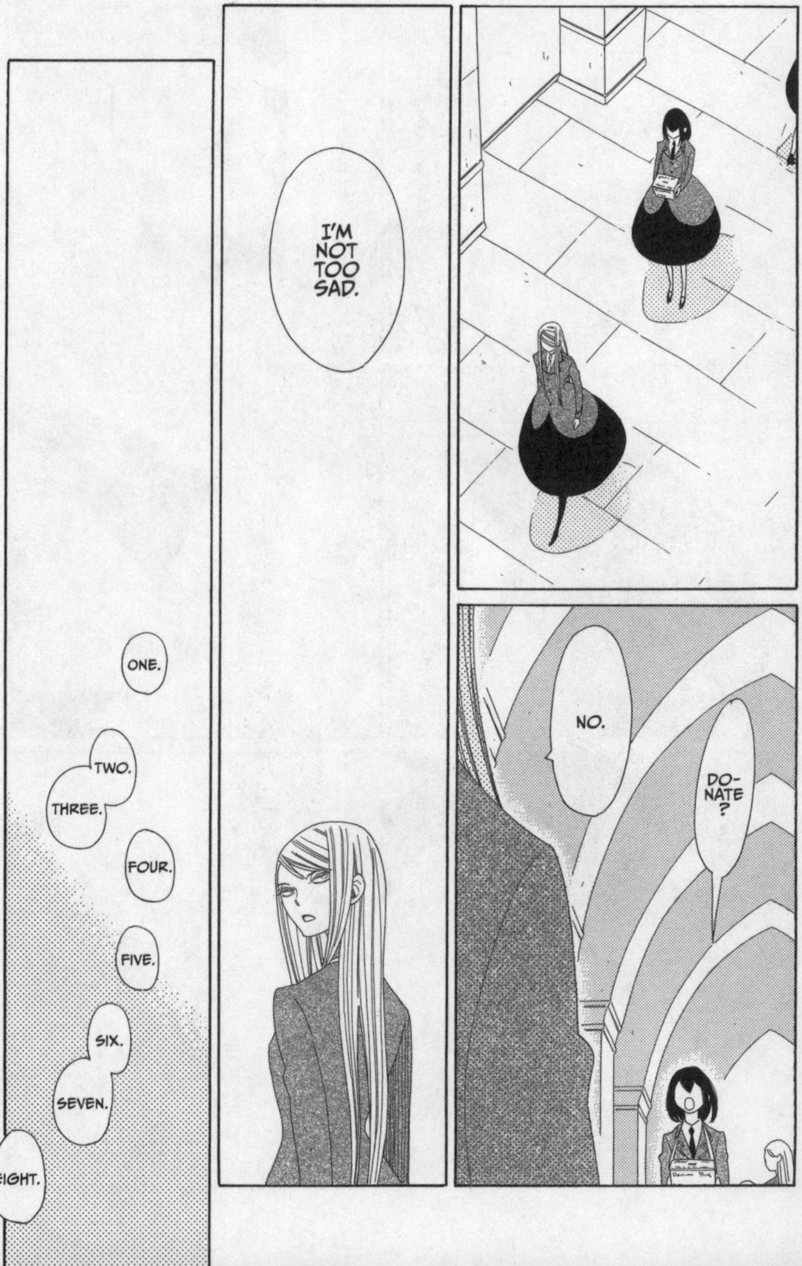
DONATE?
NO.
I'M NOT TOO SAD.
ONE.
TWO.
THREE.
FOUR.
FIVE.
SIX.
SEVEN.
EIGHT.

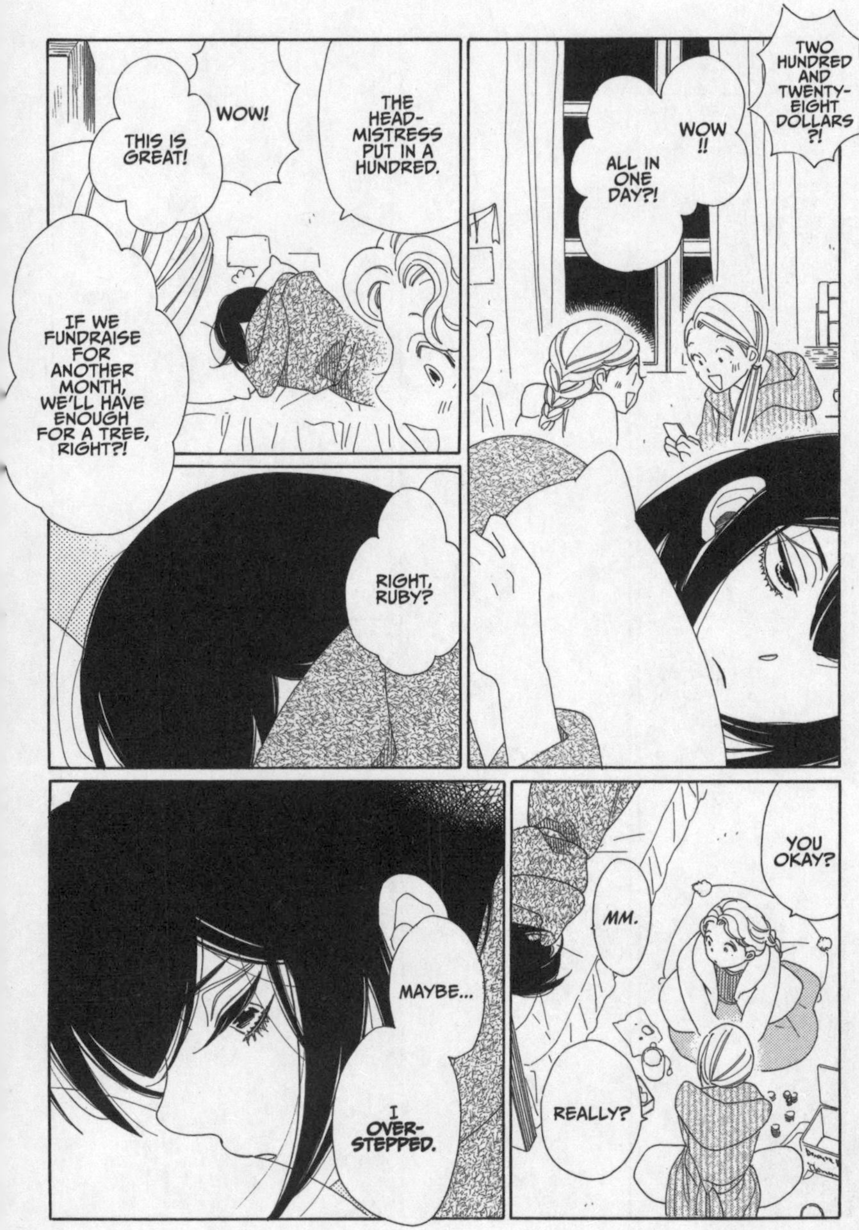
TWO HUNDRED AND TWENTY-EIGHT DOLLARS?!
WOW!!
ALL IN ONE DAY?!
THE HEAD-MISTRESS PUT IN A HUNDRED.
WOW!
THIS IS GREAT!
IF WE FUNDRAISE FOR ANOTHER MONTH, WE'LL HAVE ENOUGH FOR A TREE, RIGHT?!
RIGHT, RUBY?
YOU OKAY?
MM.
REALLY?
MAYBE...
I OVER-STEPPED.

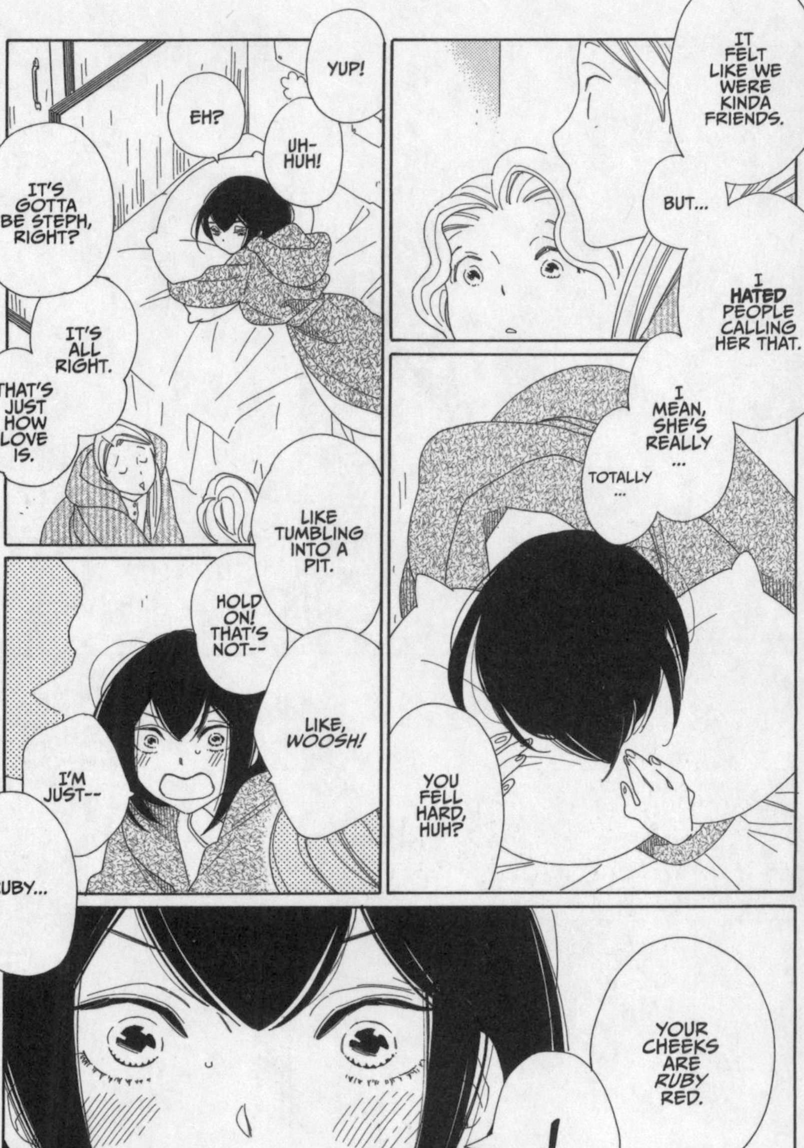
IT FELT LIKE WE WERE KINDA FRIENDS.
BUT...
I HATED PEOPLE CALLING HER THAT.
YUP!
EH?
UH-HUH!
IT'S GOTTA BE STEPH, RIGHT?
IT'S ALL RIGHT.
THAT'S JUST HOW LOVE IS.
I MEAN, SHE'S REALLY ...
TOTALLY ...
YOU FELL HARD, HUH?
LIKE TUMBLING INTO A PIT.
HOLD ON! THAT'S NOT--
LIKE, WOOSH!
I'M JUST--
RUBY...
YOUR CHEEKS ARE RUBY RED.
!

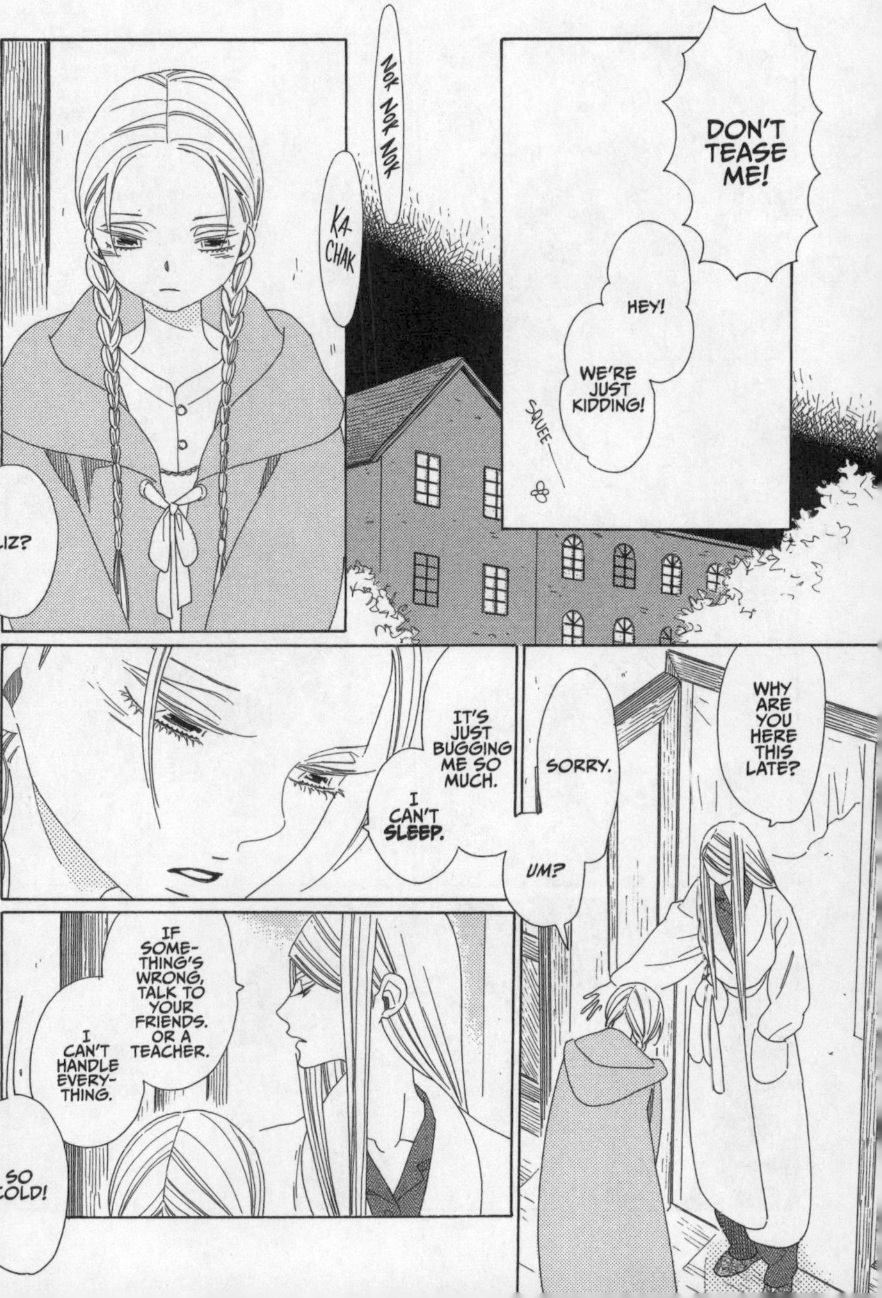
DON'T TEASE ME!
HEY!
WE'RE JUST KIDDING!
SQUEE—
NOK NOK NOK
KA-CHAK
LIZ?
WHY ARE YOU HERE THIS LATE?
SORRY.
UM?
IT'S JUST BUGGING ME SO MUCH.
I CAN'T SLEEP.
IF SOME-THING'S WRONG, TALK TO YOUR FRIENDS. OR A TEACHER.
I CAN'T HANDLE EVERY-THING.
SO COLD!

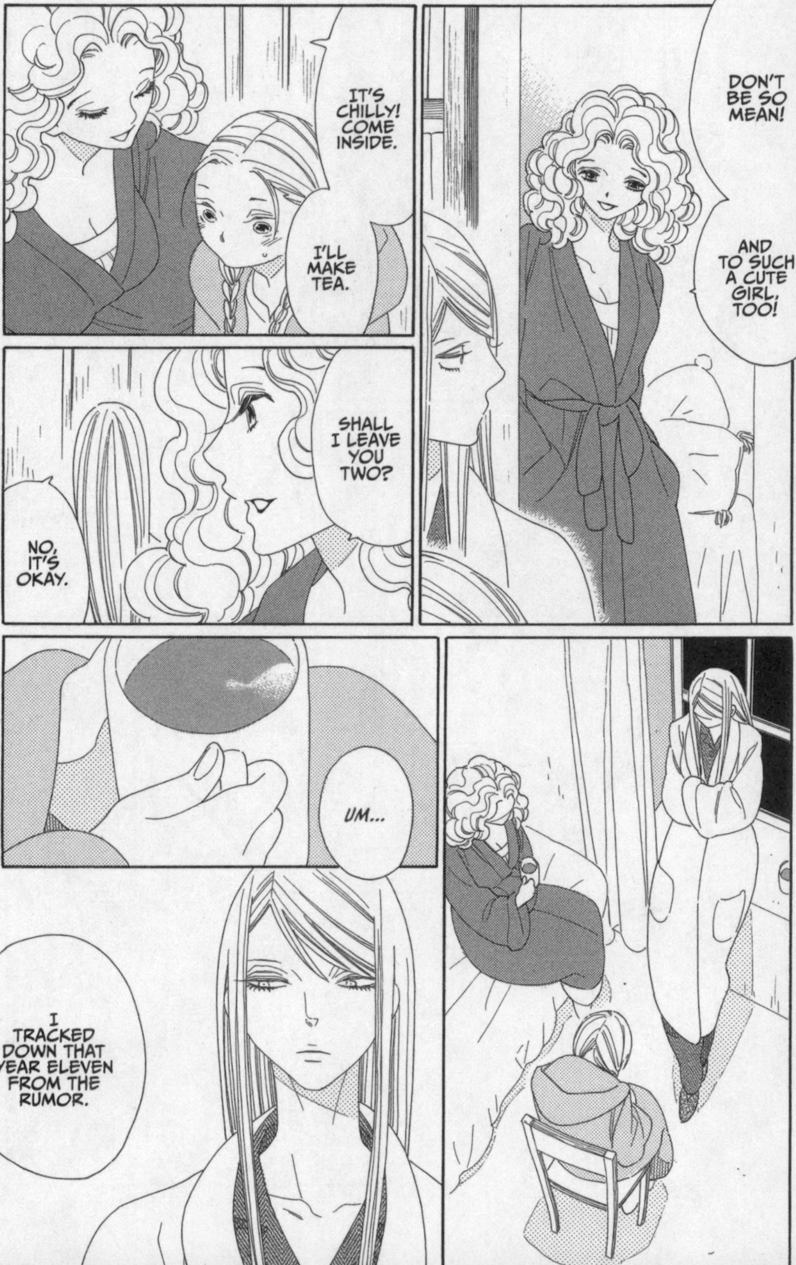
DON'T BE SO MEAN!
AND TO SUCH A CUTE GIRL, TOO!
IT'S CHILLY! COME INSIDE.
I'LL MAKE TEA.
SHALL I LEAVE YOU TWO?
NO, IT'S OKAY.
UM...
I TRACKED DOWN THAT YEAR ELEVEN FROM THE RUMOR.

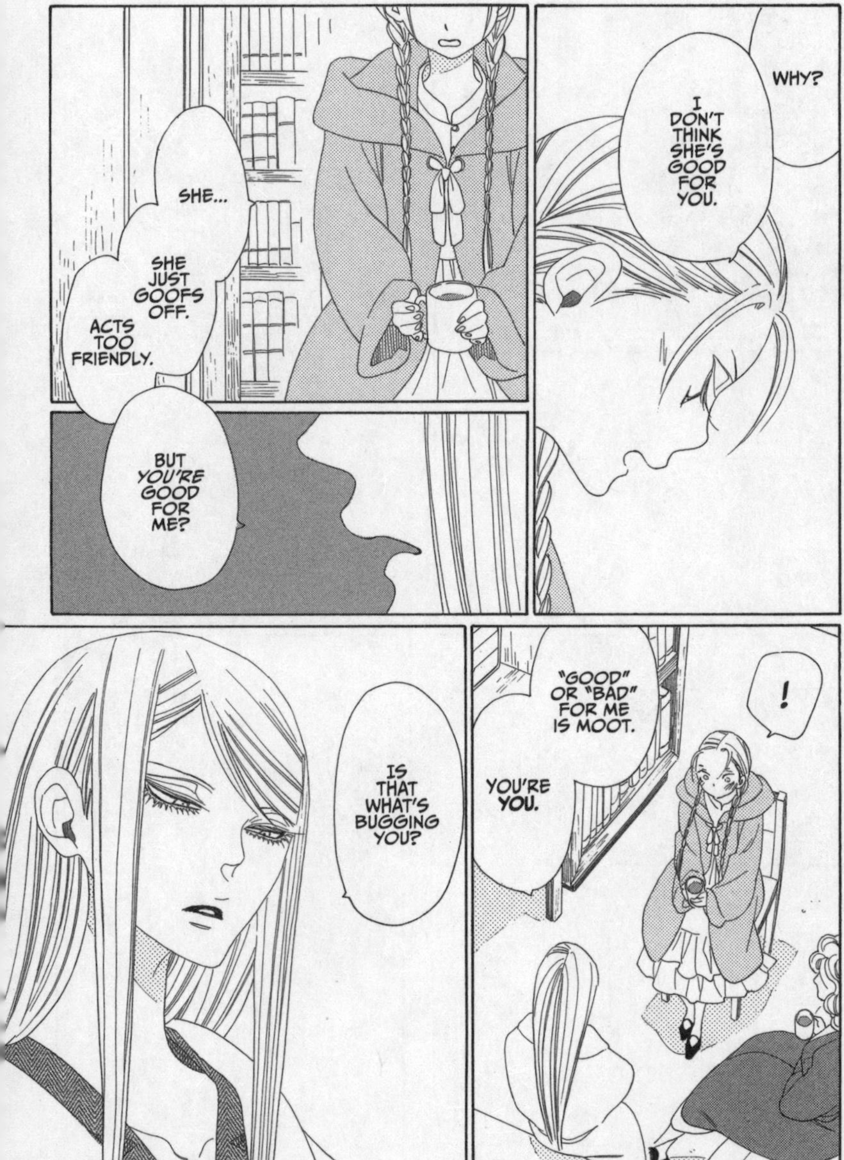
WHY?
I DON'T THINK SHE'S GOOD FOR YOU.
SHE...
SHE JUST GOOFS OFF.
ACTS TOO FRIENDLY.
BUT *YOU'RE* GOOD FOR ME?
!
"GOOD" OR "BAD" FOR ME IS MOOT.
YOU'RE **YOU.**
IS THAT WHAT'S BUGGING YOU?

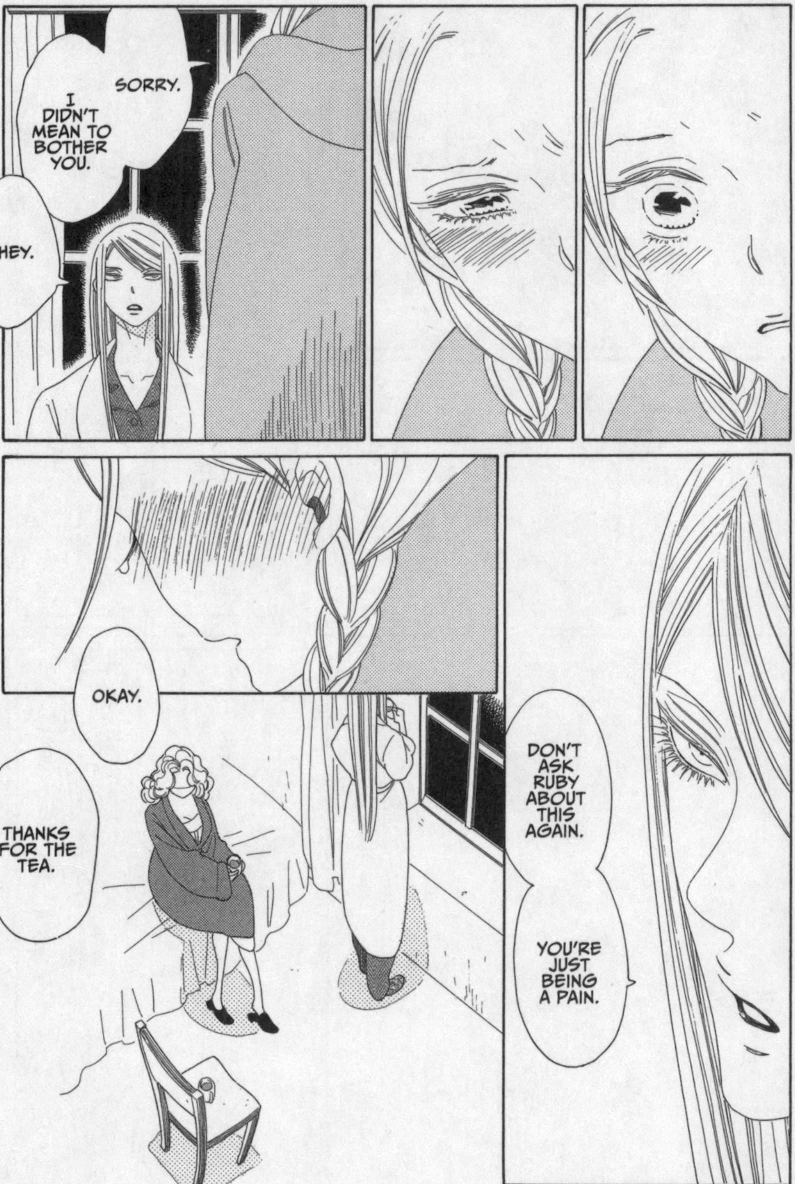
SORRY. I DIDN'T MEAN TO BOTHER YOU.
HEY.
DON'T ASK RUBY ABOUT THIS AGAIN.
YOU'RE JUST BEING A PAIN.
OKAY.
THANKS FOR THE TEA.

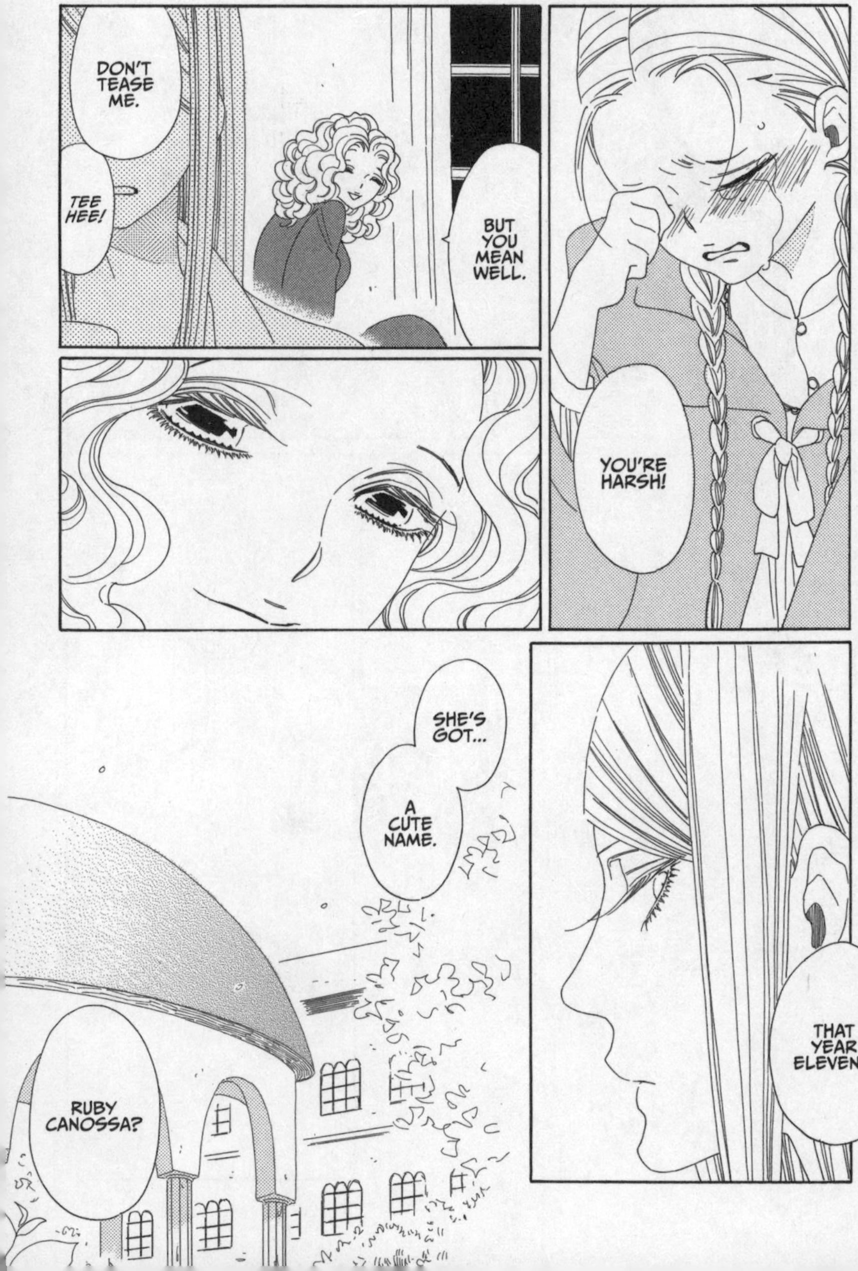
YOU'RE HARSH!
BUT YOU MEAN WELL.
DON'T TEASE ME.
TEE HEE!
THAT YEAR ELEVEN...
SHE'S GOT...
A CUTE NAME.
RUBY CANOSSA?

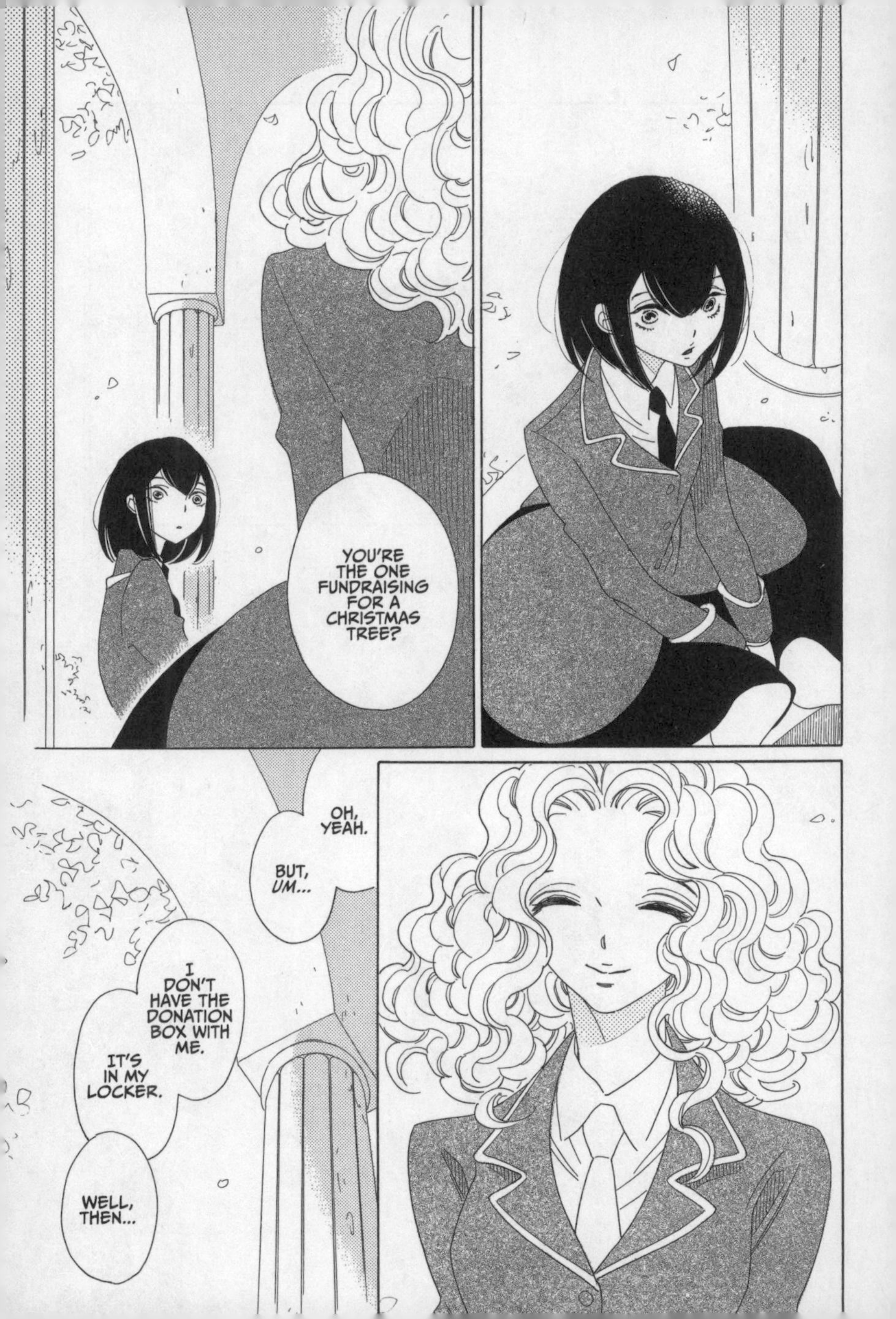
YOU'RE THE ONE FUNDRAISING FOR A CHRISTMAS TREE?
OH, YEAH.
BUT, UM...
I DON'T HAVE THE DONATION BOX WITH ME.
IT'S IN MY LOCKER.
WELL, THEN...

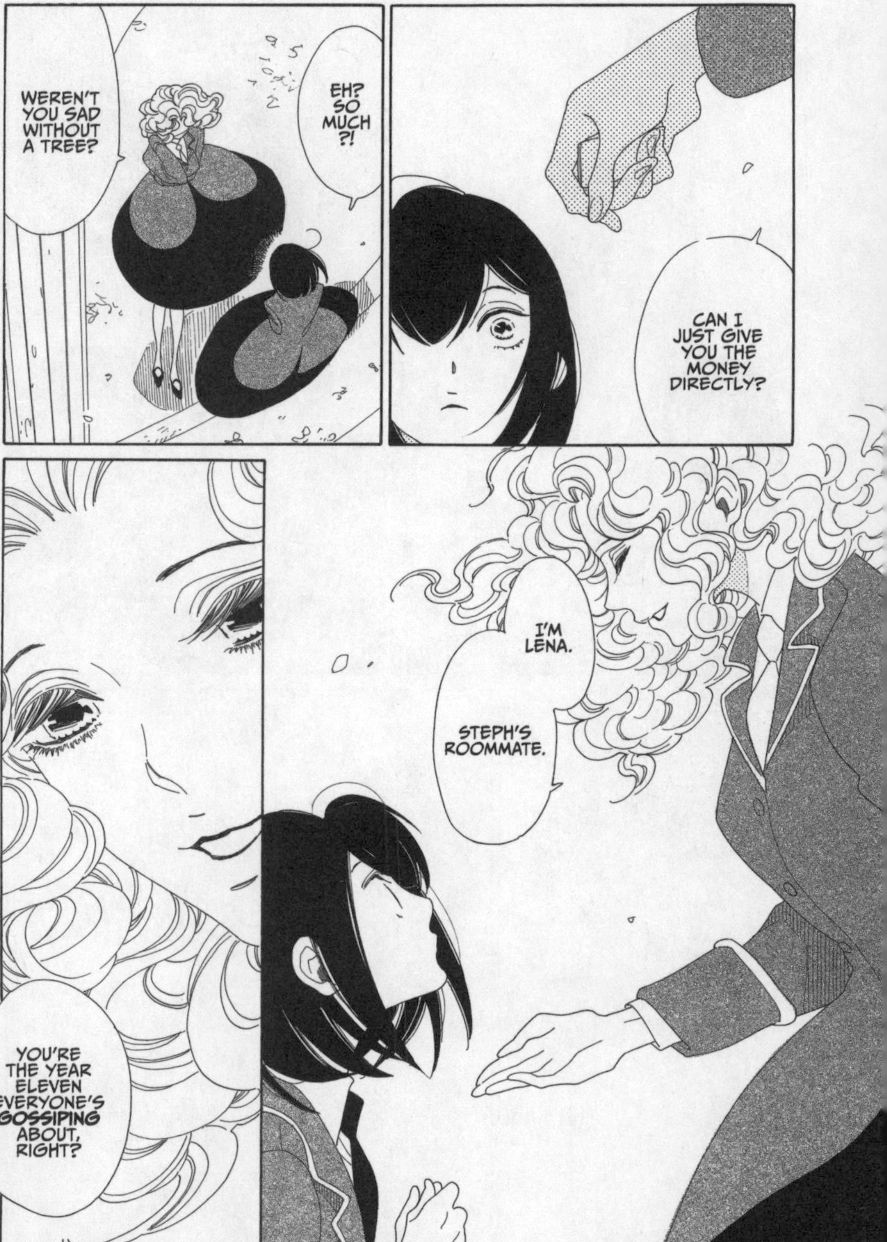
CAN I JUST GIVE YOU THE MONEY DIRECTLY?
EH? SO MUCH?!
WEREN'T YOU SAD WITHOUT A TREE?
I'M LENA.
STEPH'S ROOMMATE.
YOU'RE THE YEAR ELEVEN EVERYONE'S **GOSSIPING** ABOUT, RIGHT?

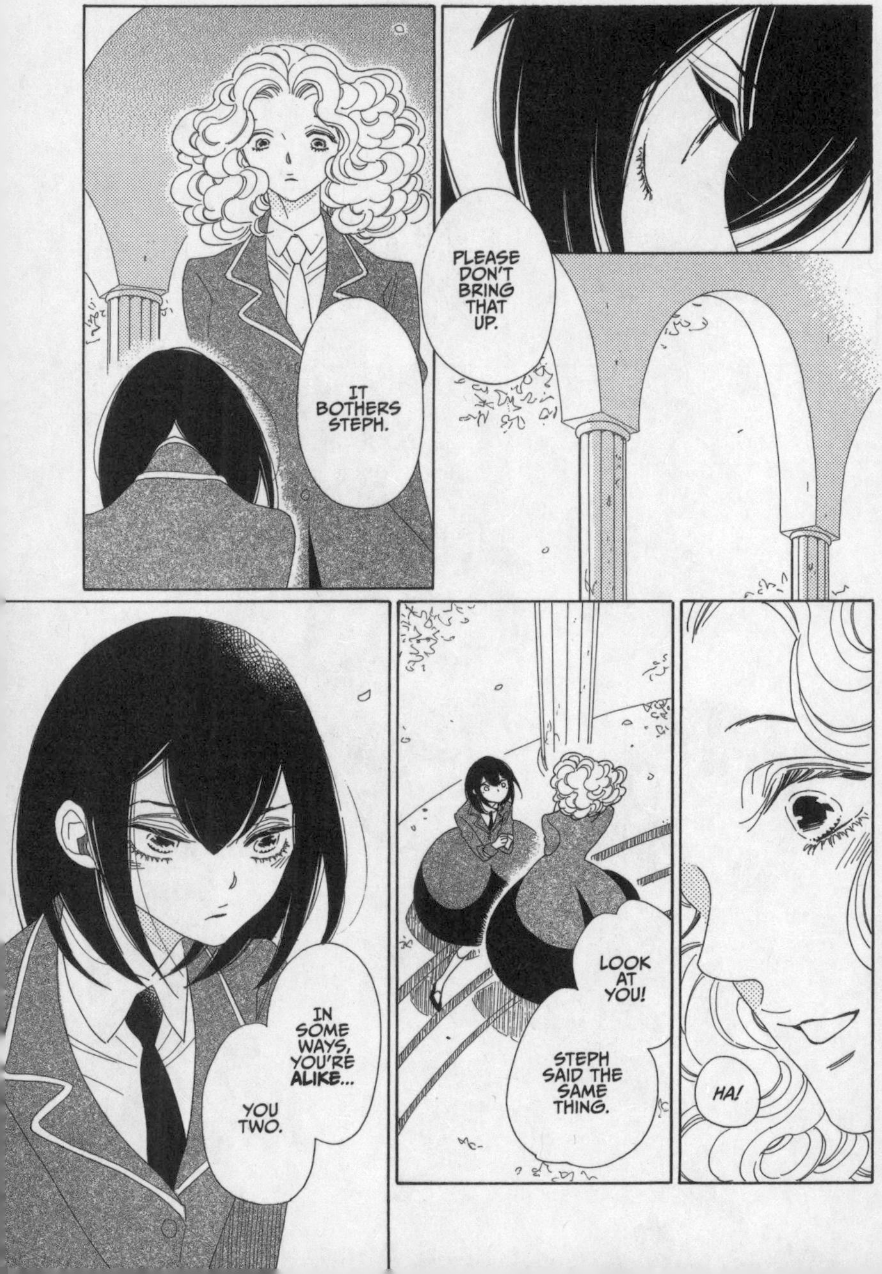
PLEASE DON'T BRING THAT UP.
IT BOTHERS STEPH.
HA!
LOOK AT YOU!
STEPH SAID THE SAME THING.
IN SOME WAYS, YOU'RE ALIKE...
YOU TWO.

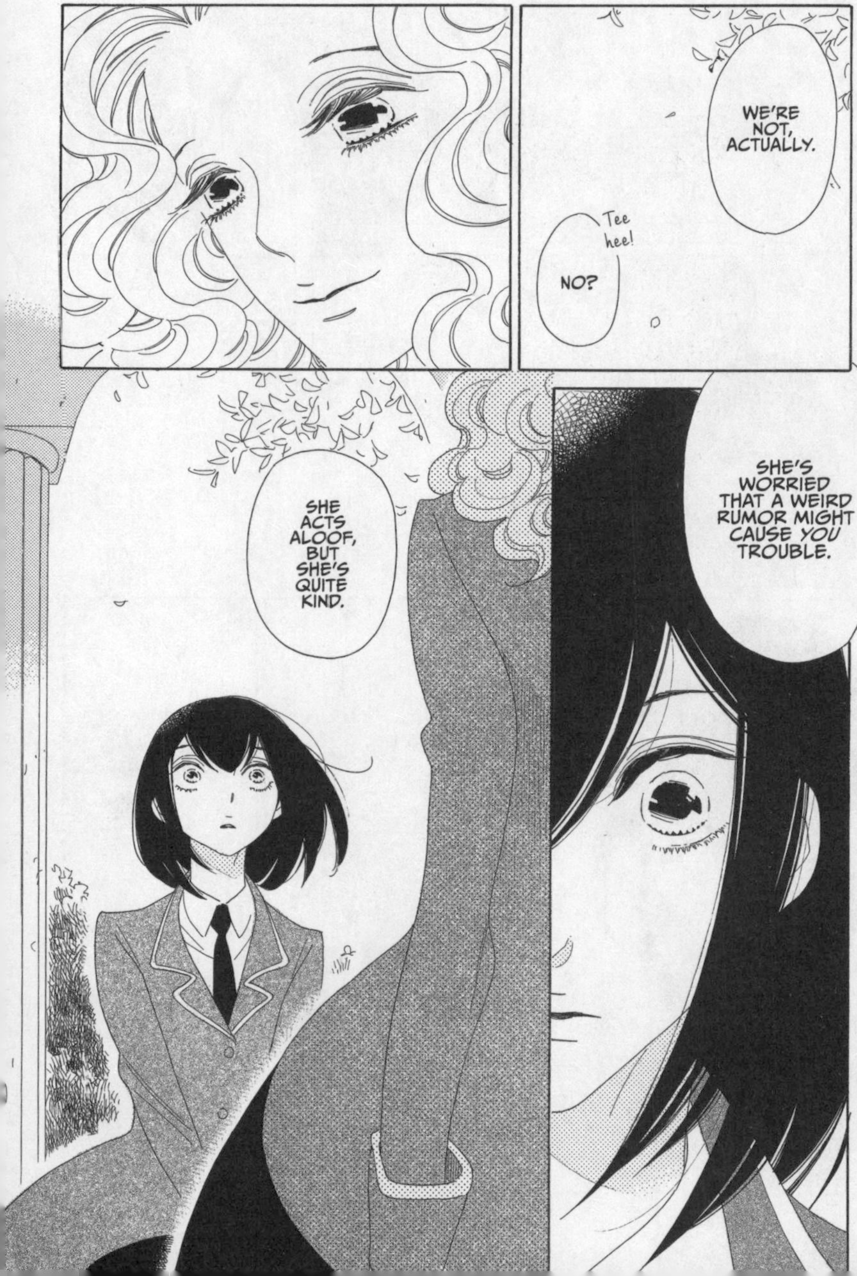
WE'RE NOT, ACTUALLY.
Tee hee!
NO?
SHE'S WORRIED THAT A WEIRD RUMOR MIGHT CAUSE *YOU* TROUBLE.
SHE ACTS ALOOF, BUT SHE'S QUITE KIND.

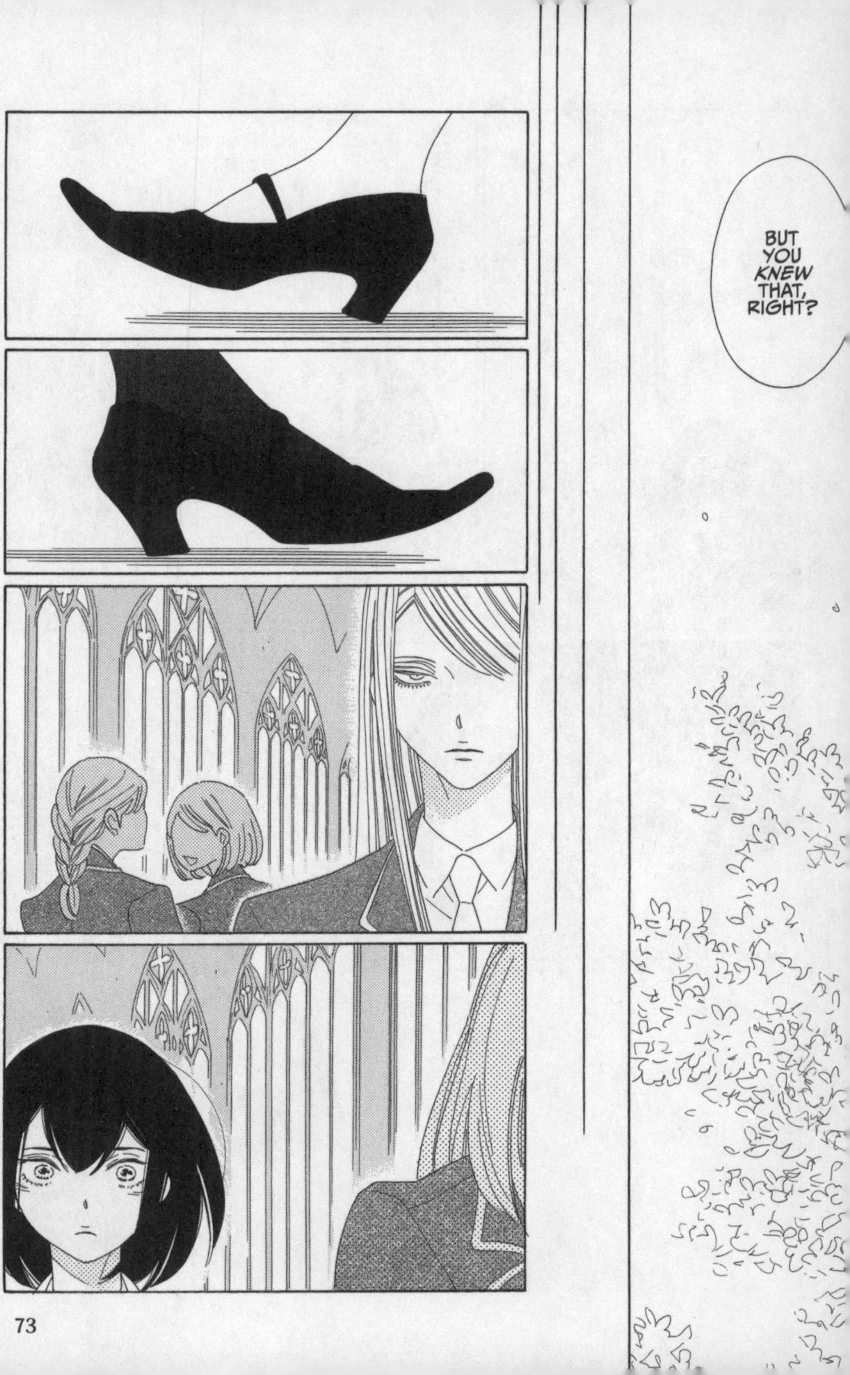
BUT YOU *KNEW* THAT, RIGHT?

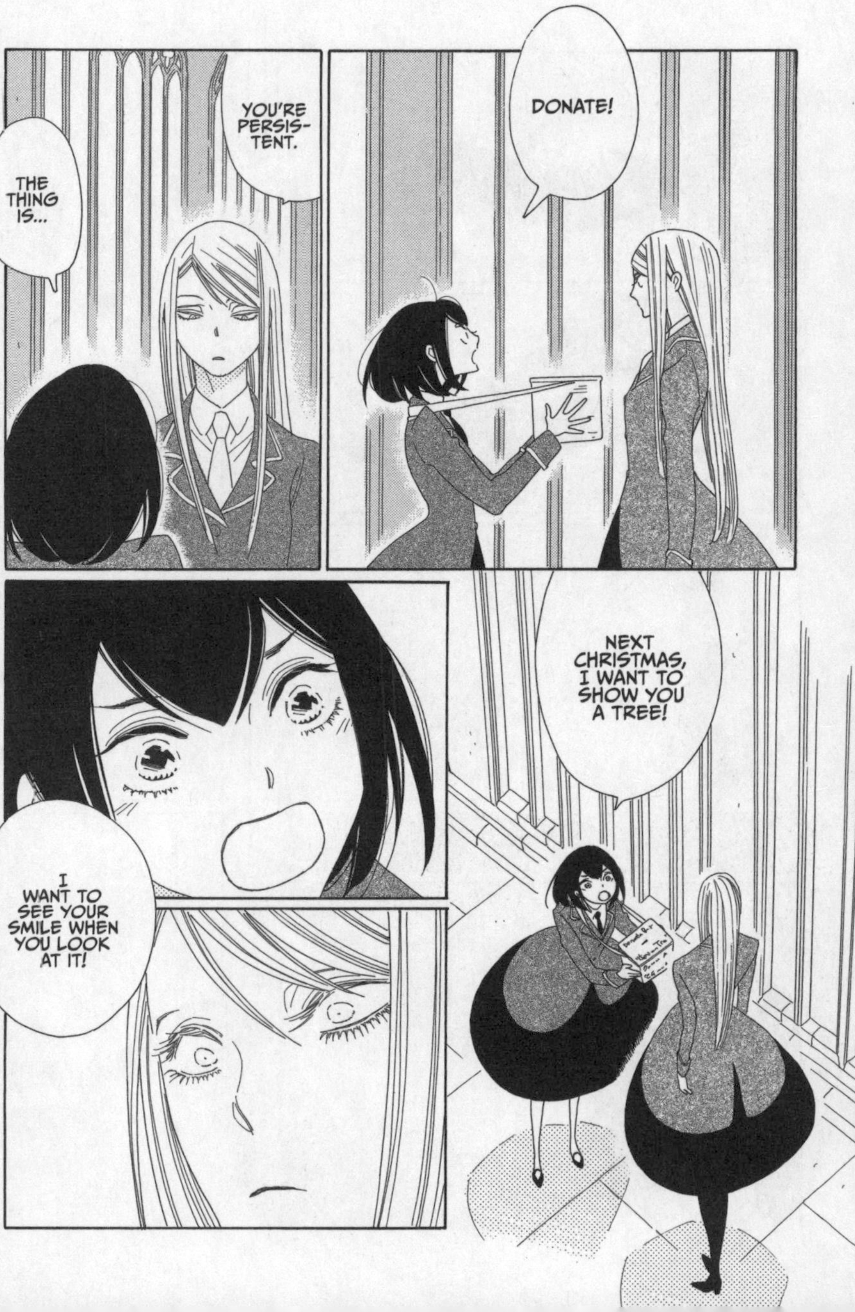
DONATE!
YOU'RE PERSIS-TENT.
THE THING IS...
NEXT CHRISTMAS, I WANT TO SHOW YOU A TREE!
I WANT TO SEE YOUR SMILE WHEN YOU LOOK AT IT!

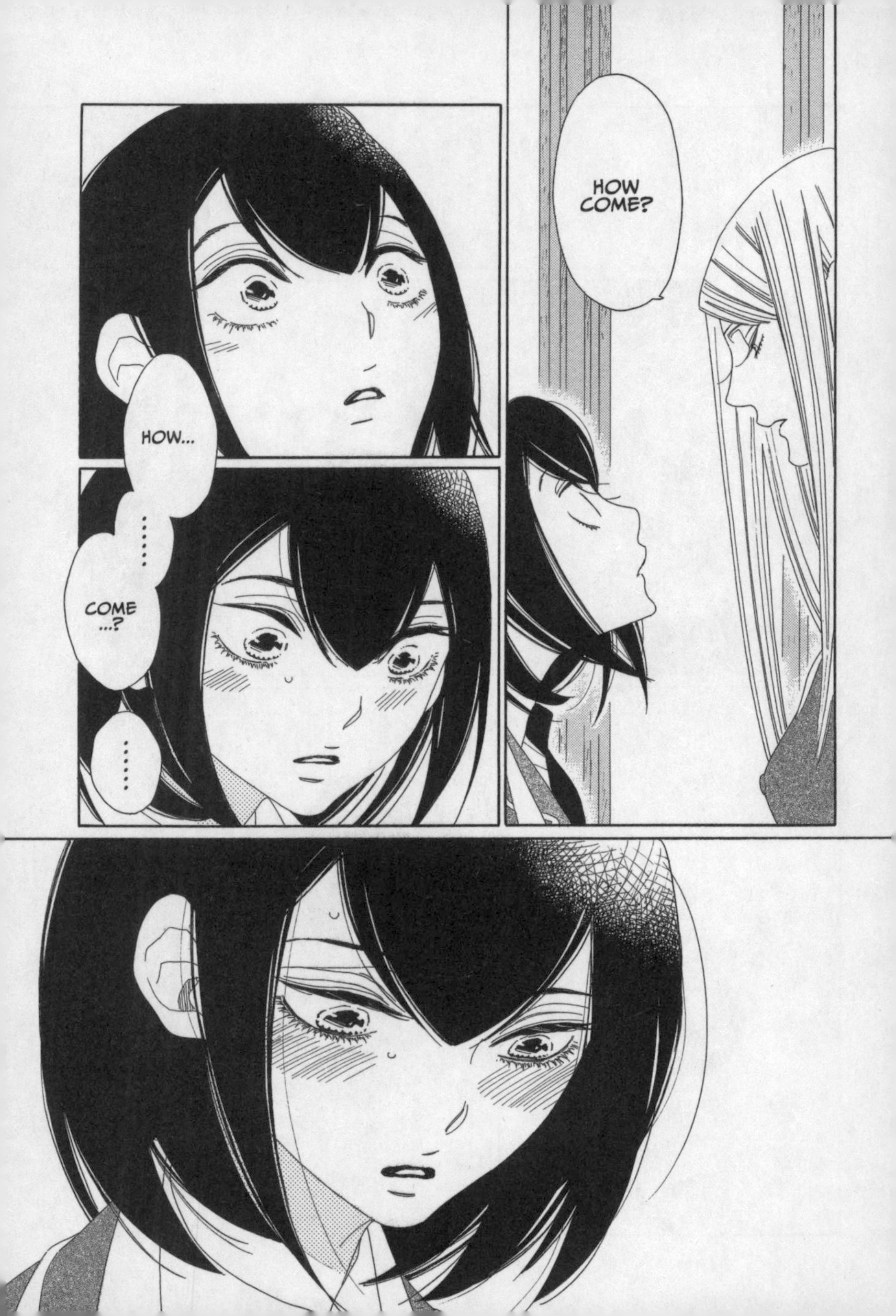
HOW COME?
HOW...
......
COME ...?
......

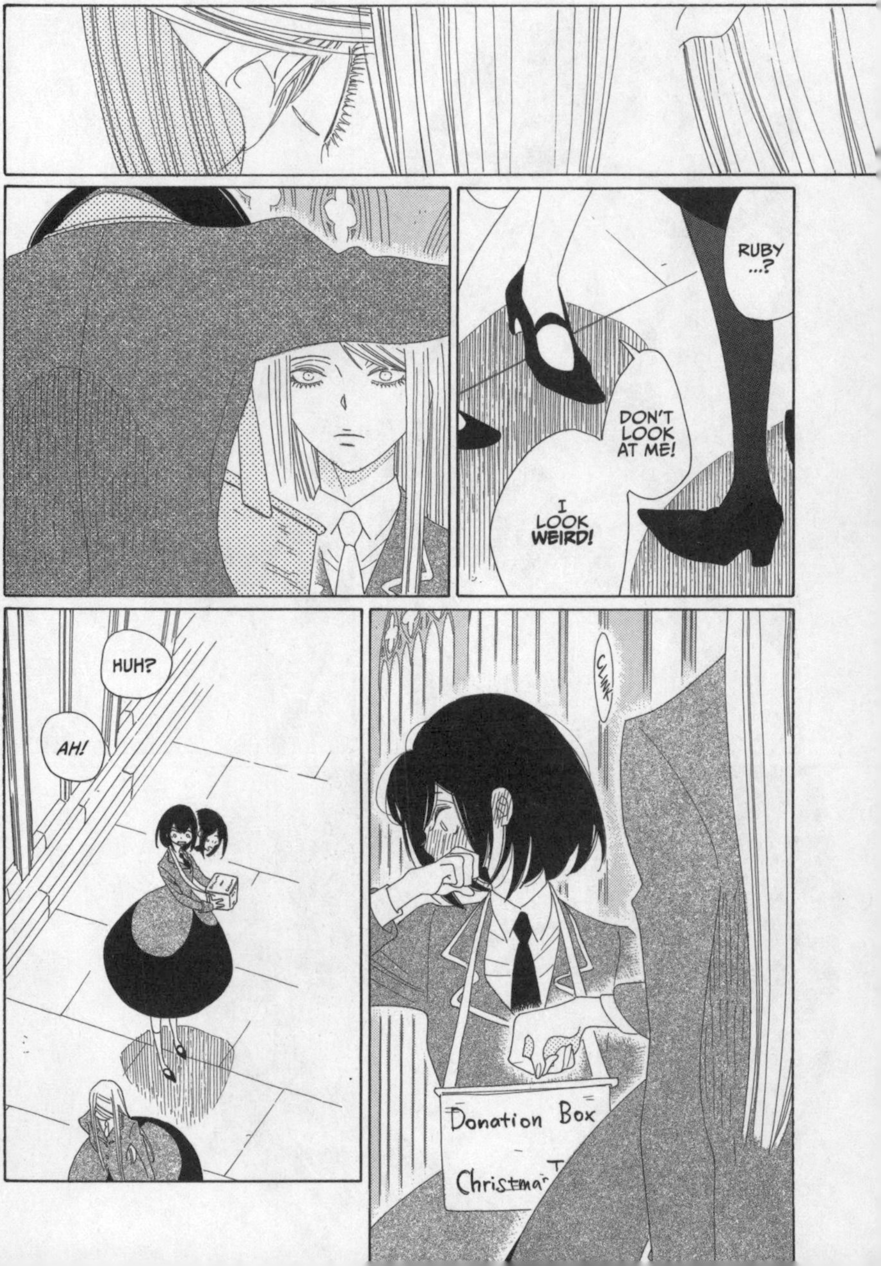
RUBY ...?
DON'T LOOK AT ME!
I LOOK WEIRD!
CLINK
Donation Box
HUH?
AH!

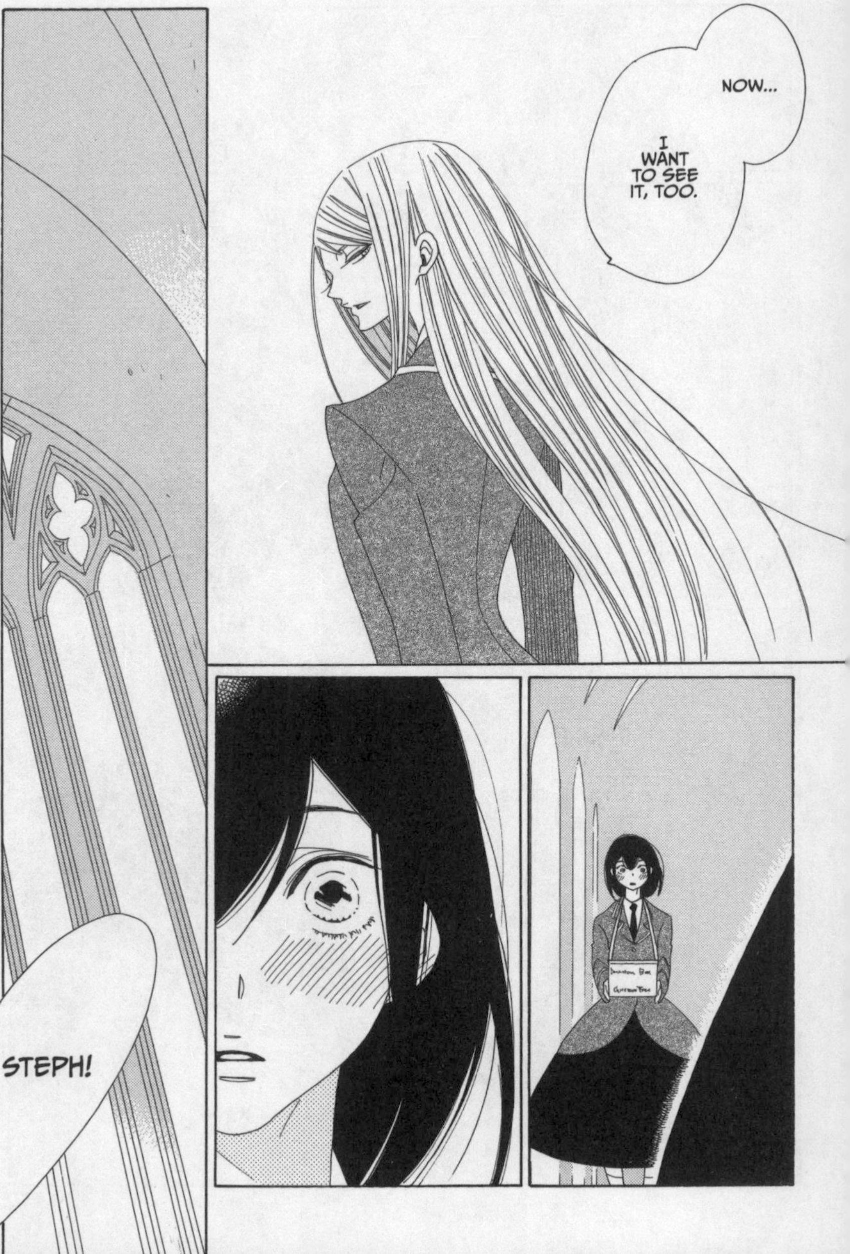
NOW...
I WANT TO SEE IT, TOO.
STEPH!

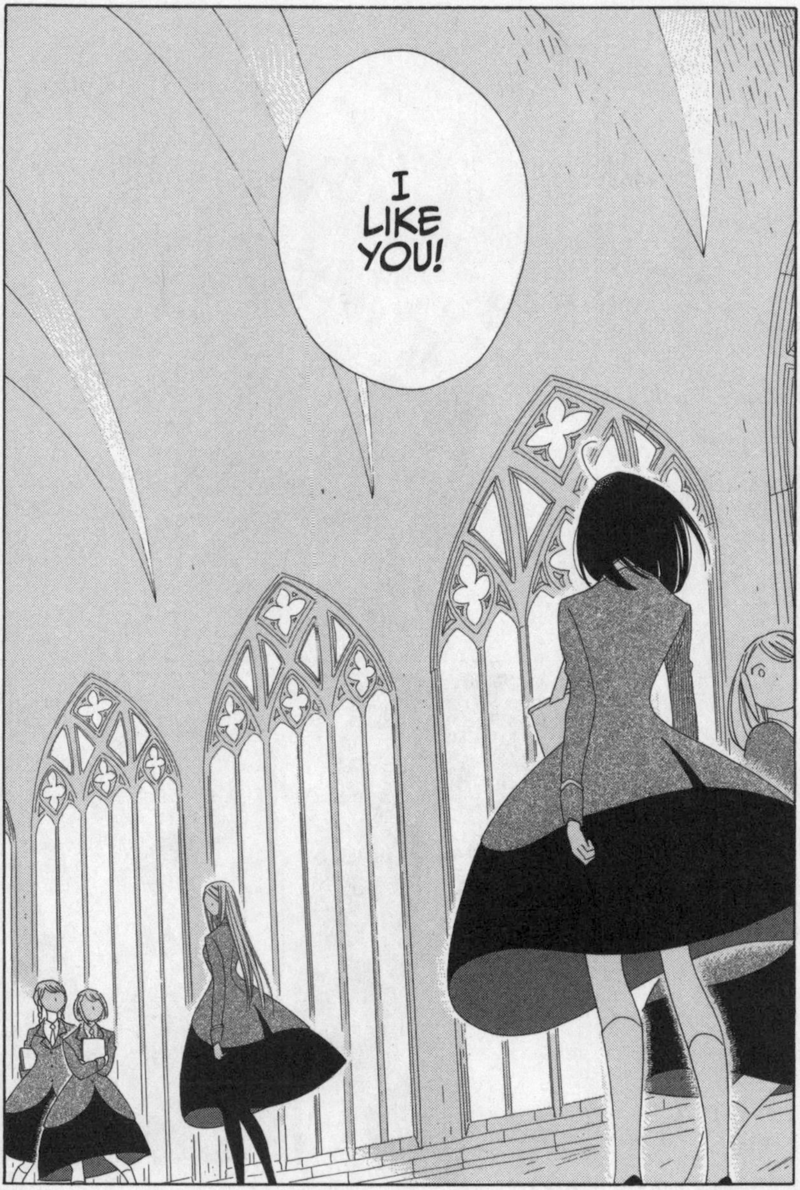
I LIKE YOU!

メジロバナの咲く

メジロバナの咲く

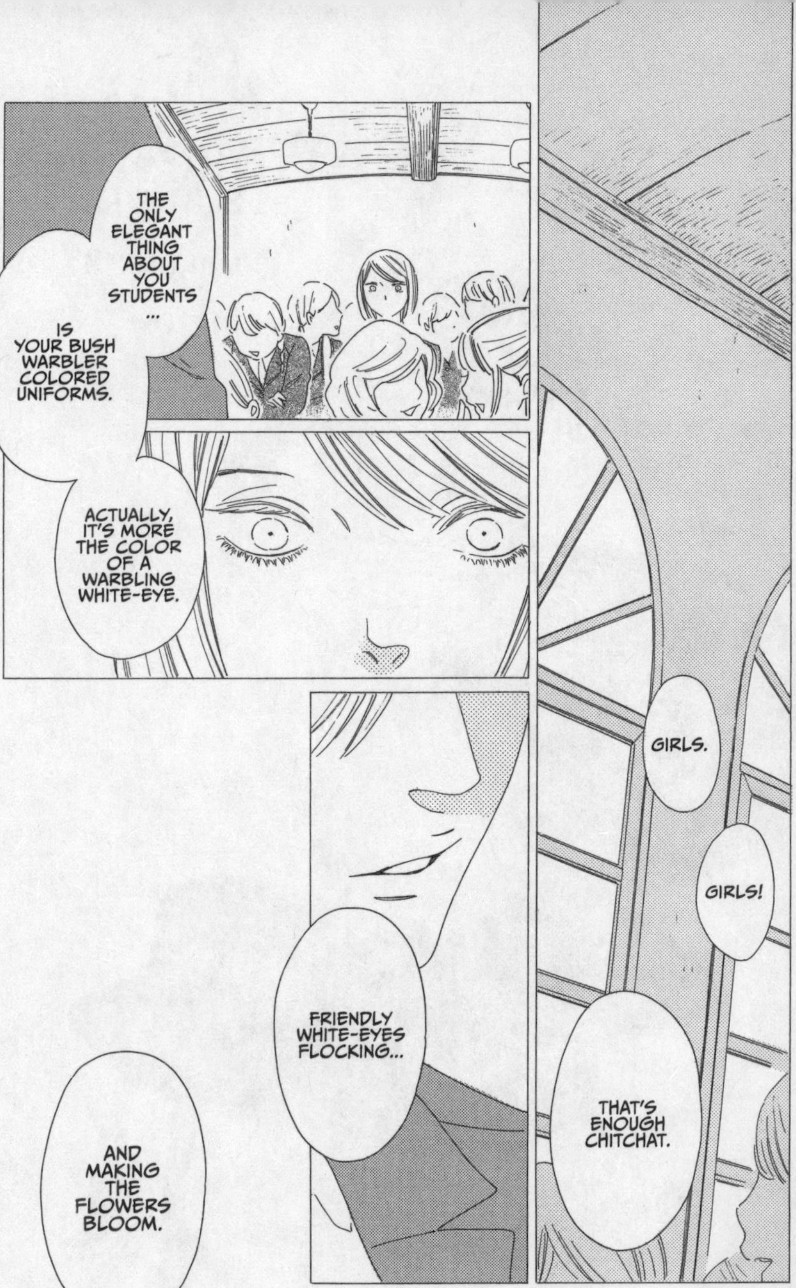
GIRLS.
GIRLS!
THAT'S ENOUGH CHITCHAT.
THE ONLY ELEGANT THING ABOUT YOU STUDENTS ...
IS YOUR BUSH WARBLER COLORED UNIFORMS.
ACTUALLY, IT'S MORE THE COLOR OF A WARBLING WHITE-EYE.
FRIENDLY WHITE-EYES FLOCKING...
AND MAKING THE FLOWERS BLOOM.

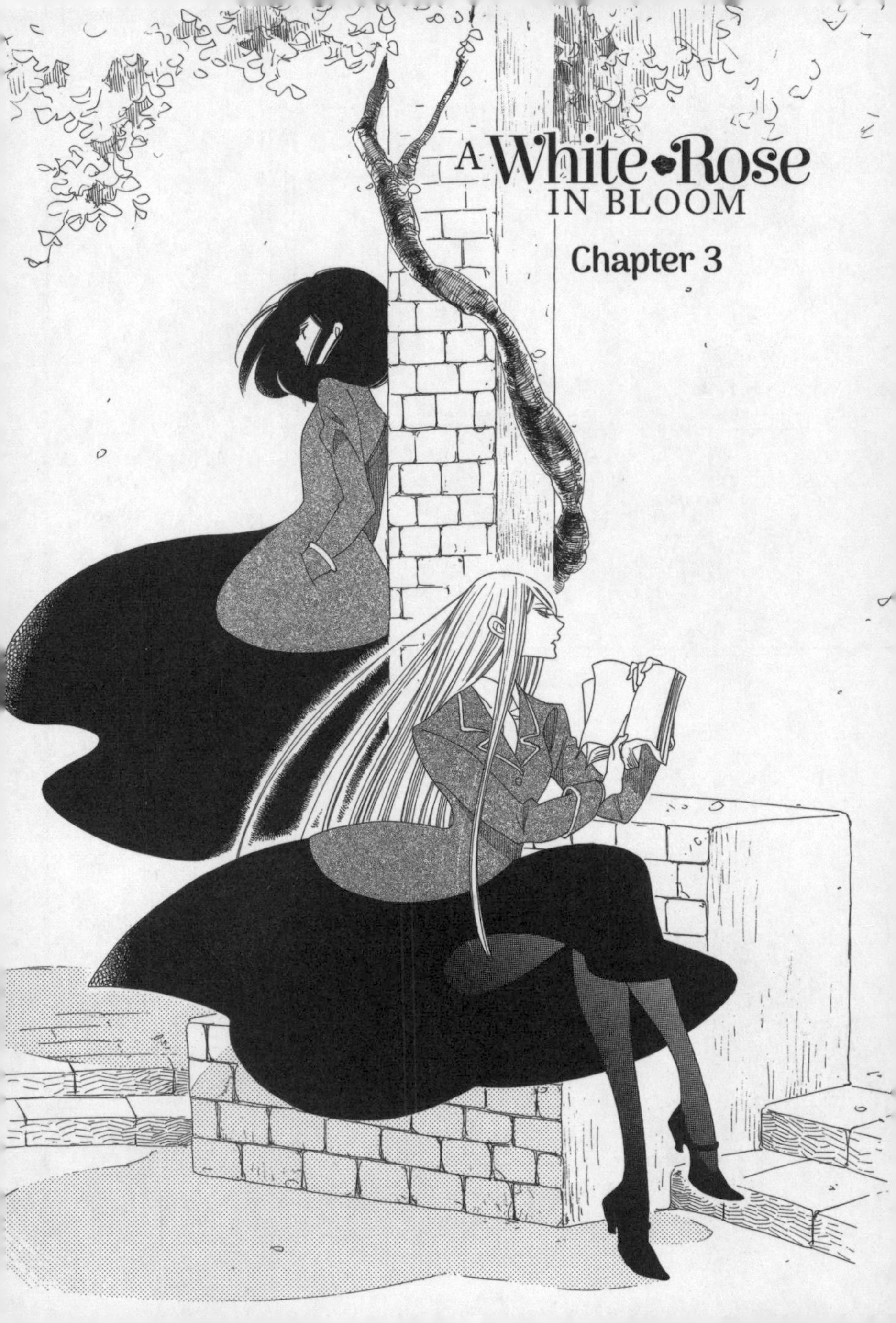
A White Rose
IN BLOOM
Chapter 3

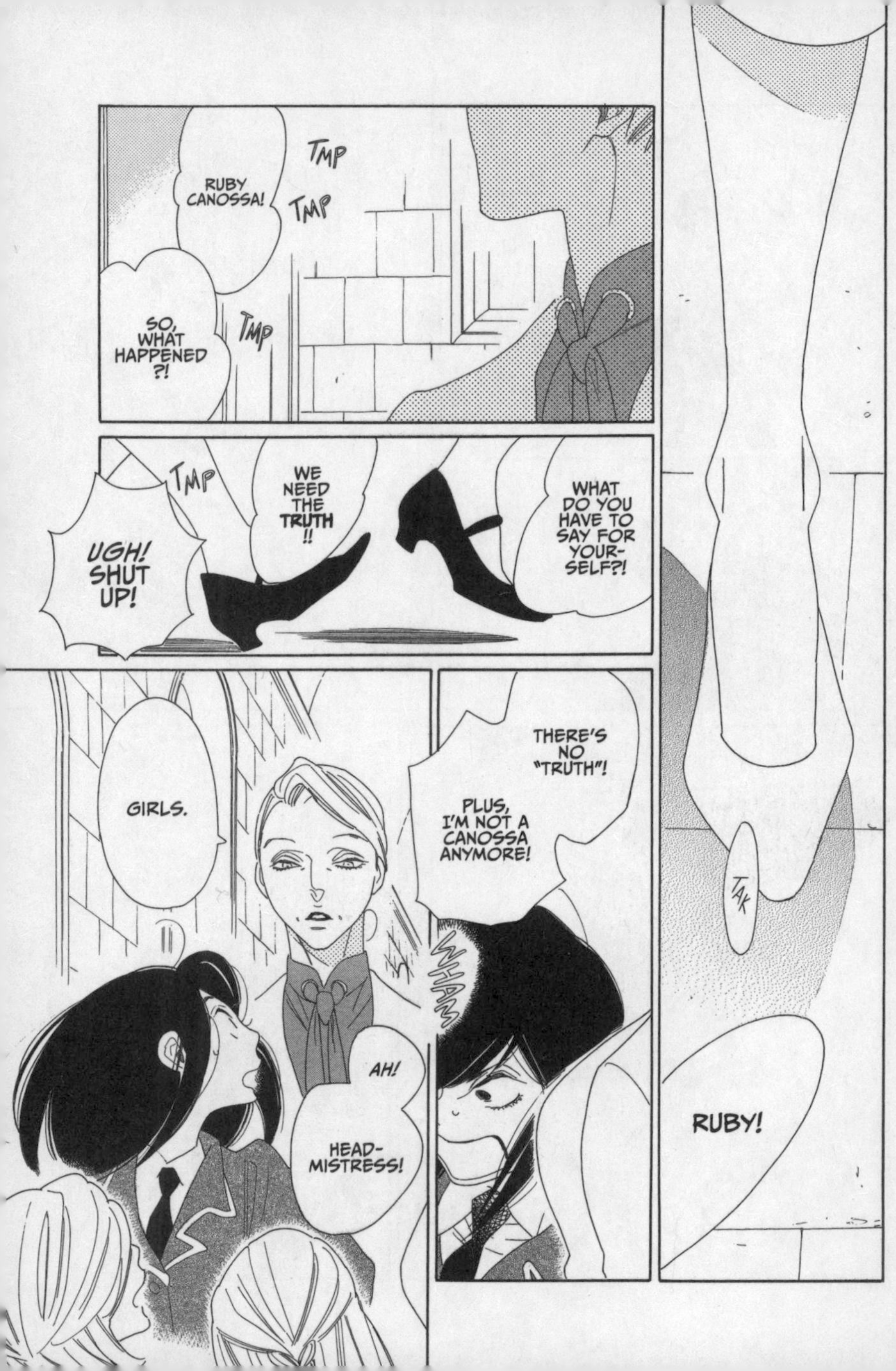
TAK
RUBY!
RUBY CANOSSA!
TMP
TMP
SO, WHAT HAPPENED?!
TMP
WHAT DO YOU HAVE TO SAY FOR YOURSELF?!
WE NEED THE TRUTH!!
TMP
UGH! SHUT UP!
THERE'S NO "TRUTH"!
PLUS, I'M NOT A CANOSSA ANYMORE!
WHAM
GIRLS.
AH!
HEADMISTRESS!

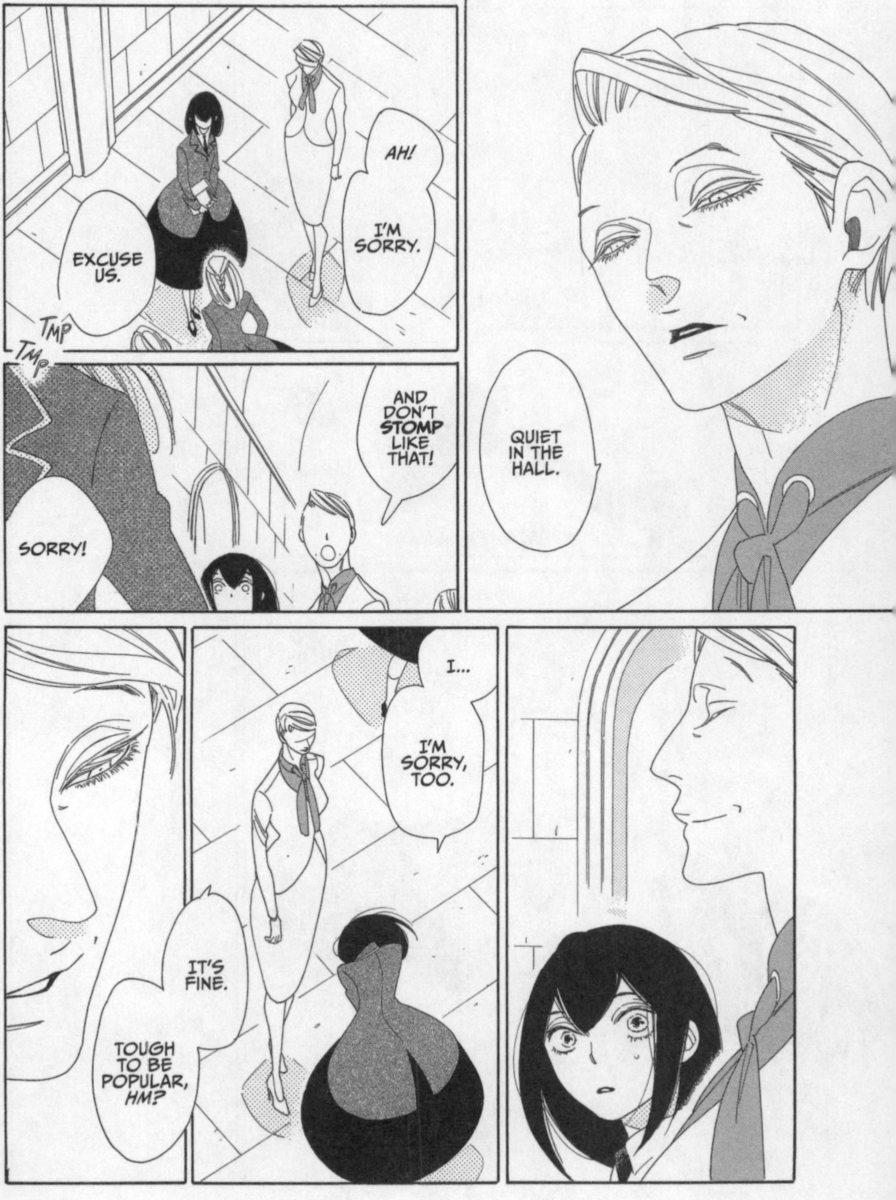
QUIET IN THE HALL.
AH!
I'M SORRY.
EXCUSE US.
TMP
TMP
AND DON'T STOMP LIKE THAT!
SORRY!
I...
I'M SORRY, TOO.
IT'S FINE.
TOUGH TO BE POPULAR, HM?

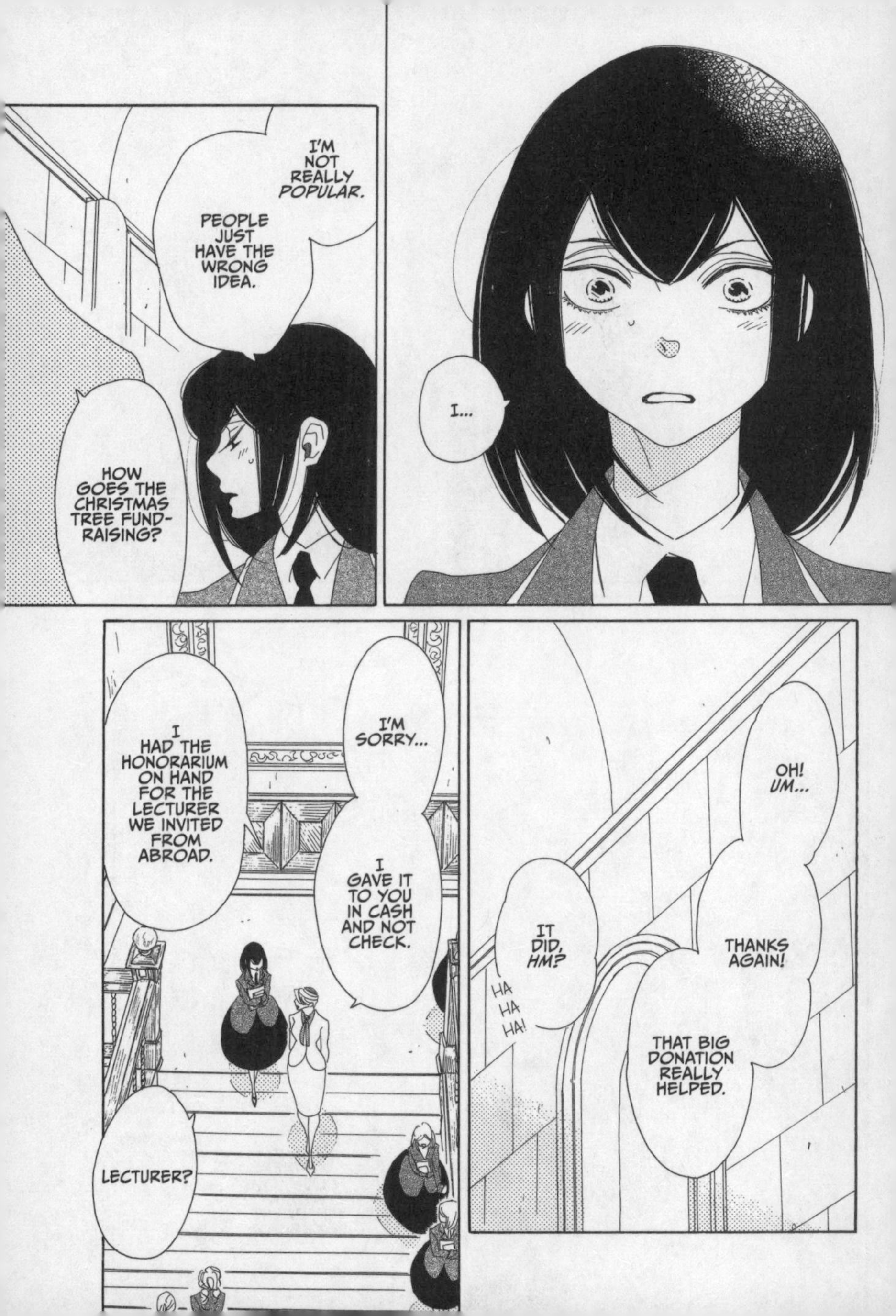
I...
I'M NOT REALLY POPULAR.
PEOPLE JUST HAVE THE WRONG IDEA.
HOW GOES THE CHRISTMAS TREE FUND-RAISING?
OH! UM...
THANKS AGAIN!
THAT BIG DONATION REALLY HELPED.
IT DID, HM?
HA HA HA!
I'M SORRY...
I HAD THE HONORARIUM ON HAND FOR THE LECTURER WE INVITED FROM ABROAD.
I GAVE IT TO YOU IN CASH AND NOT CHECK.
LECTURER?

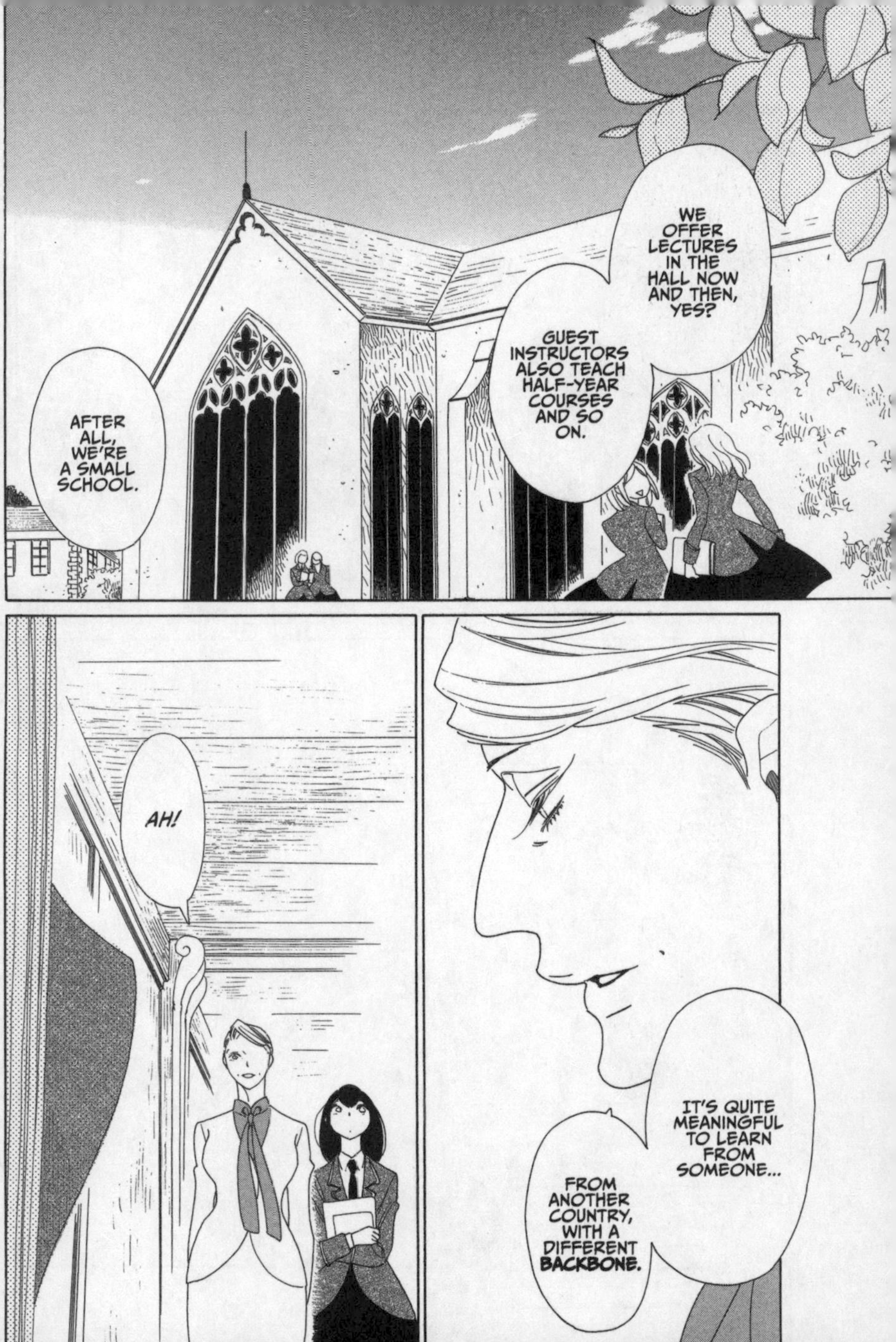
WE OFFER LECTURES IN THE HALL NOW AND THEN, YES?
GUEST INSTRUCTORS ALSO TEACH HALF-YEAR COURSES AND SO ON.
AFTER ALL, WE'RE A SMALL SCHOOL.
IT'S QUITE MEANINGFUL TO LEARN FROM SOMEONE...
FROM ANOTHER COUNTRY, WITH A DIFFERENT **BACKBONE.**
*AH!*

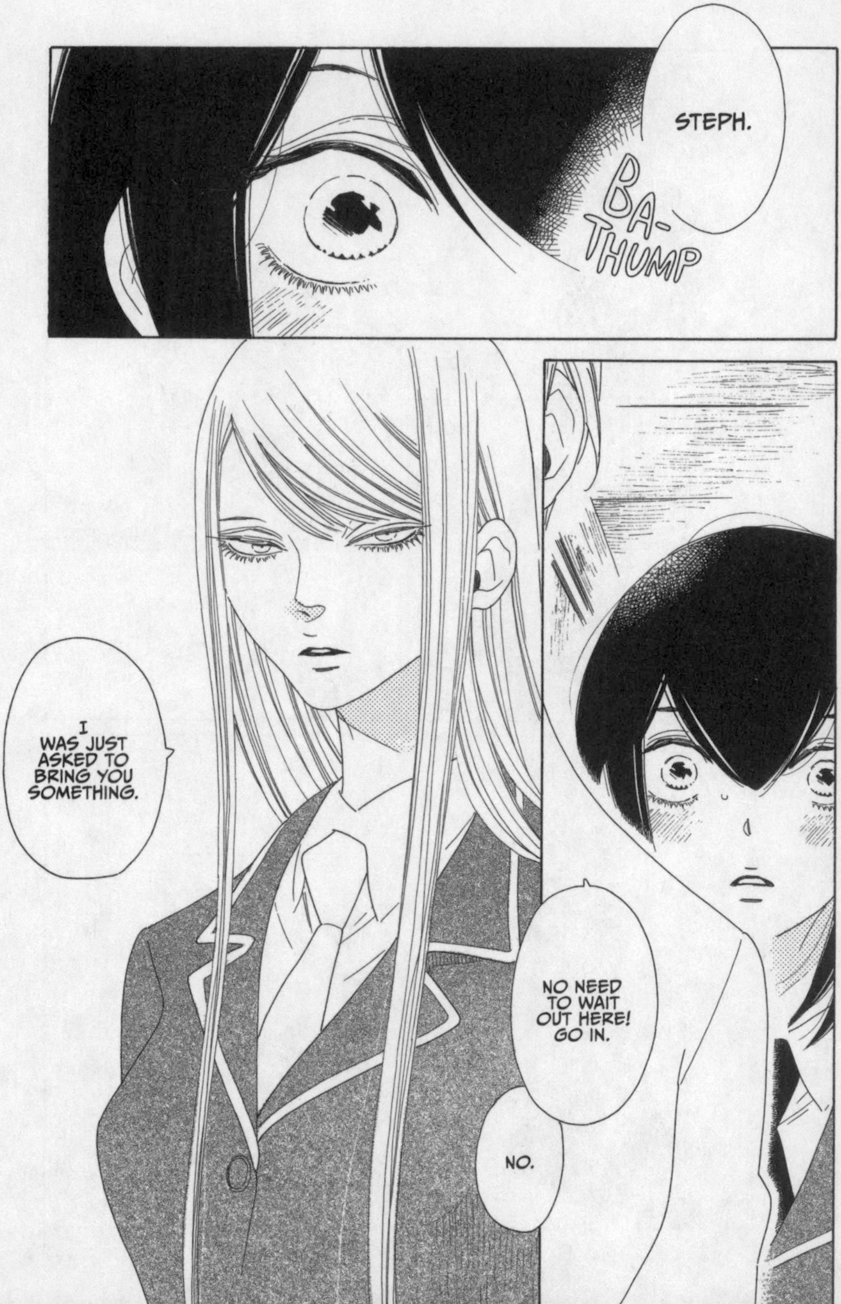
STEPH.
BA-THUMP
NO NEED TO WAIT OUT HERE! GO IN.
NO.
I WAS JUST ASKED TO BRING YOU SOMETHING.

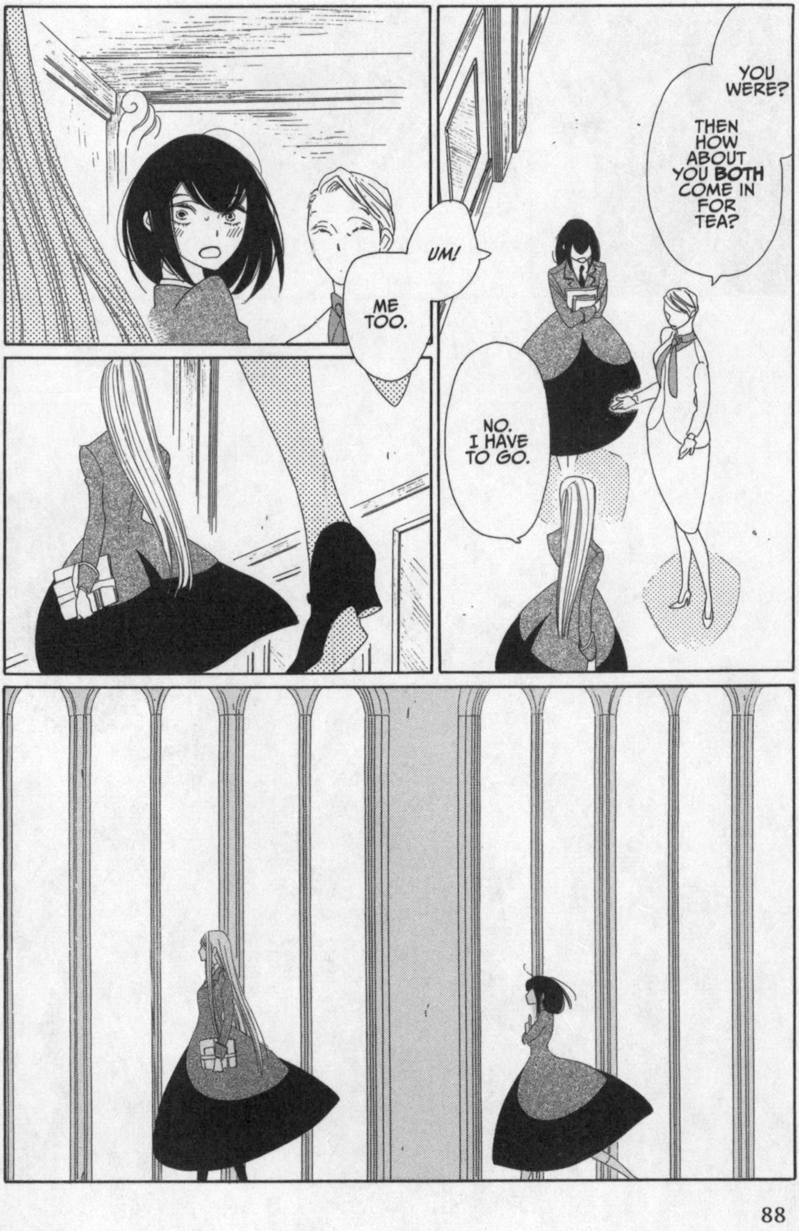
YOU WERE?
THEN HOW ABOUT YOU BOTH COME IN FOR TEA?
NO. I HAVE TO GO.
UM!
ME TOO.

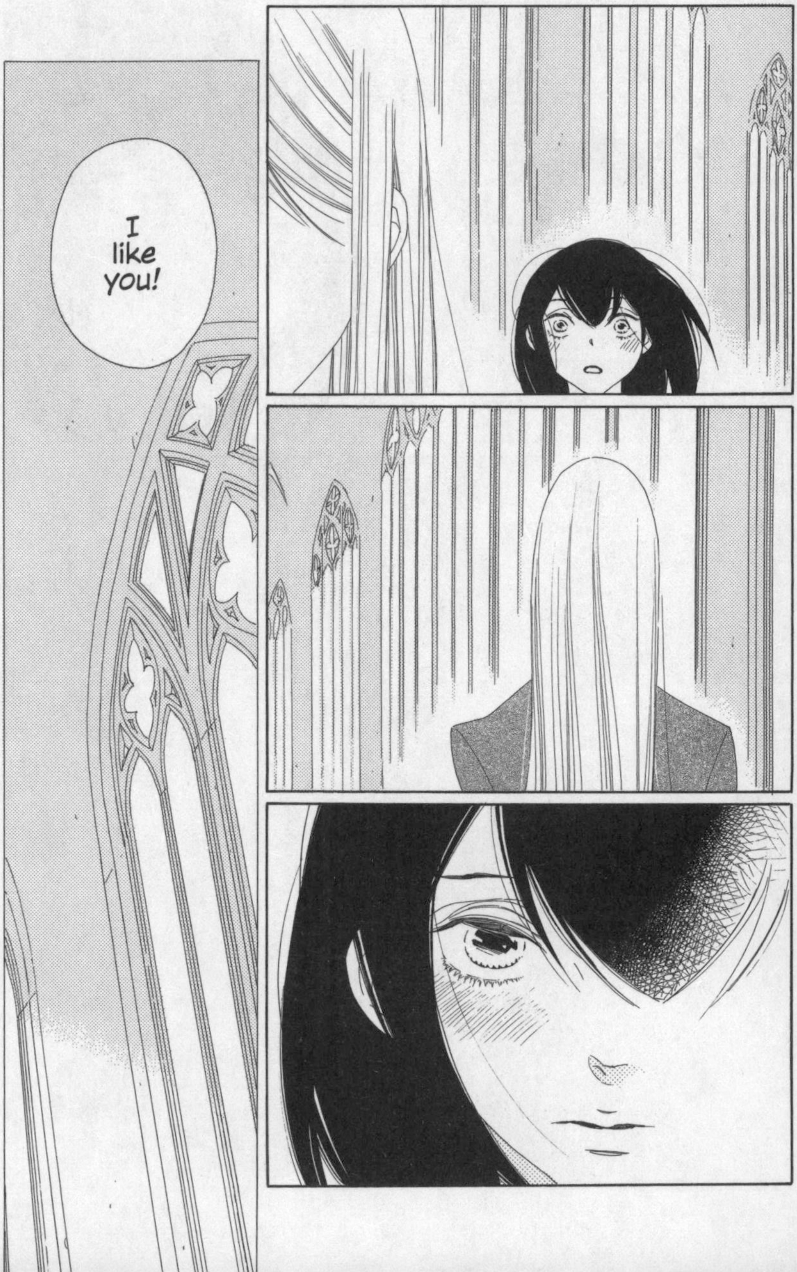
I like you!

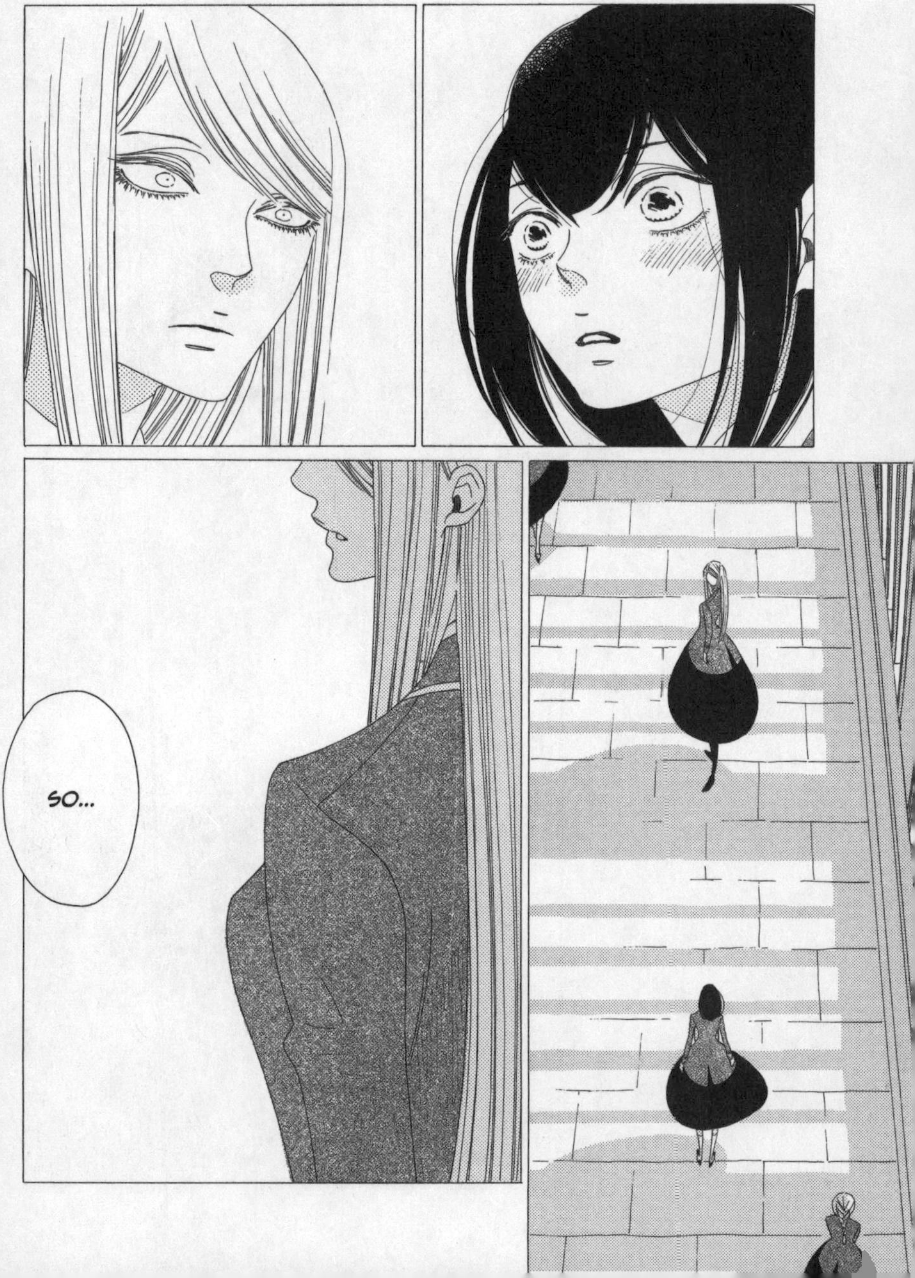
SO...

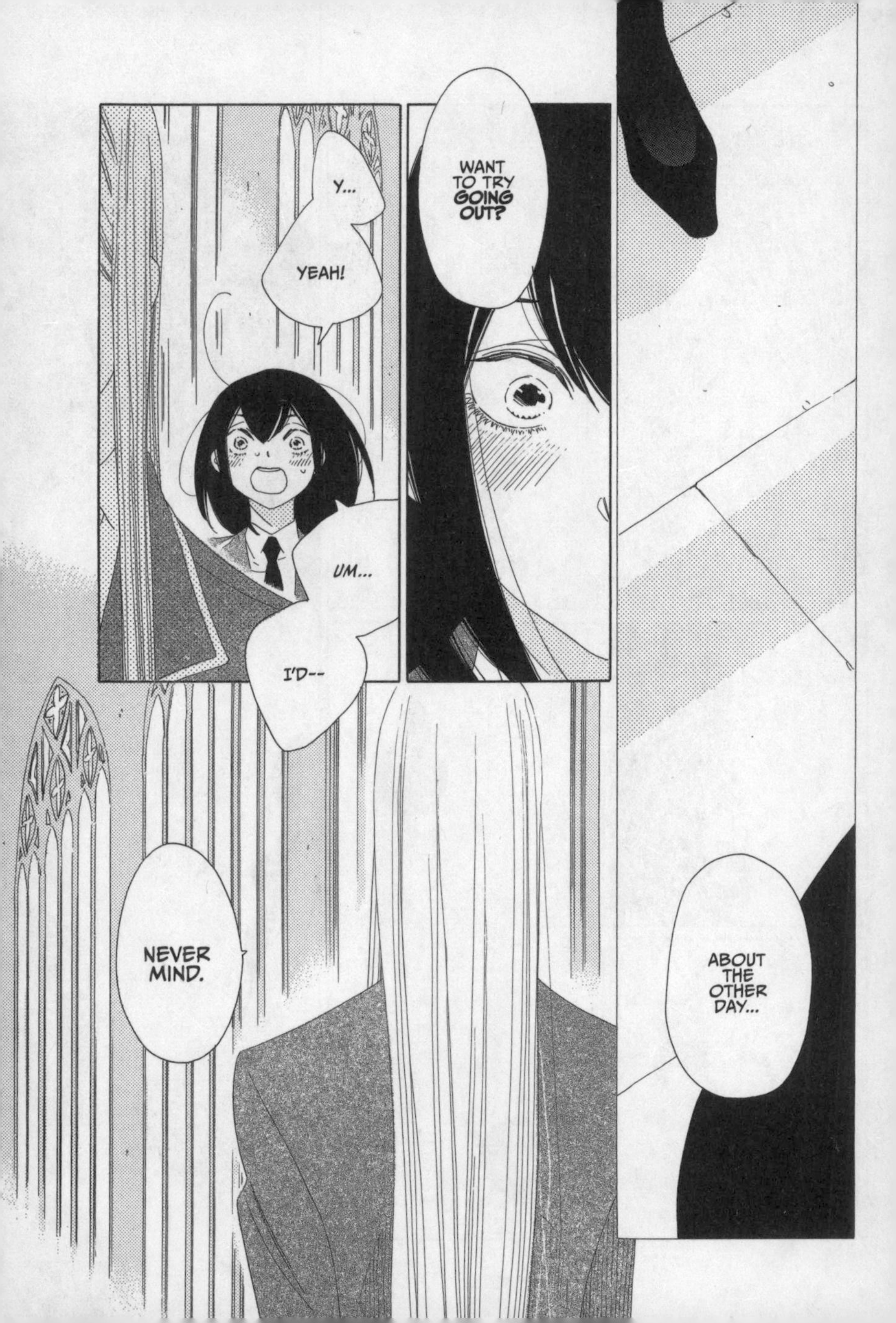
ABOUT THE OTHER DAY...
WANT TO TRY GOING OUT?
Y...
YEAH!
UM...
I'D--
NEVER MIND.

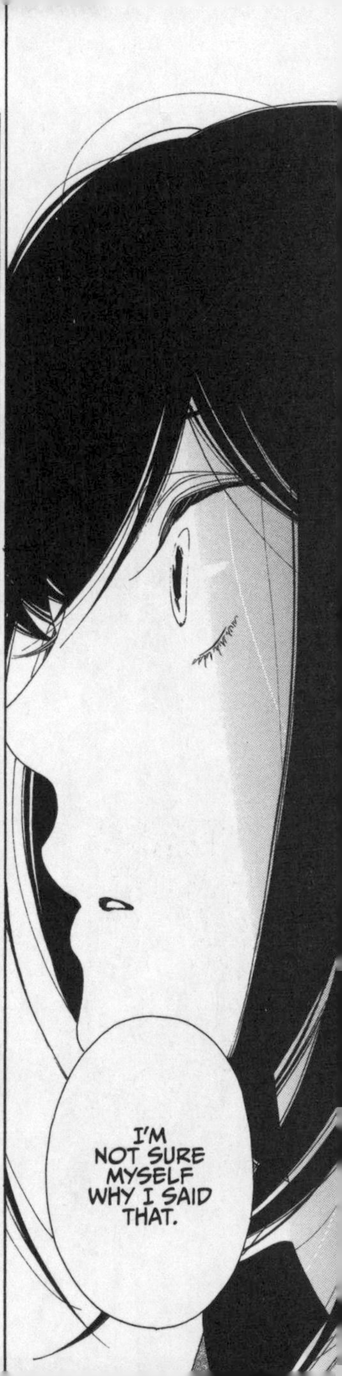
I'M NOT SURE MYSELF WHY I SAID THAT.
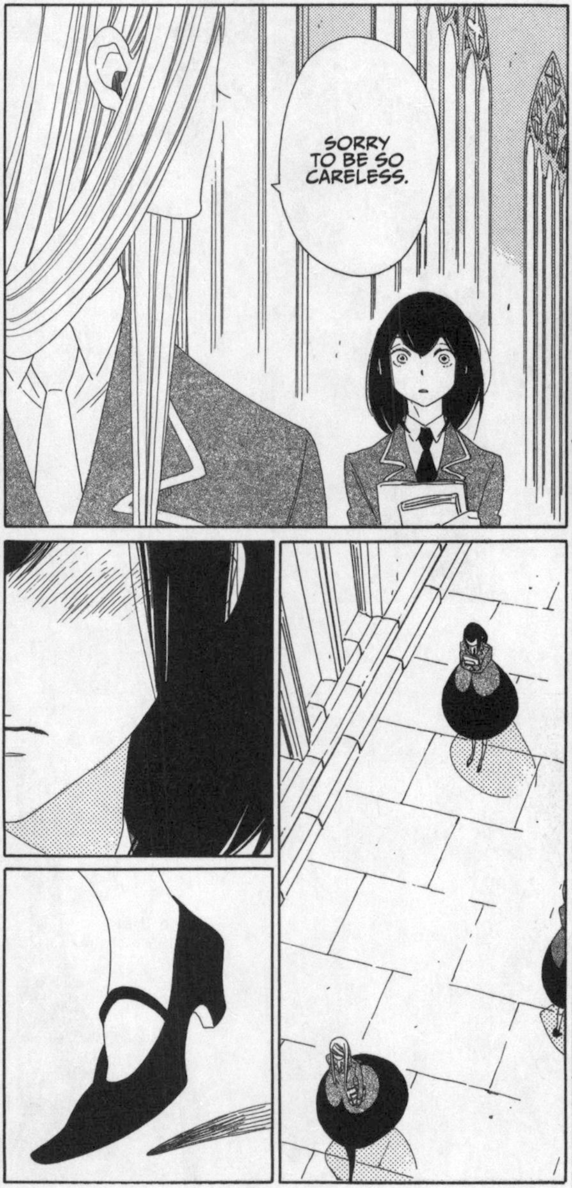
SORRY TO BE SO CARELESS.

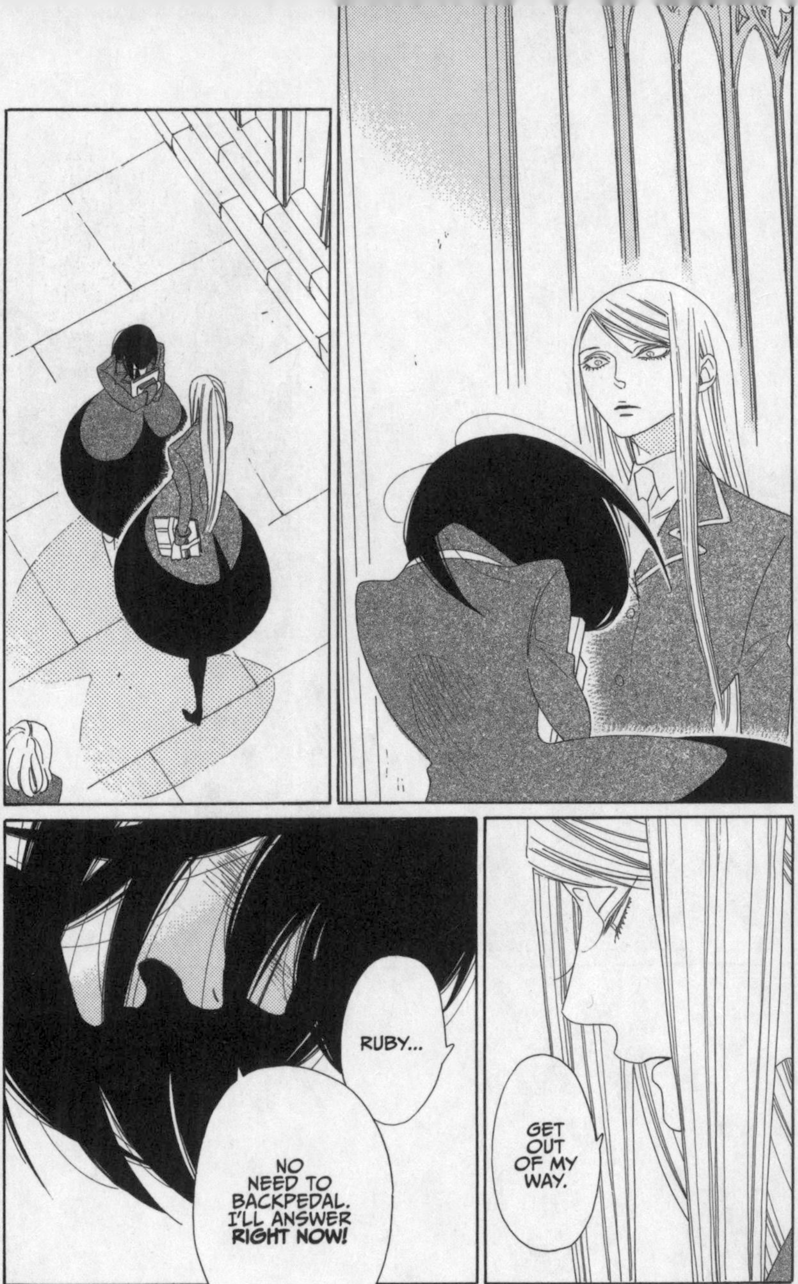
GET OUT OF MY WAY.
RUBY...
NO NEED TO BACKPEDAL. I'LL ANSWER RIGHT NOW!

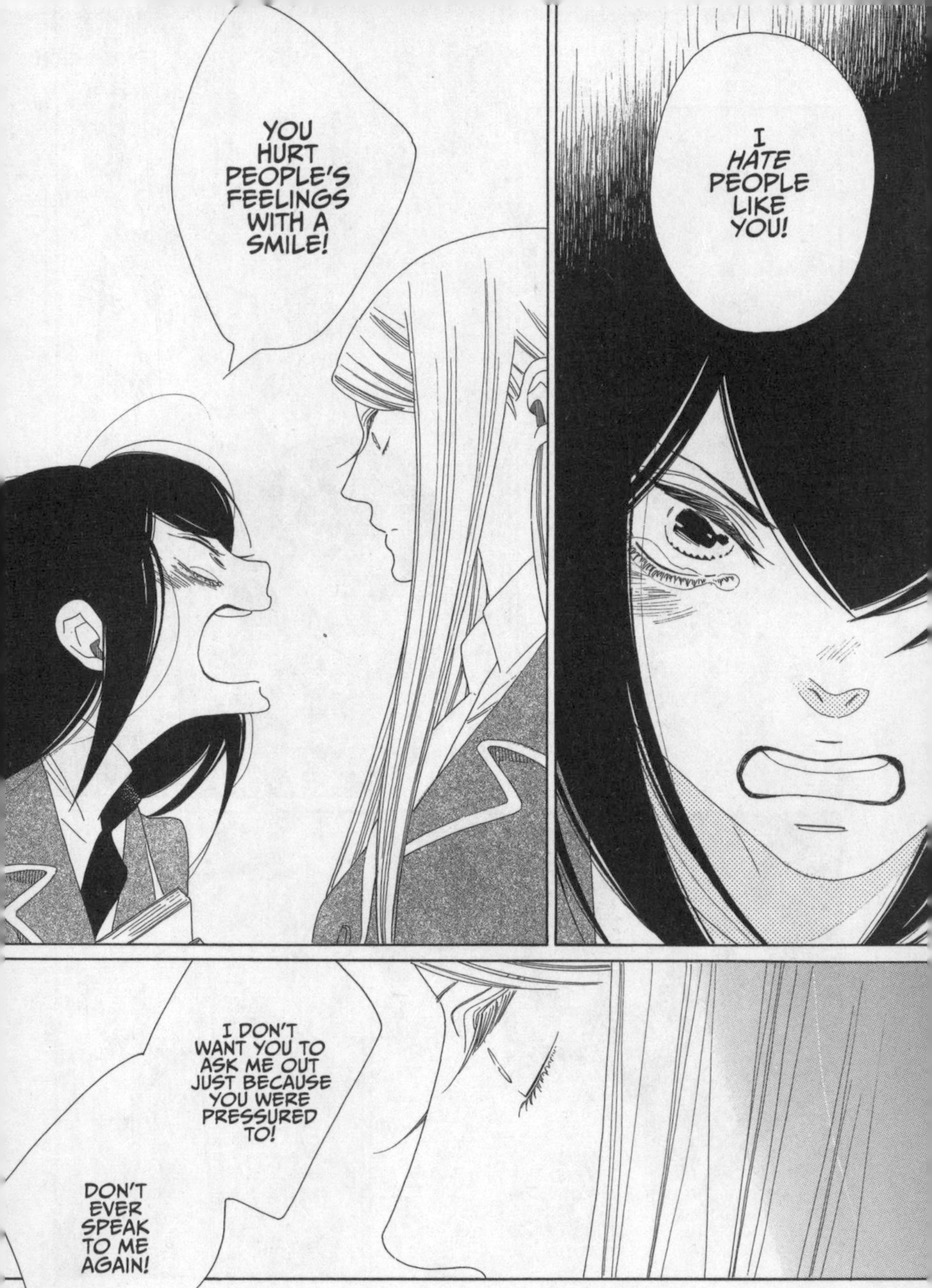
I *HATE* PEOPLE LIKE YOU!
YOU HURT PEOPLE'S FEELINGS WITH A SMILE!
I DON'T WANT YOU TO ASK ME OUT JUST BECAUSE YOU WERE PRESSURED TO!
DON'T EVER SPEAK TO ME AGAIN!

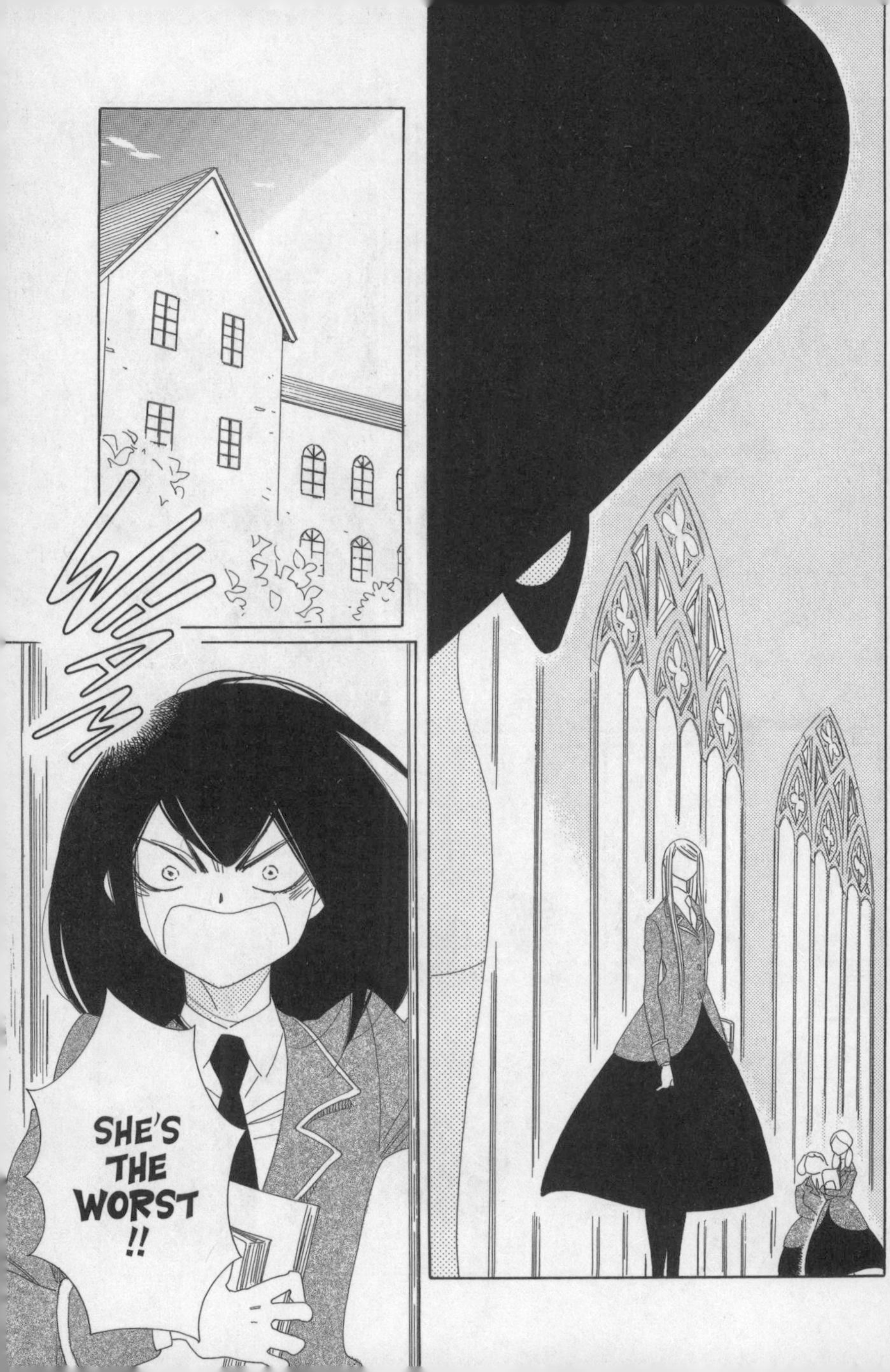
WHAM
SHE'S THE WORST!!

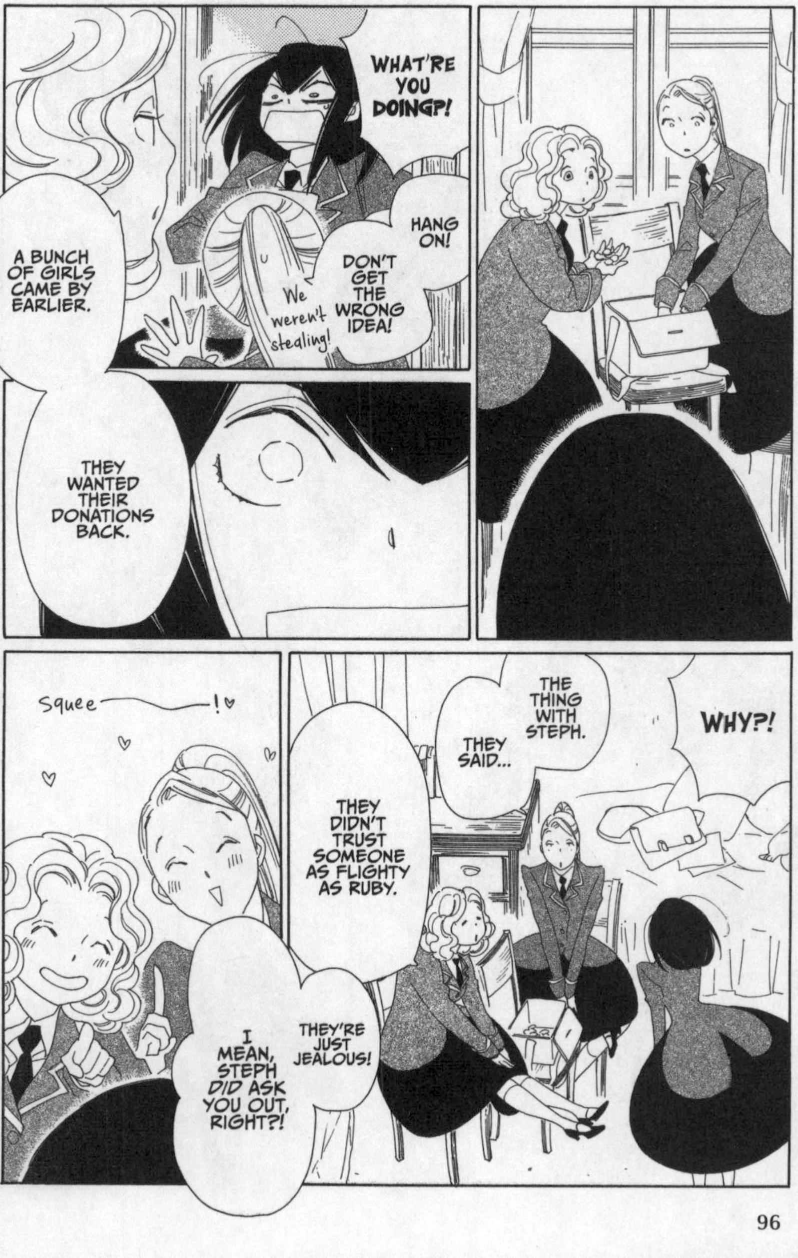
WHAT'RE YOU DOING?!
HANG ON!
DON'T GET THE WRONG IDEA!
We weren't stealing!
A BUNCH OF GIRLS CAME BY EARLIER.
THEY WANTED THEIR DONATIONS BACK.
WHY?!
THE THING WITH STEPH.
THEY SAID...
THEY DIDN'T TRUST SOMEONE AS FLIGHTY AS RUBY.
Squee—!♡
THEY'RE JUST JEALOUS!
I MEAN, STEPH *DID* ASK YOU OUT, RIGHT?!

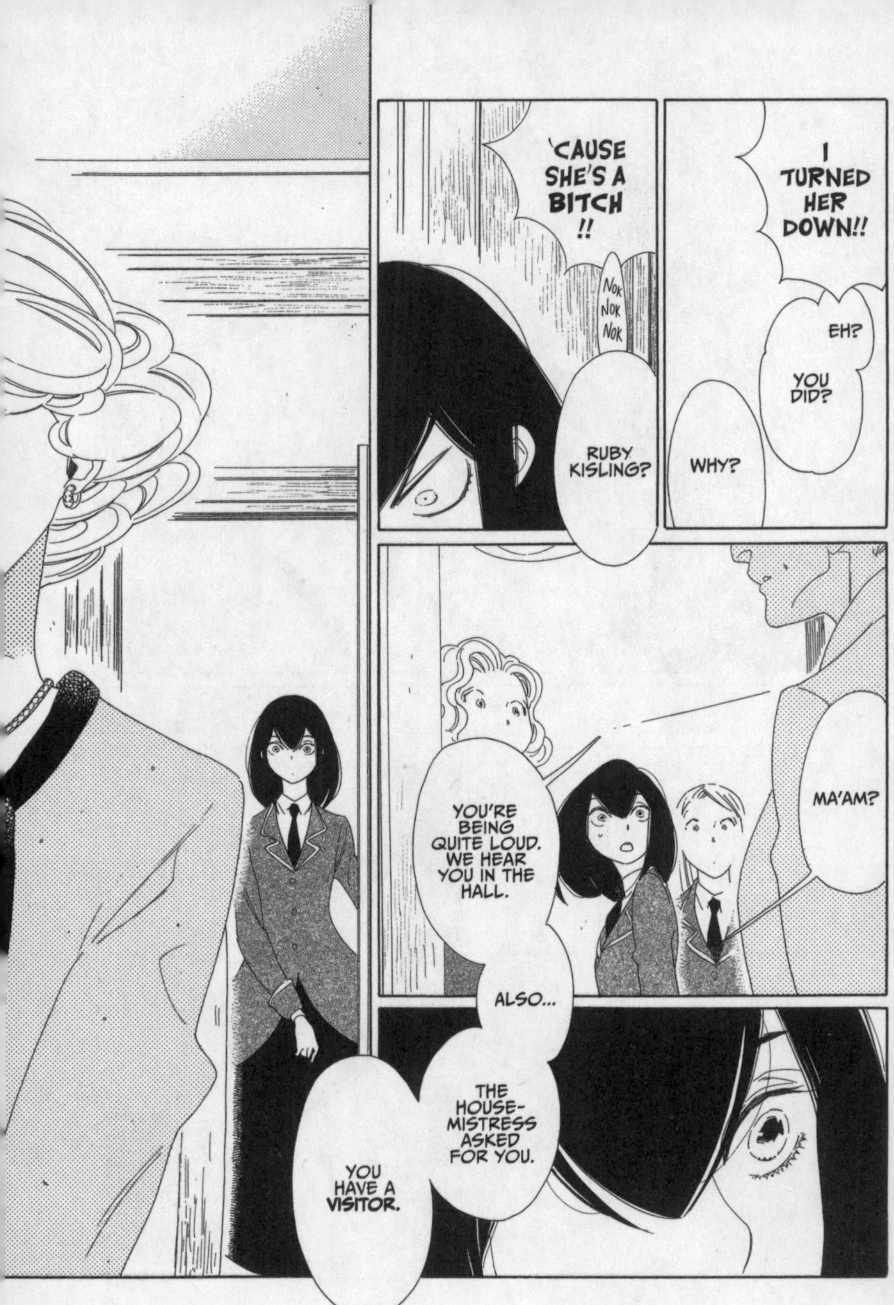
I TURNED HER DOWN!!
EH?
YOU DID?
WHY?
'CAUSE SHE'S A BITCH!!
NOK NOK NOK
RUBY KISLING?
MA'AM?
YOU'RE BEING QUITE LOUD. WE HEAR YOU IN THE HALL.
ALSO...
THE HOUSE-MISTRESS ASKED FOR YOU.
YOU HAVE A VISITOR.

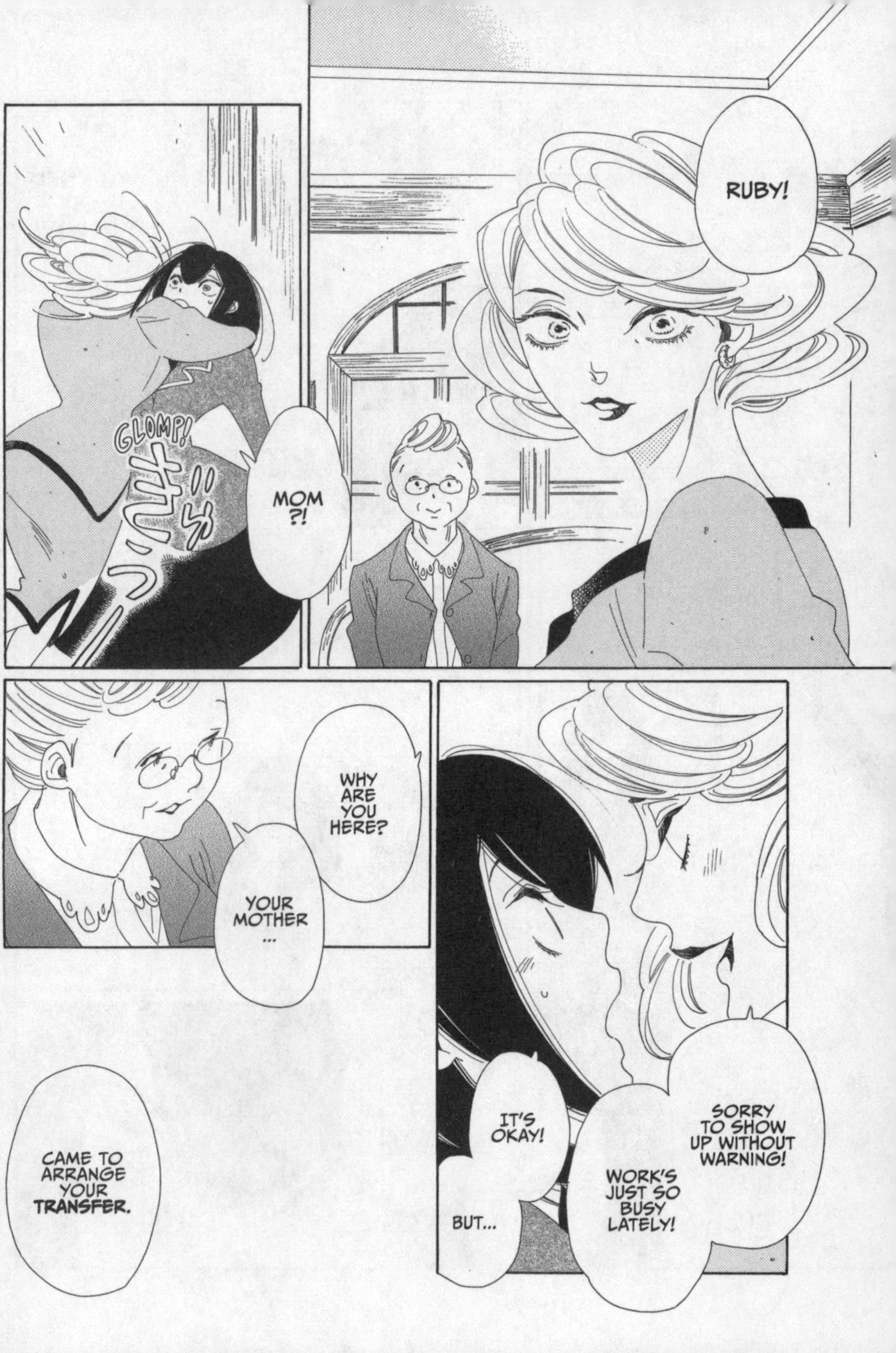
RUBY!
MOM ?!
GLOMP!
SORRY TO SHOW UP WITHOUT WARNING!
WORK'S JUST SO BUSY LATELY!
IT'S OKAY!
BUT...
WHY ARE YOU HERE?
YOUR MOTHER ...
CAME TO ARRANGE YOUR TRANSFER.

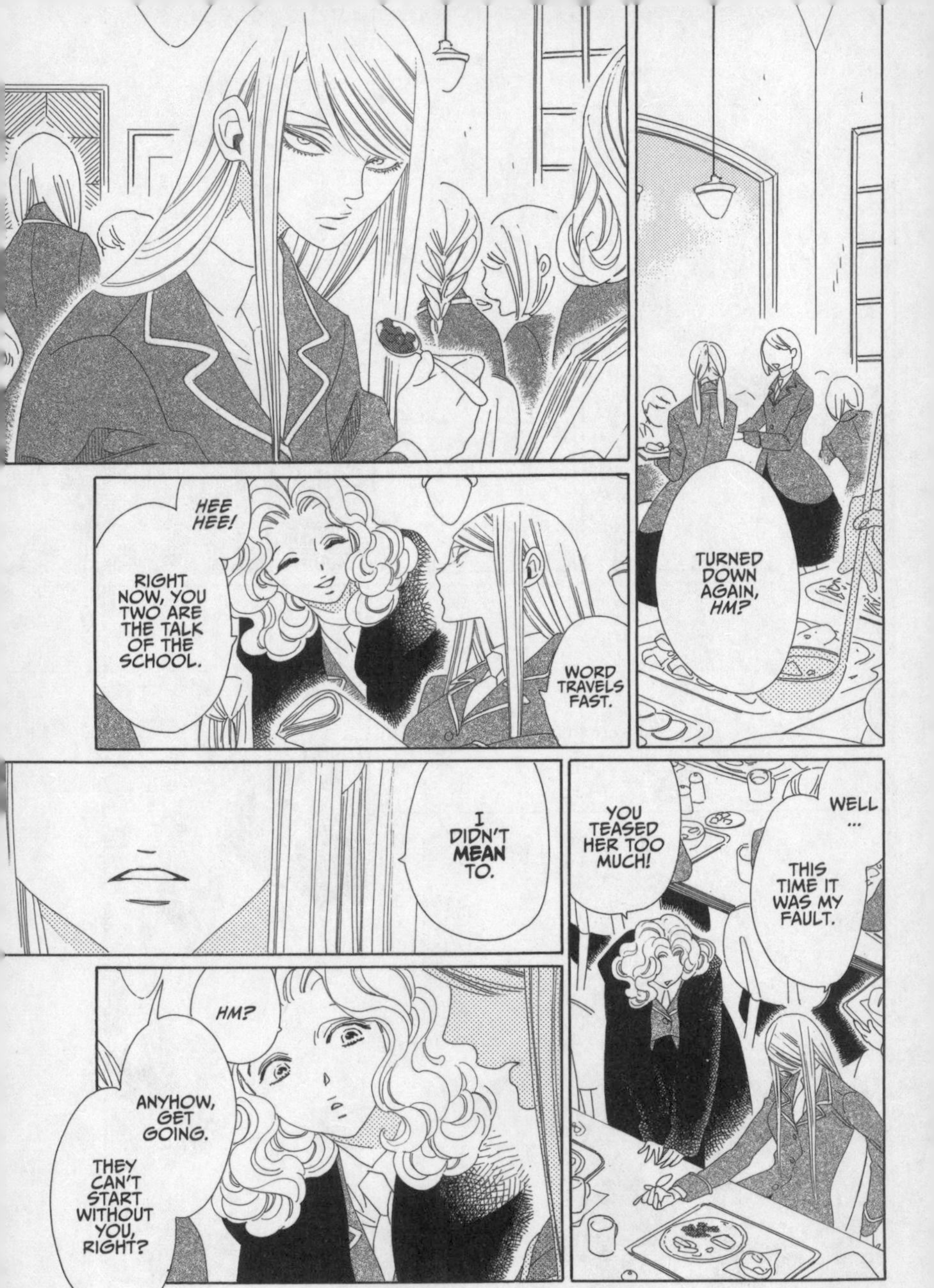
TURNED DOWN AGAIN, HM?
HEE HEE!
RIGHT NOW, YOU TWO ARE THE TALK OF THE SCHOOL.
WORD TRAVELS FAST.
WELL ... THIS TIME IT WAS MY FAULT.
YOU TEASED HER TOO MUCH!
I DIDN'T MEAN TO.
HM?
ANYHOW, GET GOING.
THEY CAN'T START WITHOUT YOU, RIGHT?

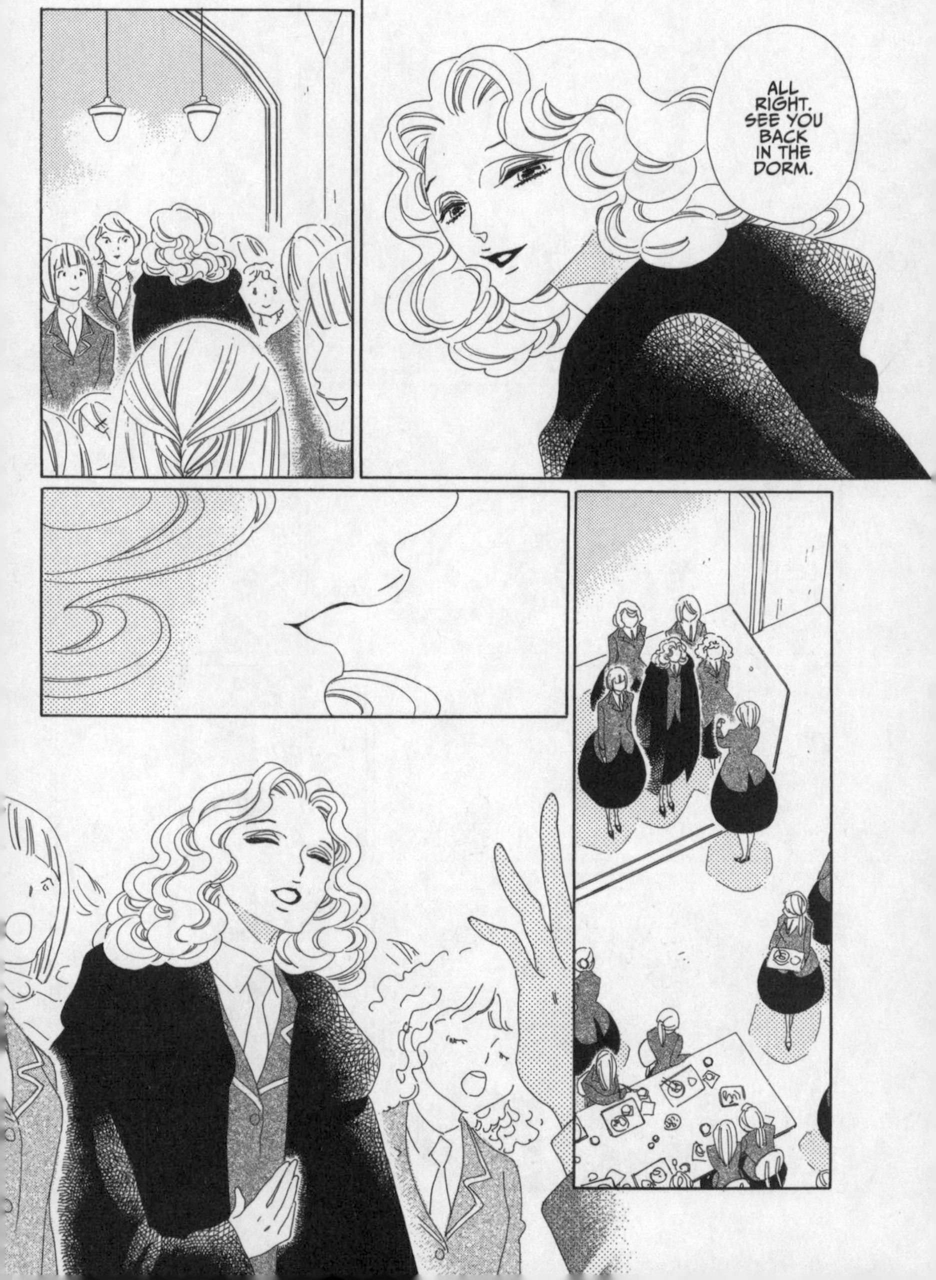
ALL RIGHT. SEE YOU BACK IN THE DORM.

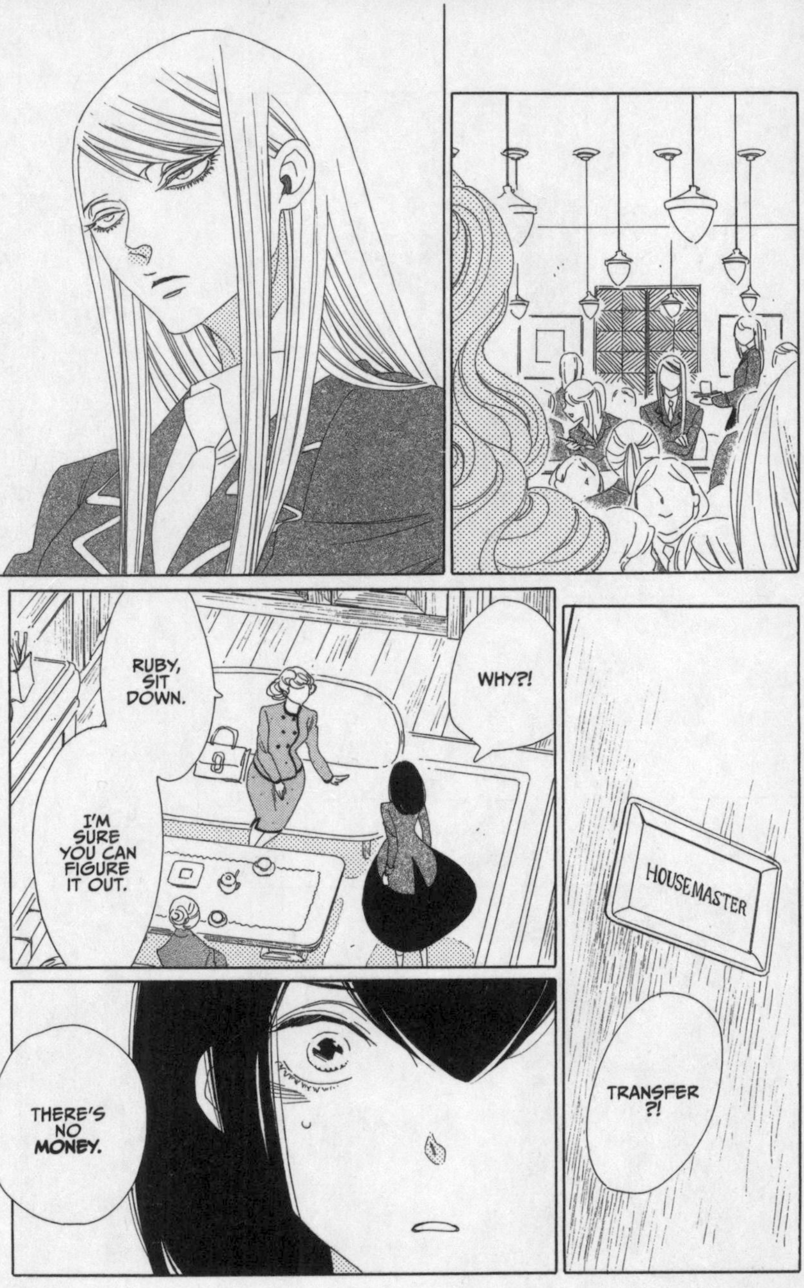
HOUSEMASTER
TRANSFER ?!
WHY?!
RUBY, SIT DOWN.
I'M SURE YOU CAN FIGURE IT OUT.
THERE'S NO MONEY.

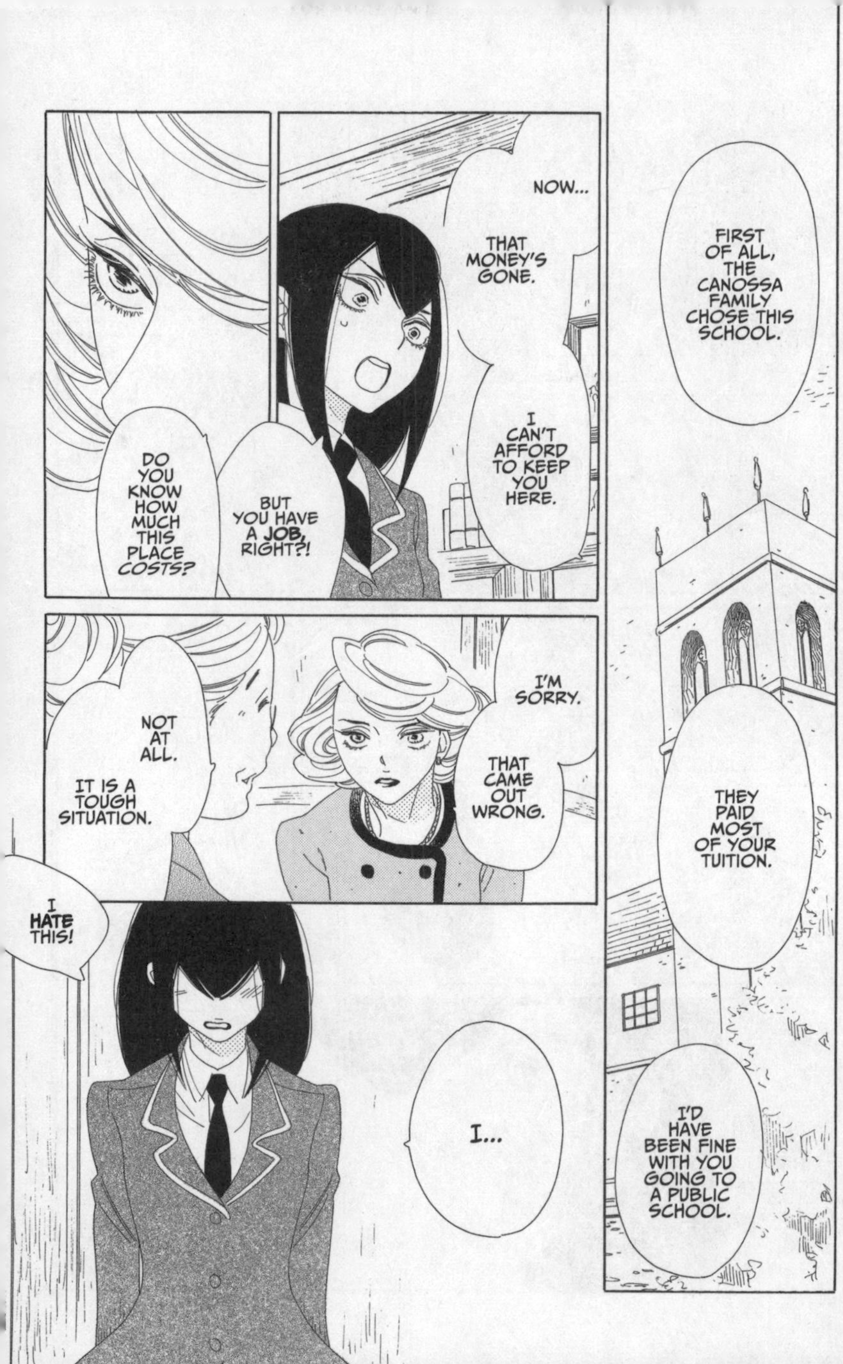
FIRST OF ALL, THE CANOSSA FAMILY CHOSE THIS SCHOOL.
THEY PAID MOST OF YOUR TUITION.
I'D HAVE BEEN FINE WITH YOU GOING TO A PUBLIC SCHOOL.
NOW...
THAT MONEY'S GONE.
I CAN'T AFFORD TO KEEP YOU HERE.
BUT YOU HAVE A JOB, RIGHT?!
DO YOU KNOW HOW MUCH THIS PLACE COSTS?
I'M SORRY.
THAT CAME OUT WRONG.
NOT AT ALL.
IT IS A TOUGH SITUATION.
I...
I HATE THIS!

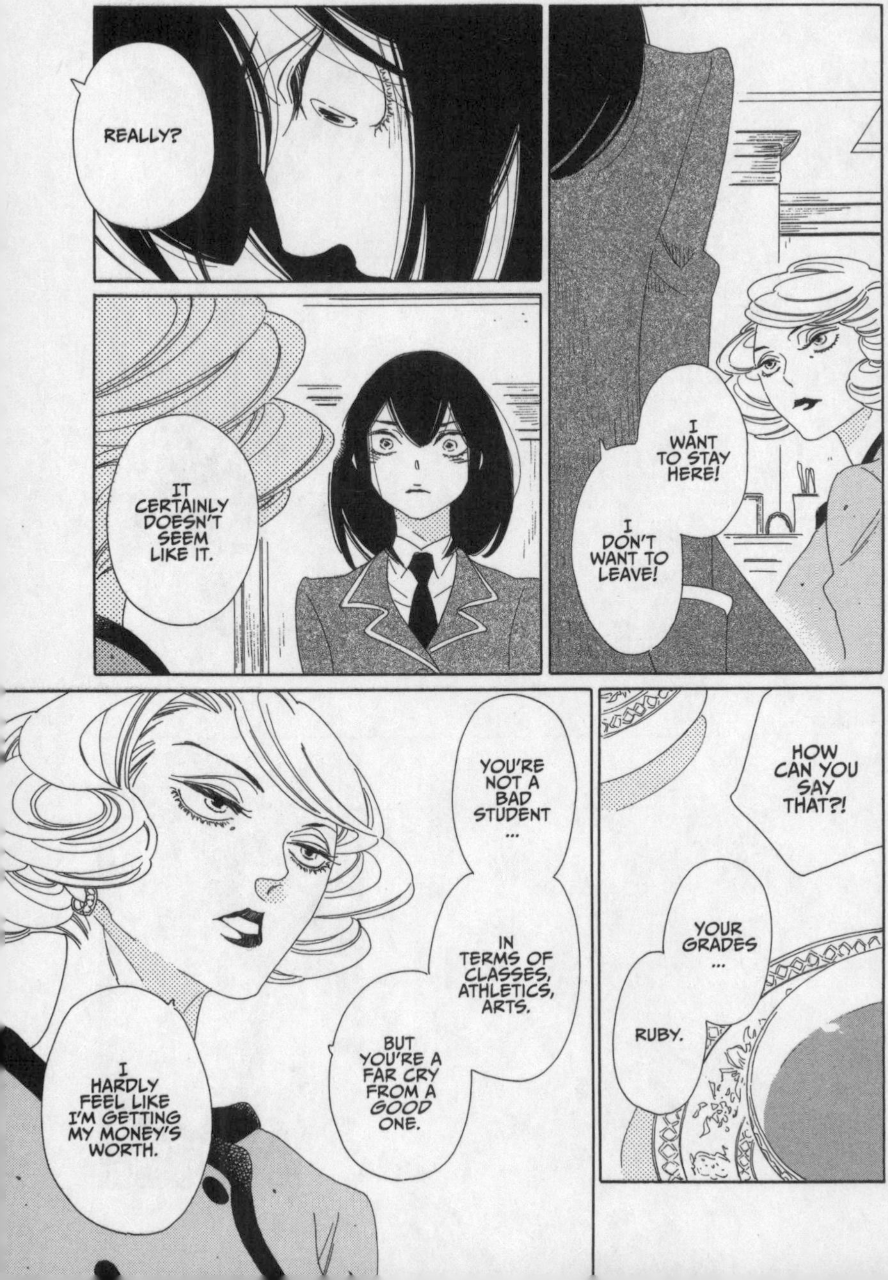
I WANT TO STAY HERE!
I DON'T WANT TO LEAVE!
REALLY?
IT CERTAINLY DOESN'T SEEM LIKE IT.
HOW CAN YOU SAY THAT?!
YOUR GRADES ...
RUBY.
YOU'RE NOT A BAD STUDENT ...
IN TERMS OF CLASSES, ATHLETICS, ARTS.
BUT YOU'RE A FAR CRY FROM A *GOOD* ONE.
I HARDLY FEEL LIKE I'M GETTING MY MONEY'S WORTH.

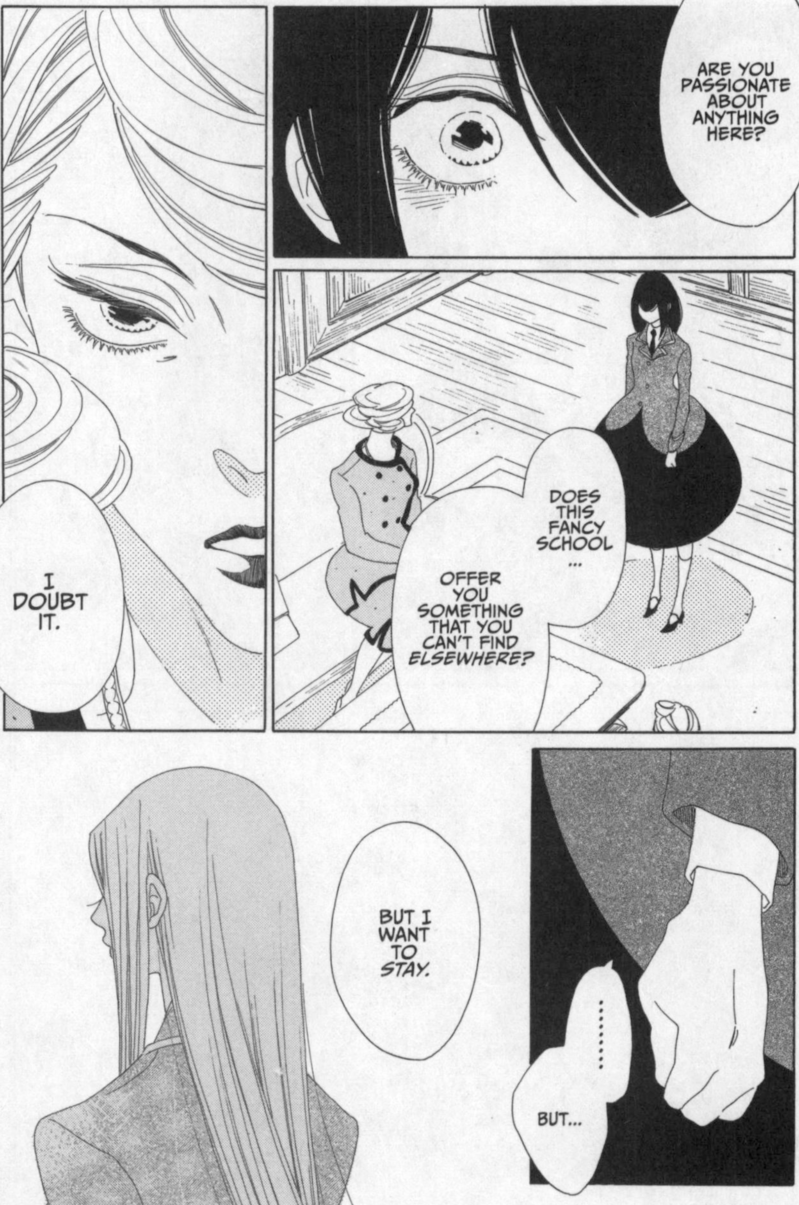
ARE YOU PASSIONATE ABOUT ANYTHING HERE?
DOES THIS FANCY SCHOOL ...
OFFER YOU SOMETHING THAT YOU CAN'T FIND *ELSEWHERE?*
I DOUBT IT.
......
BUT...
BUT I WANT TO *STAY.*

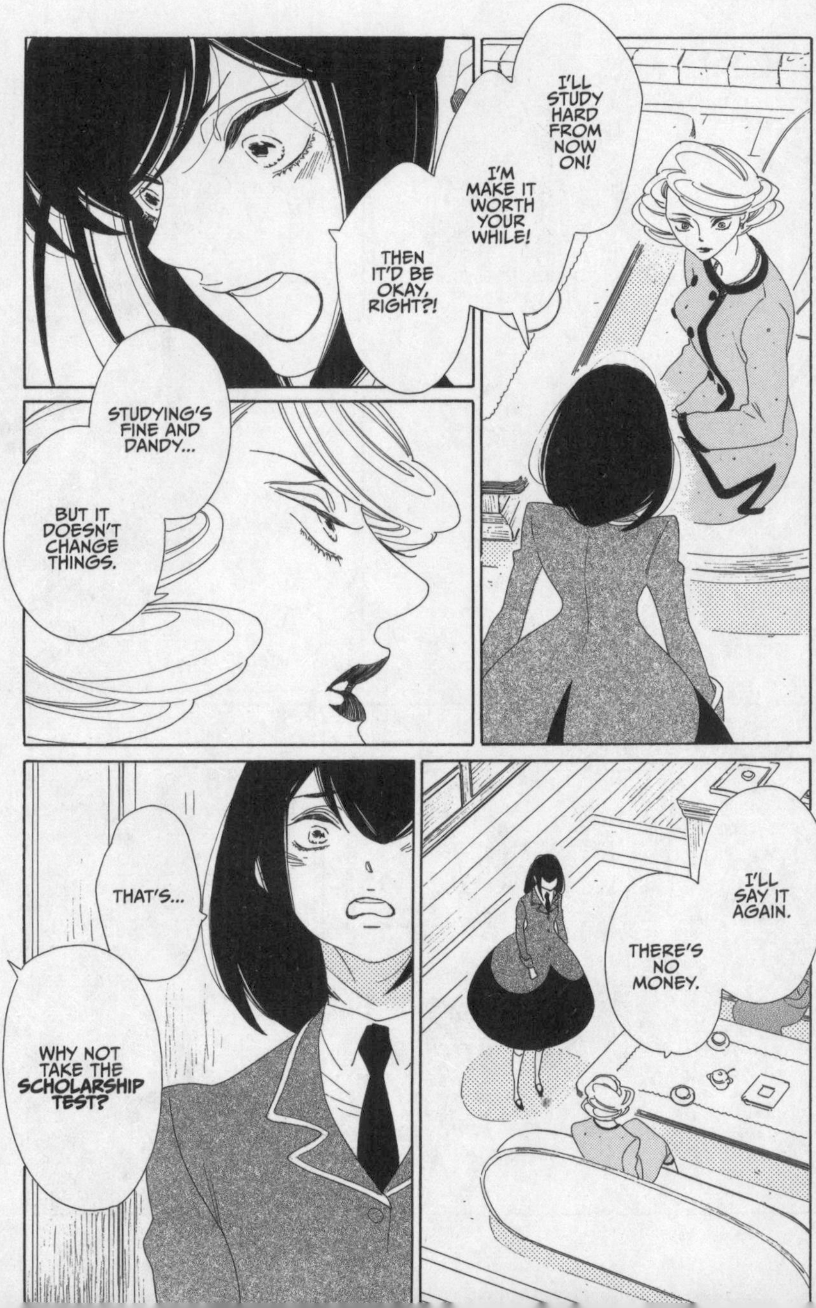
I'LL STUDY HARD FROM NOW ON!
I'M MAKE IT WORTH YOUR WHILE!
THEN IT'D BE OKAY, RIGHT?!
STUDYING'S FINE AND DANDY...
BUT IT DOESN'T CHANGE THINGS.
I'LL SAY IT AGAIN.
THERE'S NO MONEY.
THAT'S...
WHY NOT TAKE THE SCHOLARSHIP TEST?

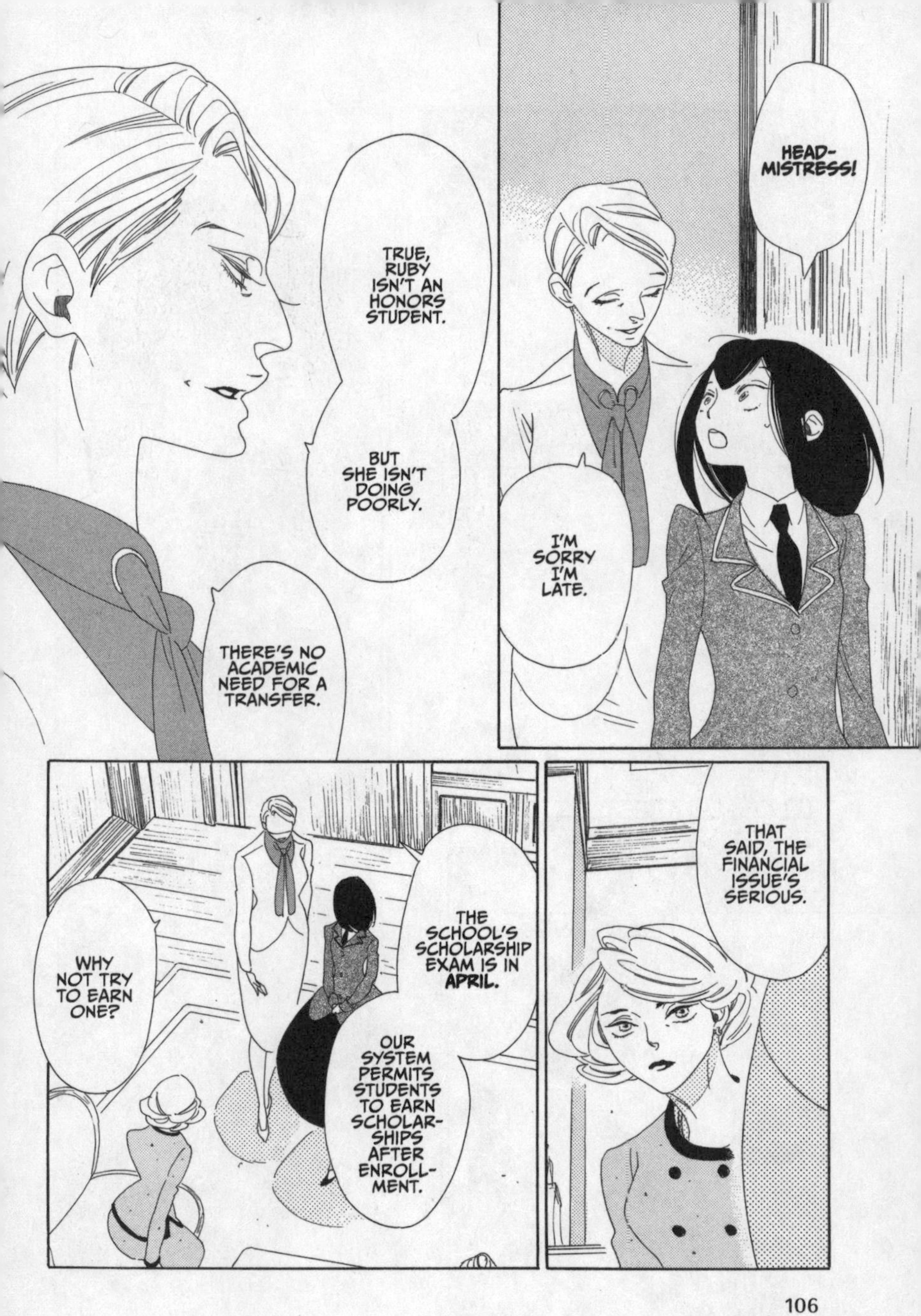
HEAD-MISTRESS!
I'M SORRY I'M LATE.
TRUE, RUBY ISN'T AN HONORS STUDENT.
BUT SHE ISN'T DOING POORLY.
THERE'S NO ACADEMIC NEED FOR A TRANSFER.
THAT SAID, THE FINANCIAL ISSUE'S SERIOUS.
THE SCHOOL'S SCHOLARSHIP EXAM IS IN **APRIL.**
OUR SYSTEM PERMITS STUDENTS TO EARN SCHOLAR-SHIPS AFTER ENROLL-MENT.
WHY NOT TRY TO EARN ONE?

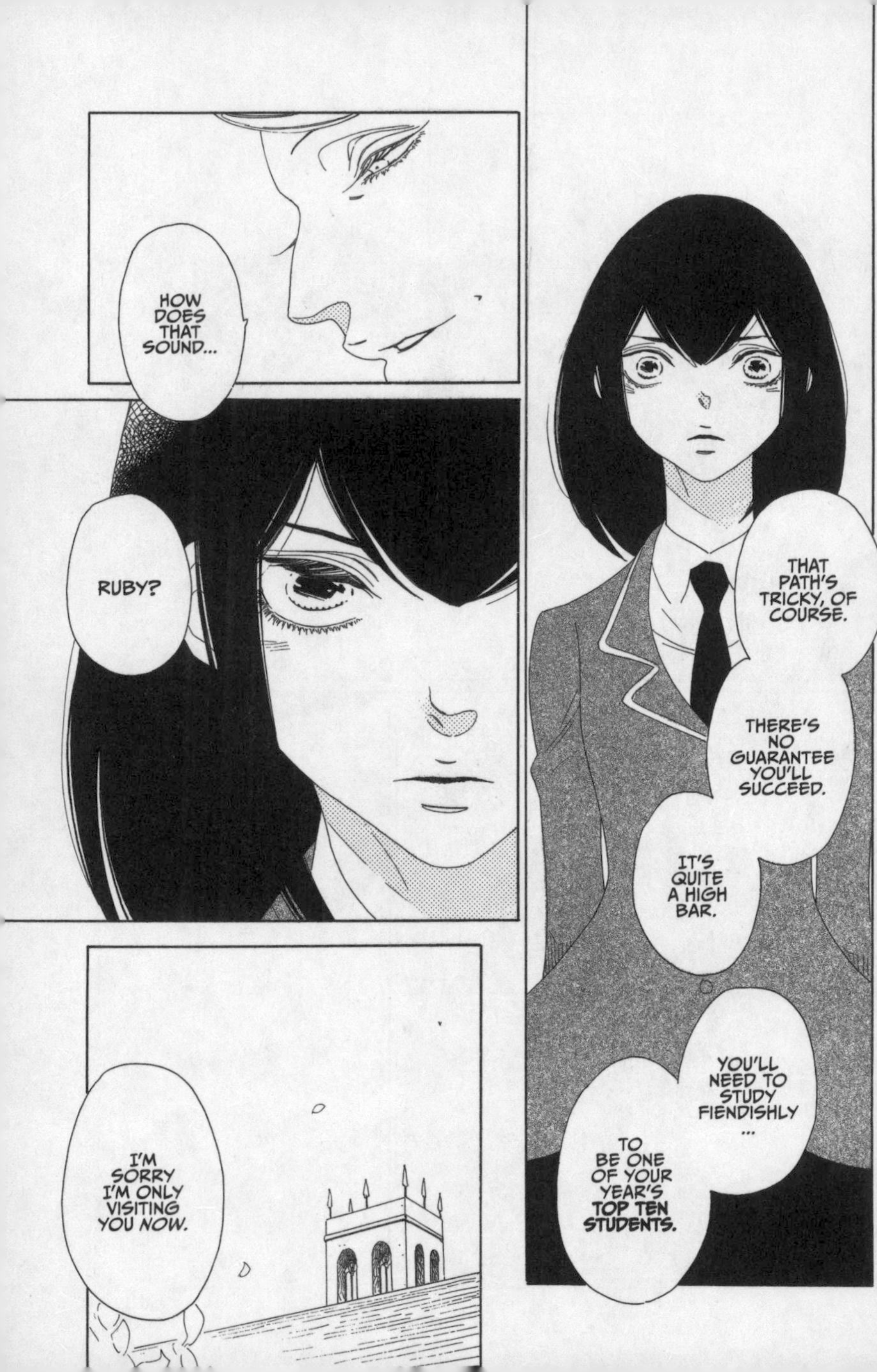
THAT PATH'S TRICKY, OF COURSE.
THERE'S NO GUARANTEE YOU'LL SUCCEED.
IT'S QUITE A HIGH BAR.
YOU'LL NEED TO STUDY FIENDISHLY ...
TO BE ONE OF YOUR YEAR'S TOP TEN STUDENTS.
HOW DOES THAT SOUND...
RUBY?
I'M SORRY I'M ONLY VISITING YOU NOW.

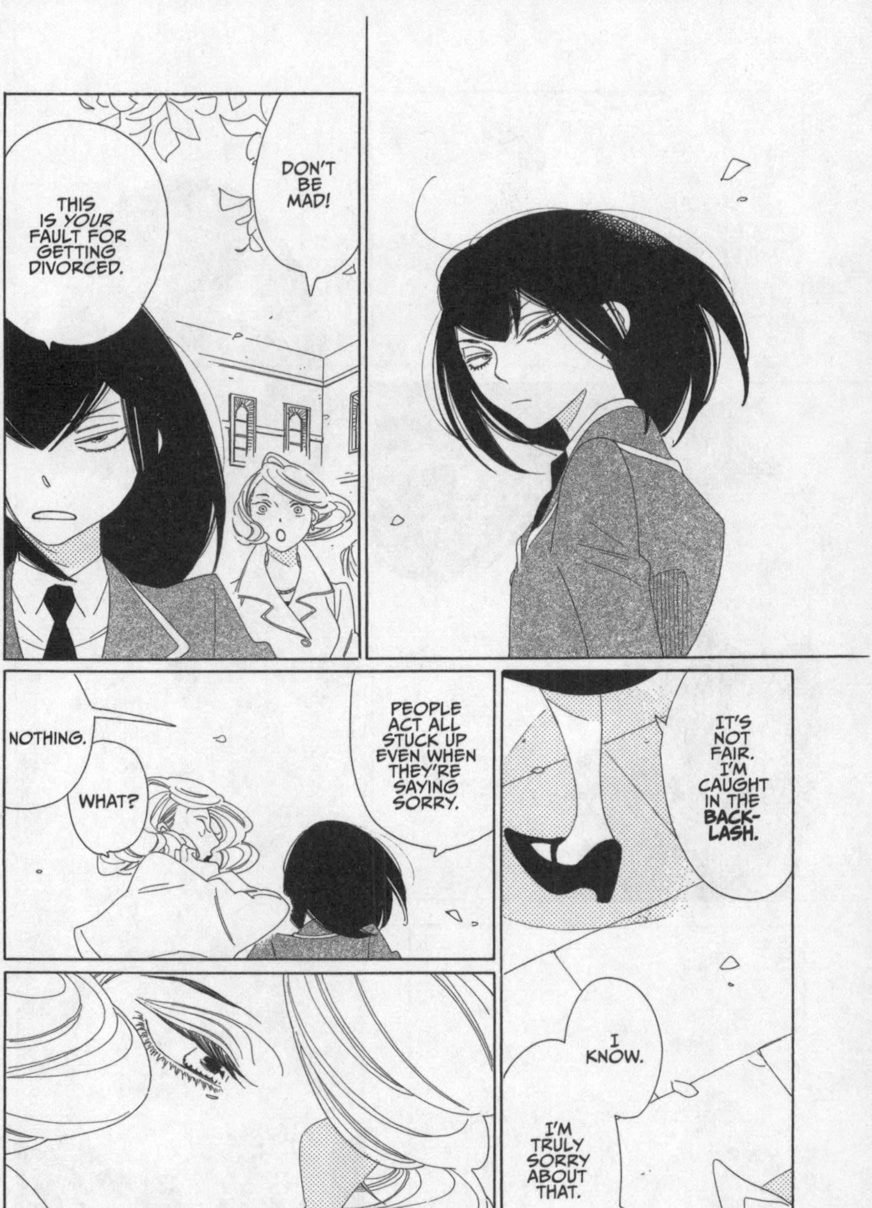
DON'T BE MAD!
THIS IS *YOUR* FAULT FOR GETTING DIVORCED.
IT'S NOT FAIR. I'M CAUGHT IN THE **BACK-LASH.**
I KNOW.
I'M TRULY SORRY ABOUT THAT.
PEOPLE ACT ALL STUCK UP EVEN WHEN THEY'RE SAYING SORRY.
WHAT?
NOTHING.

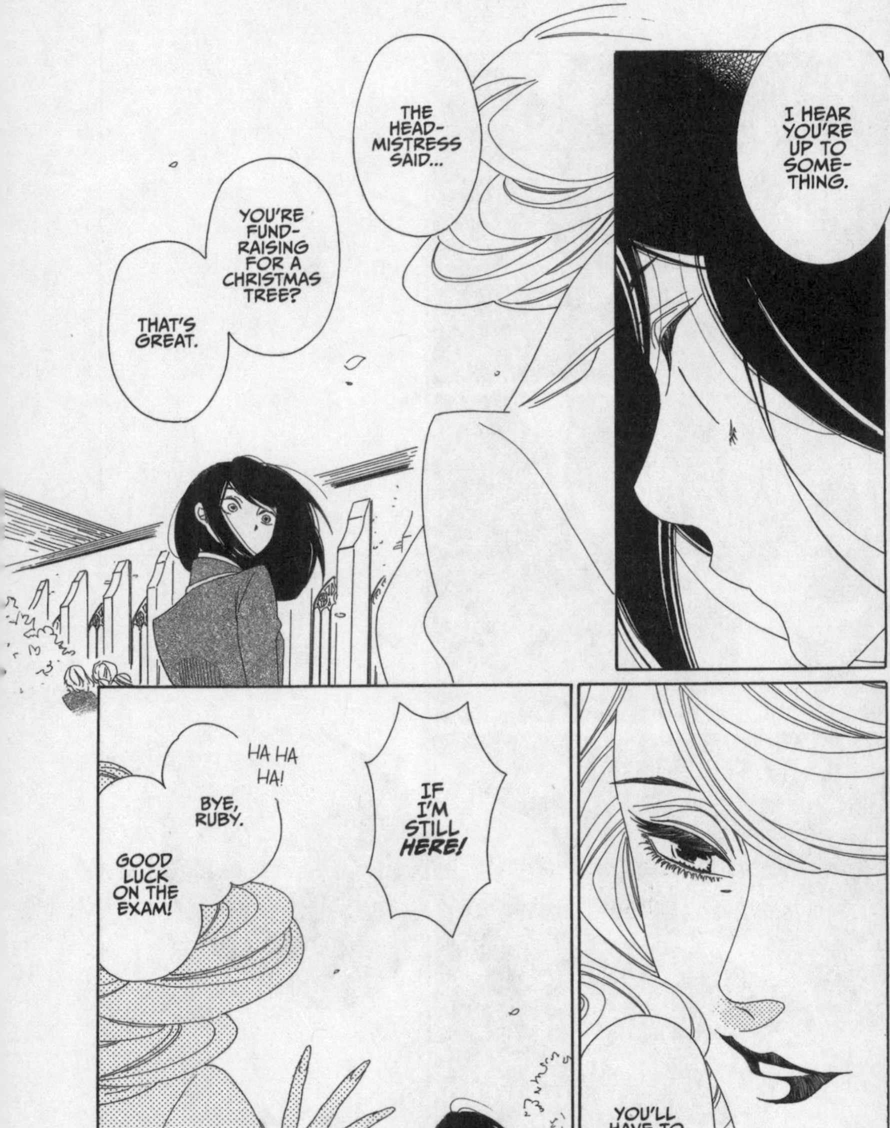
I HEAR YOU'RE UP TO SOME-THING.
THE HEAD-MISTRESS SAID...
YOU'RE FUND-RAISING FOR A CHRISTMAS TREE?
THAT'S GREAT.
YOU'LL HAVE TO LET ME SEE IT.
IF I'M STILL *HERE!*
HA HA HA!
BYE, RUBY.
GOOD LUCK ON THE EXAM!

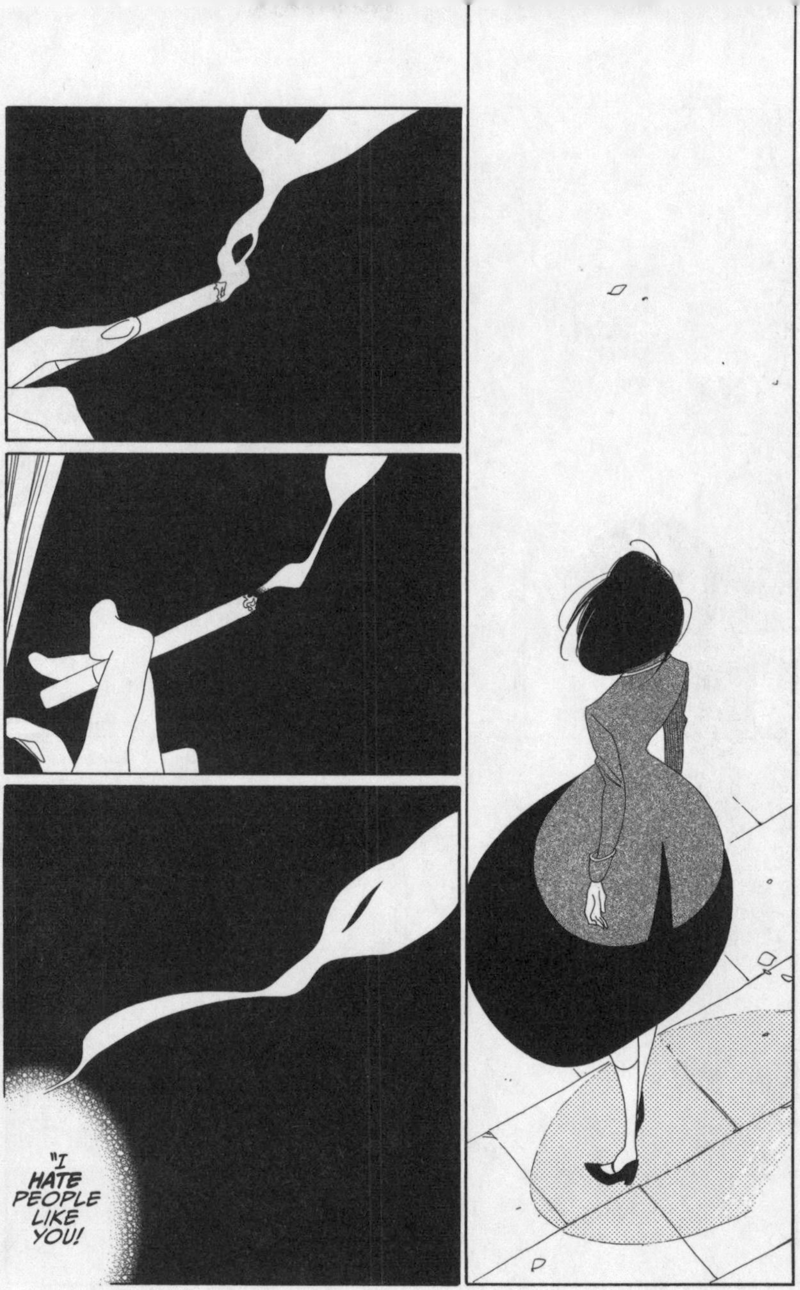
"I HATE PEOPLE LIKE YOU!

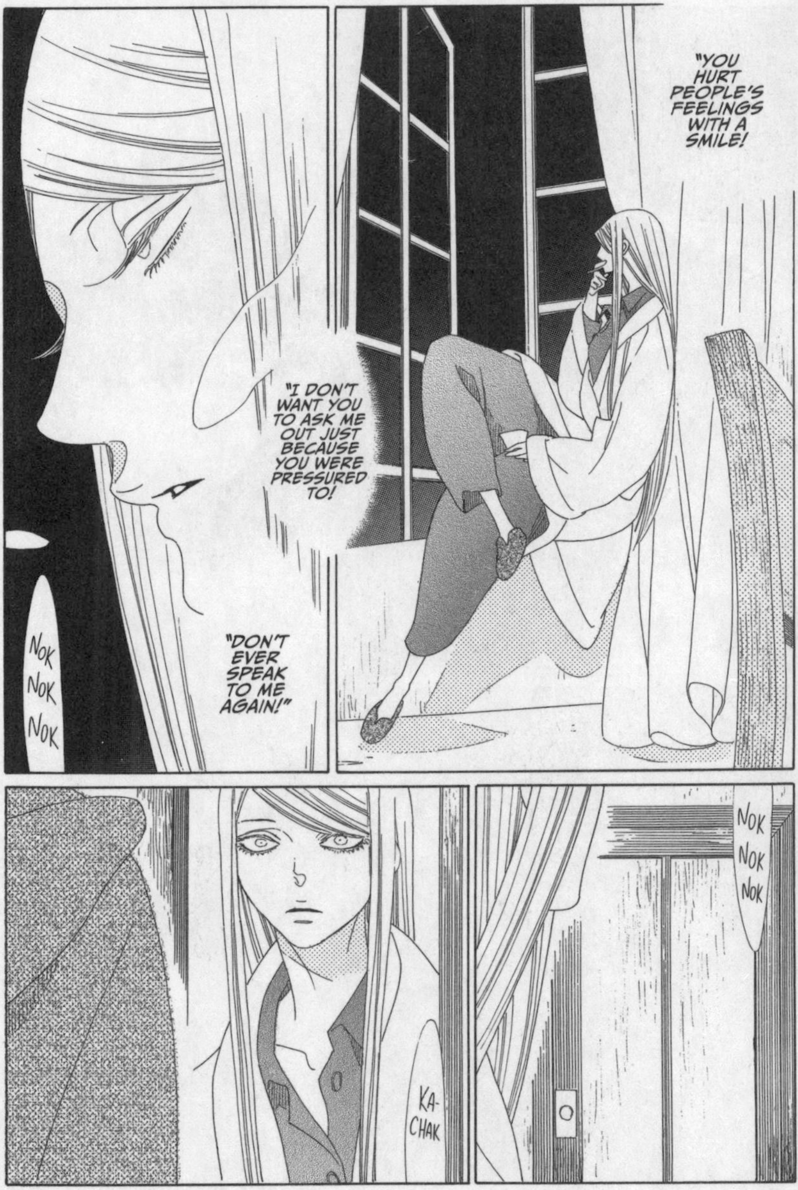
"YOU HURT PEOPLE'S FEELINGS WITH A SMILE!
"I DON'T WANT YOU TO ASK ME OUT JUST BECAUSE YOU WERE PRESSURED TO!
"DON'T EVER SPEAK TO ME AGAIN!"
NOK NOK NOK
NOK NOK NOK
KA-CHAK

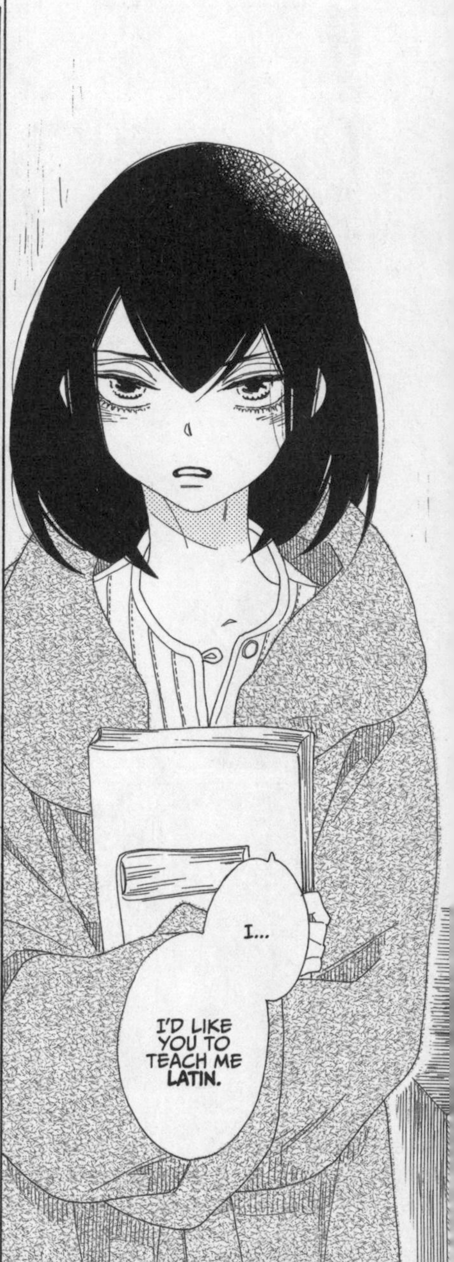
I...
I'D LIKE YOU TO TEACH ME LATIN.

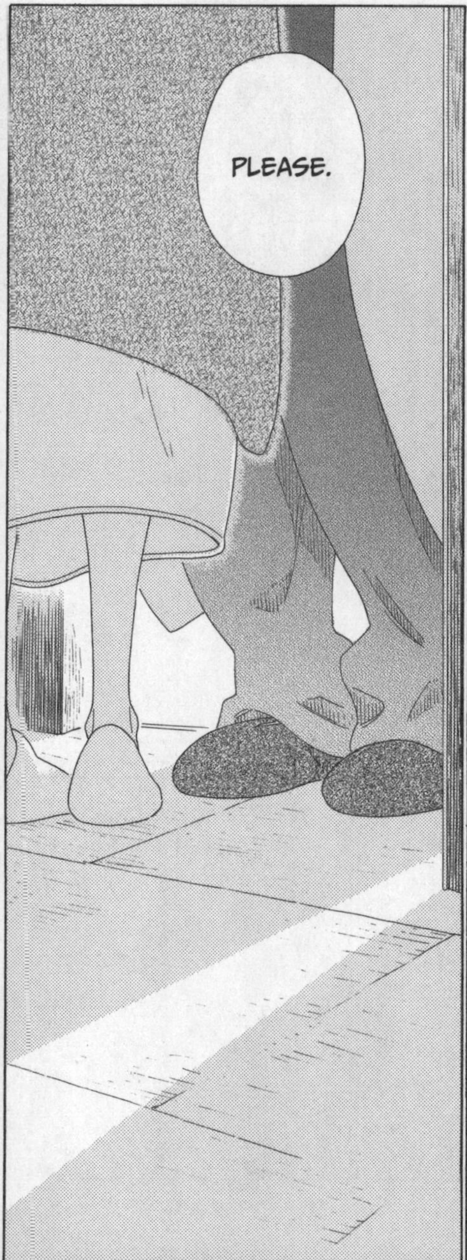
PLEASE.

メジロバナの咲く

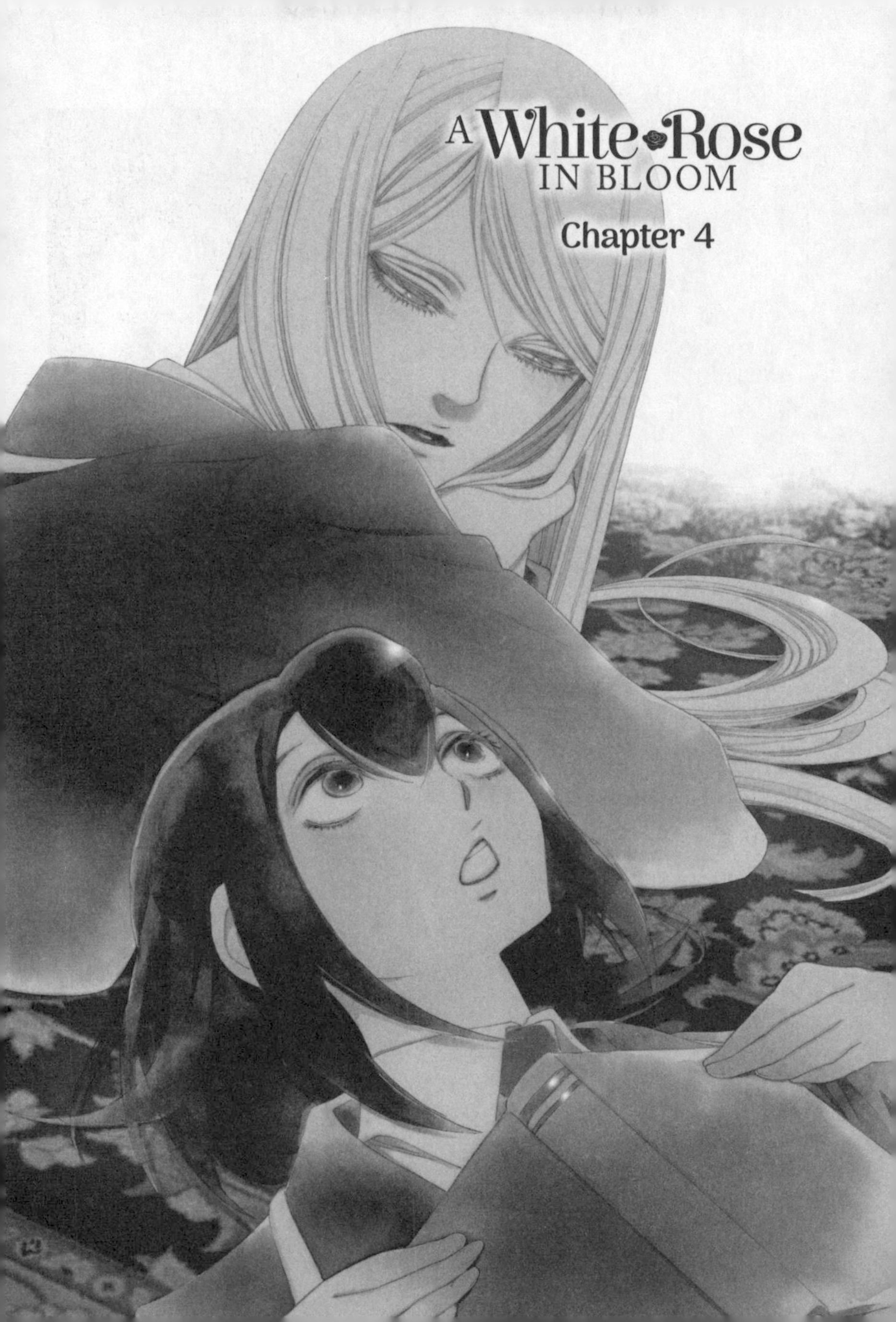
A White Rose IN BLOOM
Chapter 4

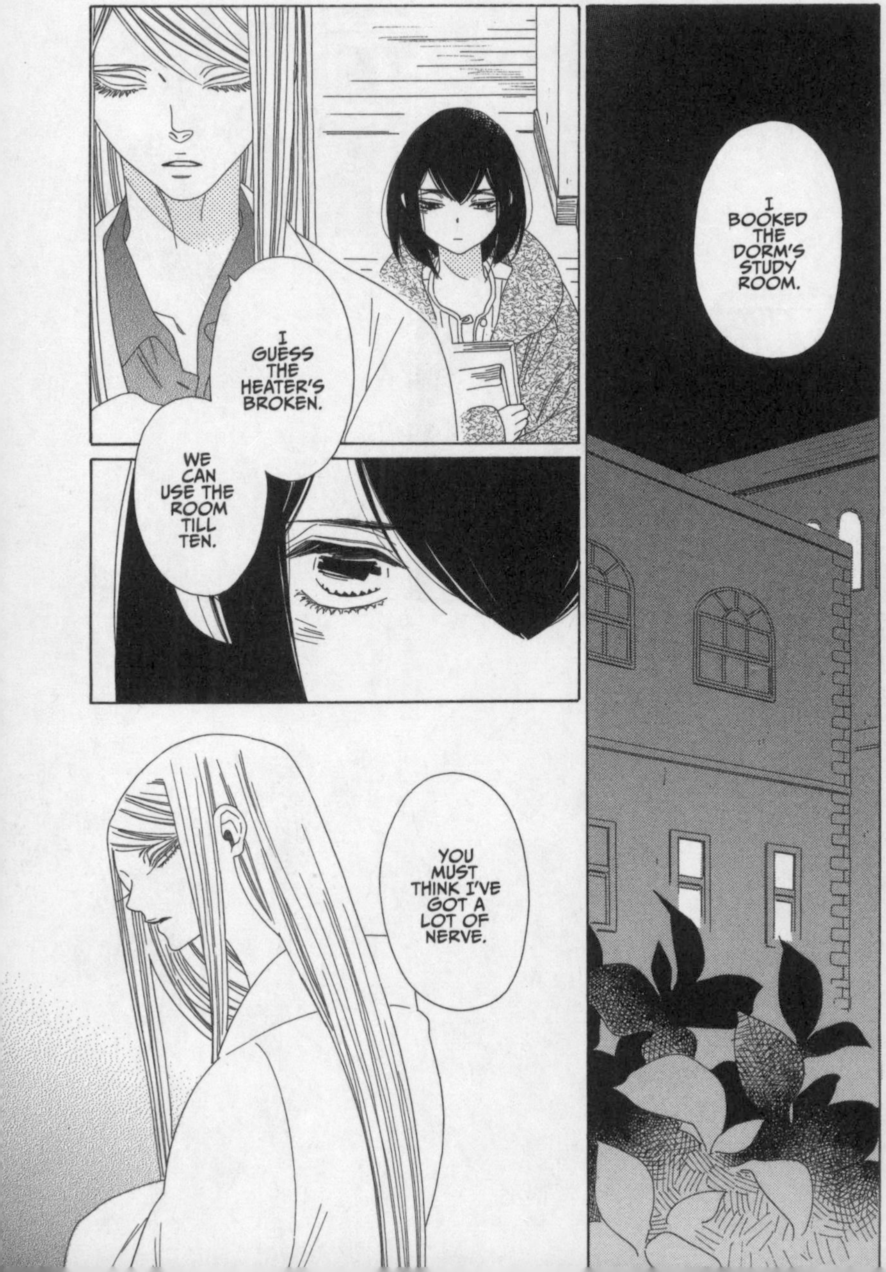
I BOOKED THE DORM'S STUDY ROOM.
I GUESS THE HEATER'S BROKEN.
WE CAN USE THE ROOM TILL TEN.
YOU MUST THINK I'VE GOT A LOT OF NERVE.

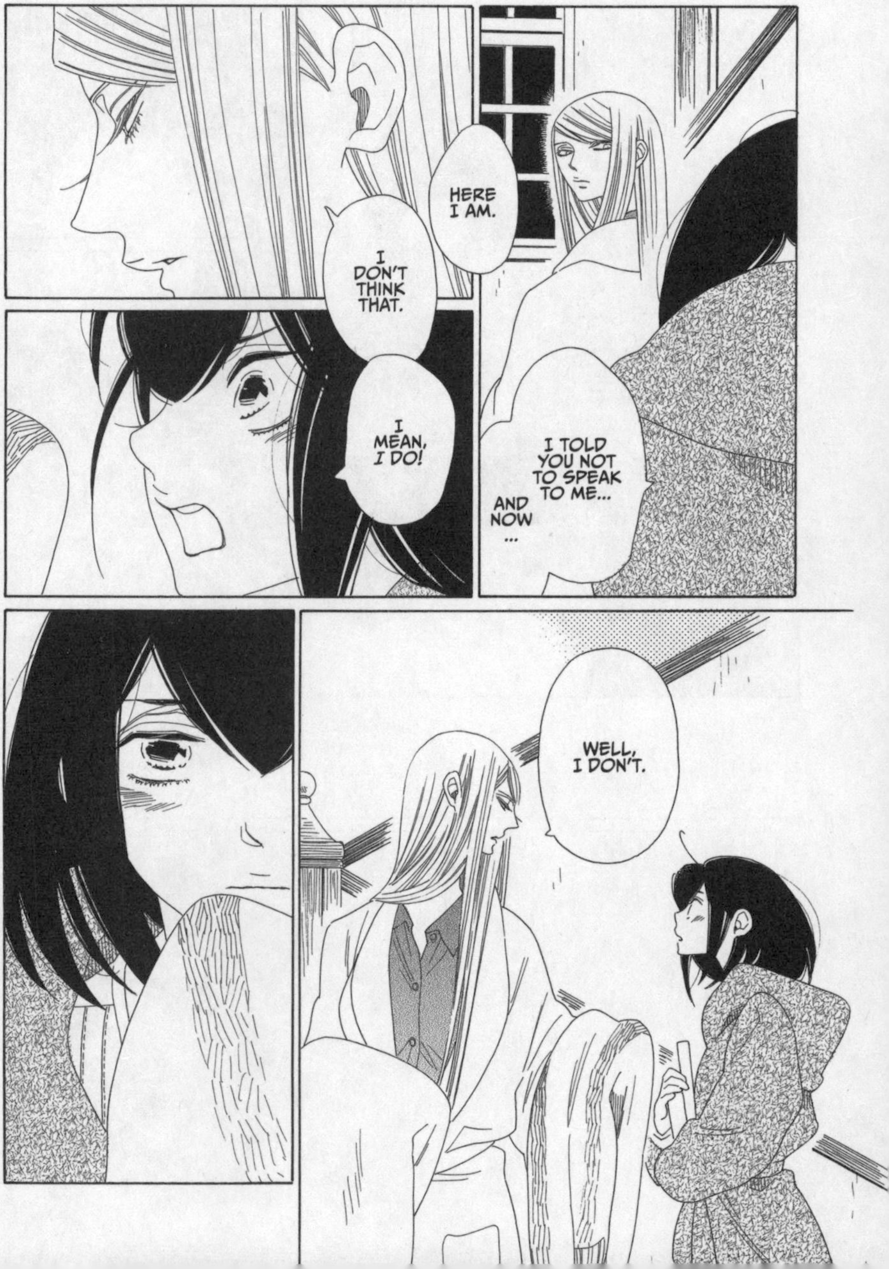
HERE I AM.
I TOLD YOU NOT TO SPEAK TO ME...
AND NOW ...
I DON'T THINK THAT.
I MEAN, I DO!
WELL, I DON'T.

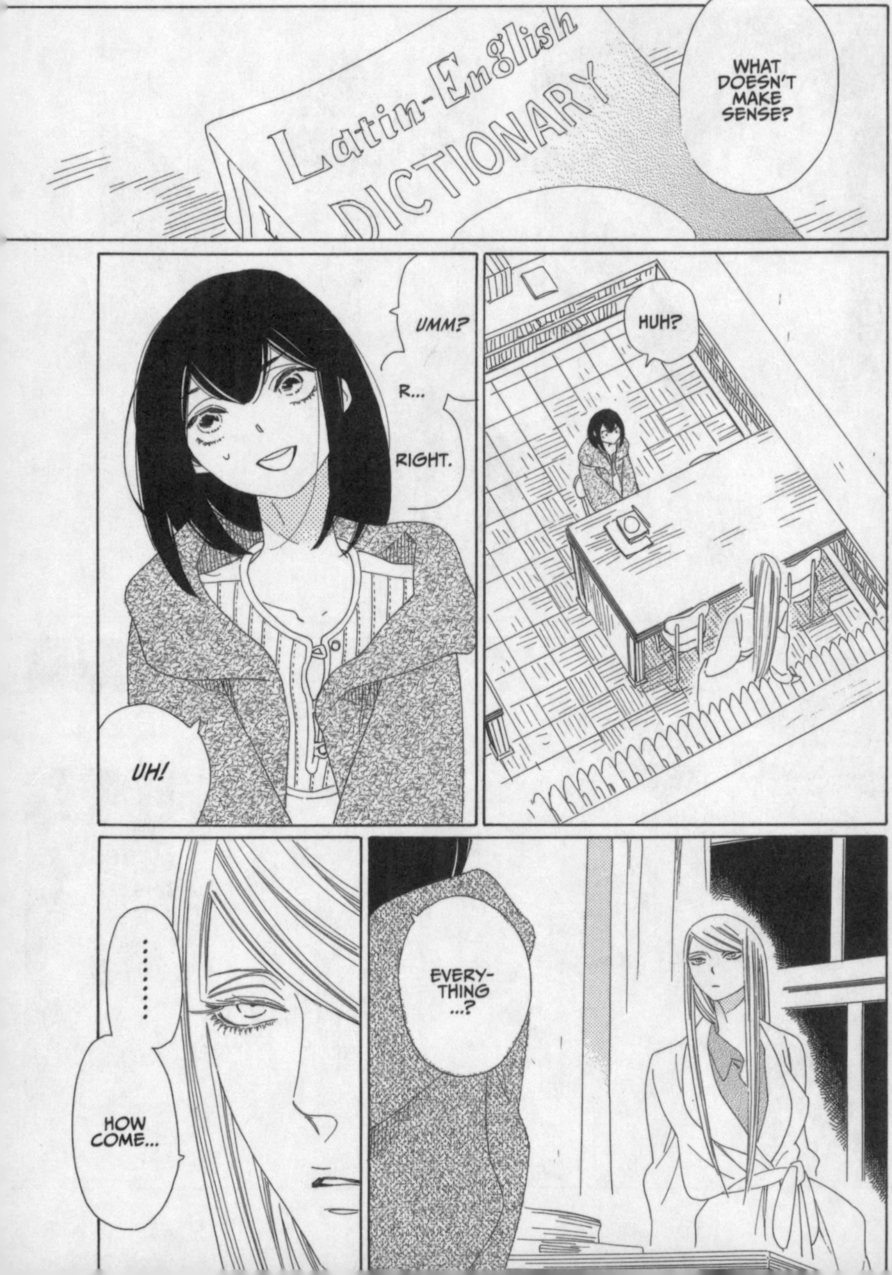
WHAT DOESN'T MAKE SENSE?
Latin-English
DICTIONARY
HUH?
UMM?
R...
RIGHT.
UH!
EVERY-THING ...?
......
HOW COME...

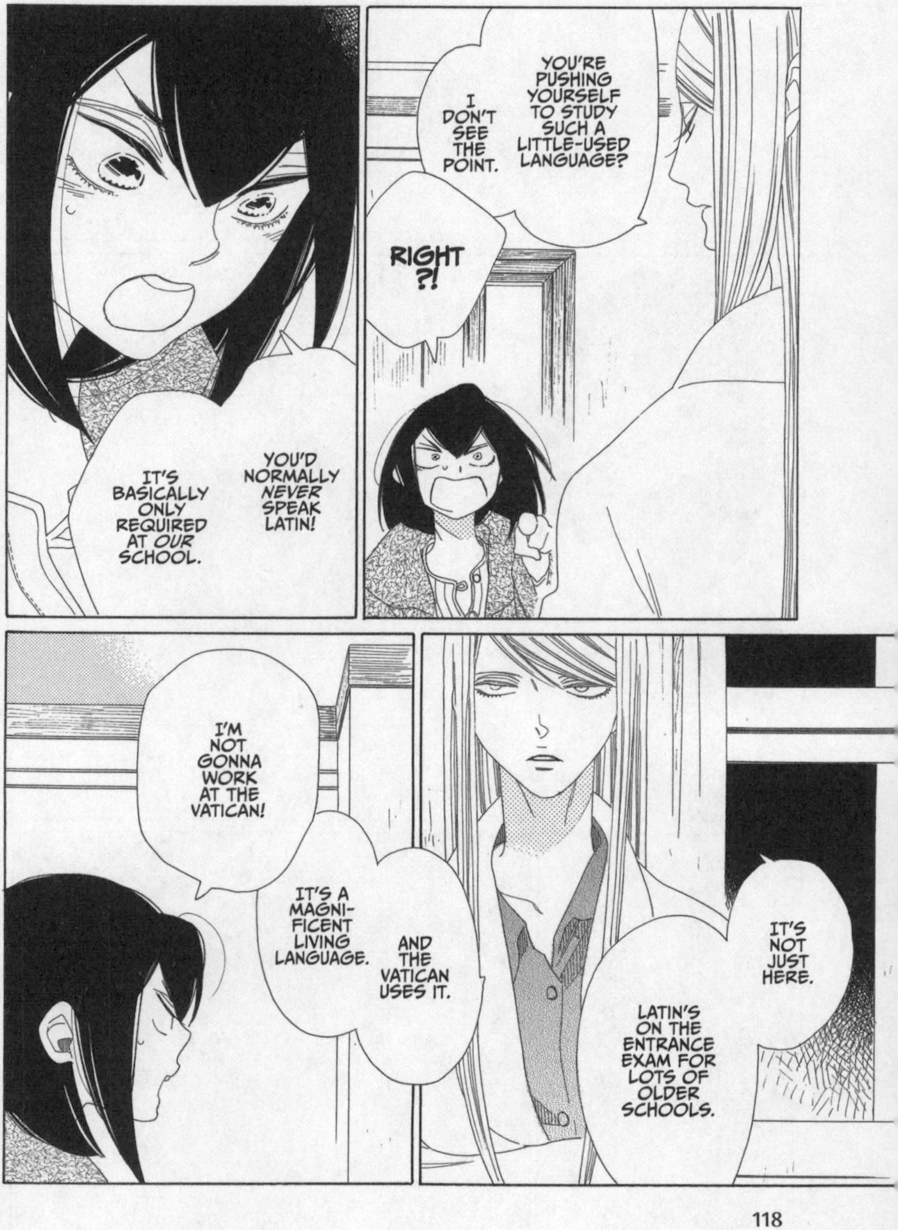
YOU'RE PUSHING YOURSELF TO STUDY SUCH A LITTLE-USED LANGUAGE?
I DON'T SEE THE POINT.
RIGHT ?!
YOU'D NORMALLY *NEVER* SPEAK LATIN!
IT'S BASICALLY ONLY REQUIRED AT *OUR* SCHOOL.
IT'S NOT JUST HERE.
LATIN'S ON THE ENTRANCE EXAM FOR LOTS OF OLDER SCHOOLS.
IT'S A MAGNIFICENT LIVING LANGUAGE.
AND THE VATICAN USES IT.
I'M NOT GONNA WORK AT THE VATICAN!

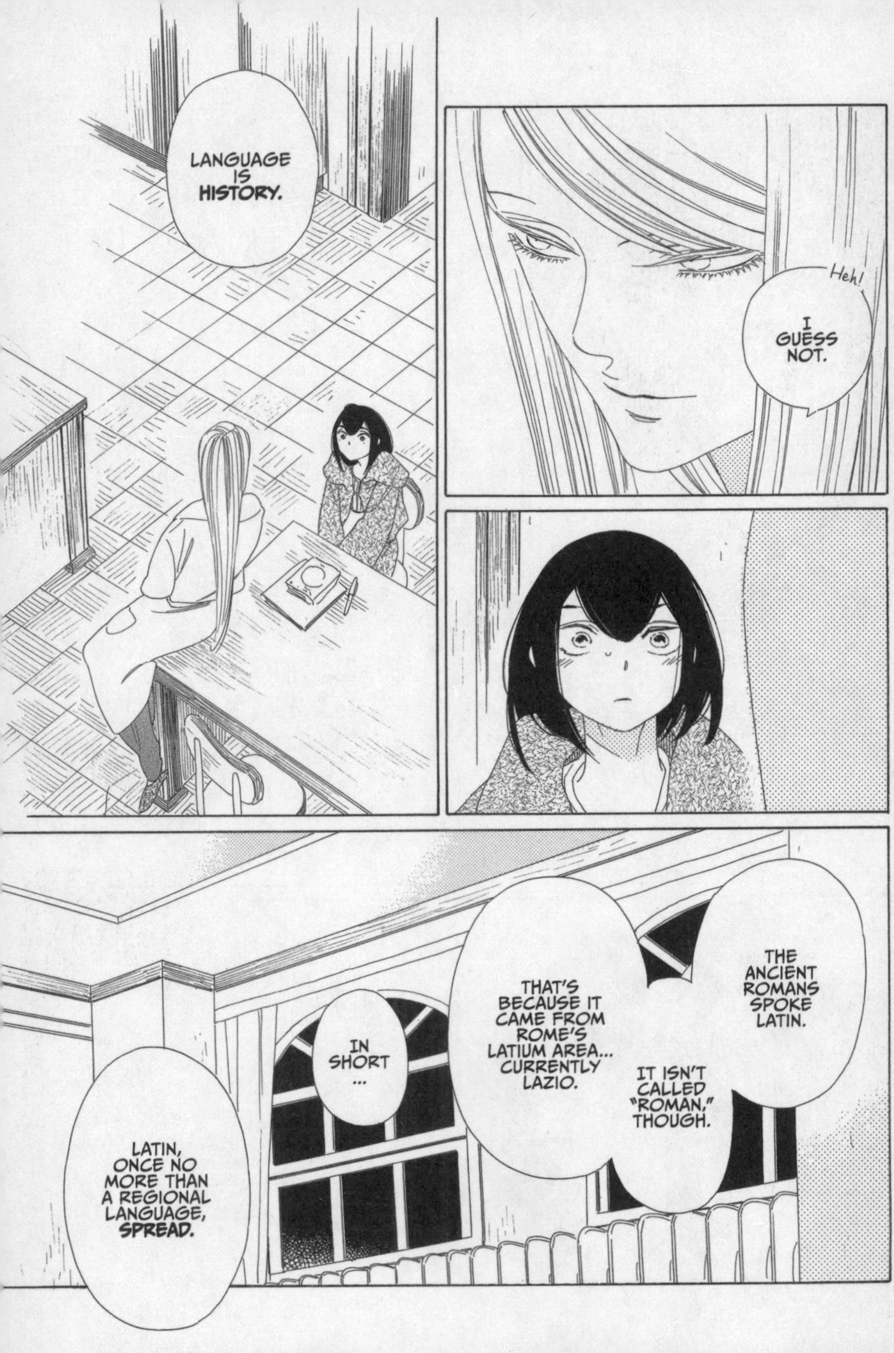
Heh!
I GUESS NOT.
LANGUAGE IS HISTORY.
THE ANCIENT ROMANS SPOKE LATIN.
IT ISN'T CALLED "ROMAN," THOUGH.
THAT'S BECAUSE IT CAME FROM ROME'S LATIUM AREA... CURRENTLY LAZIO.
IN SHORT...
LATIN, ONCE NO MORE THAN A REGIONAL LANGUAGE, SPREAD.

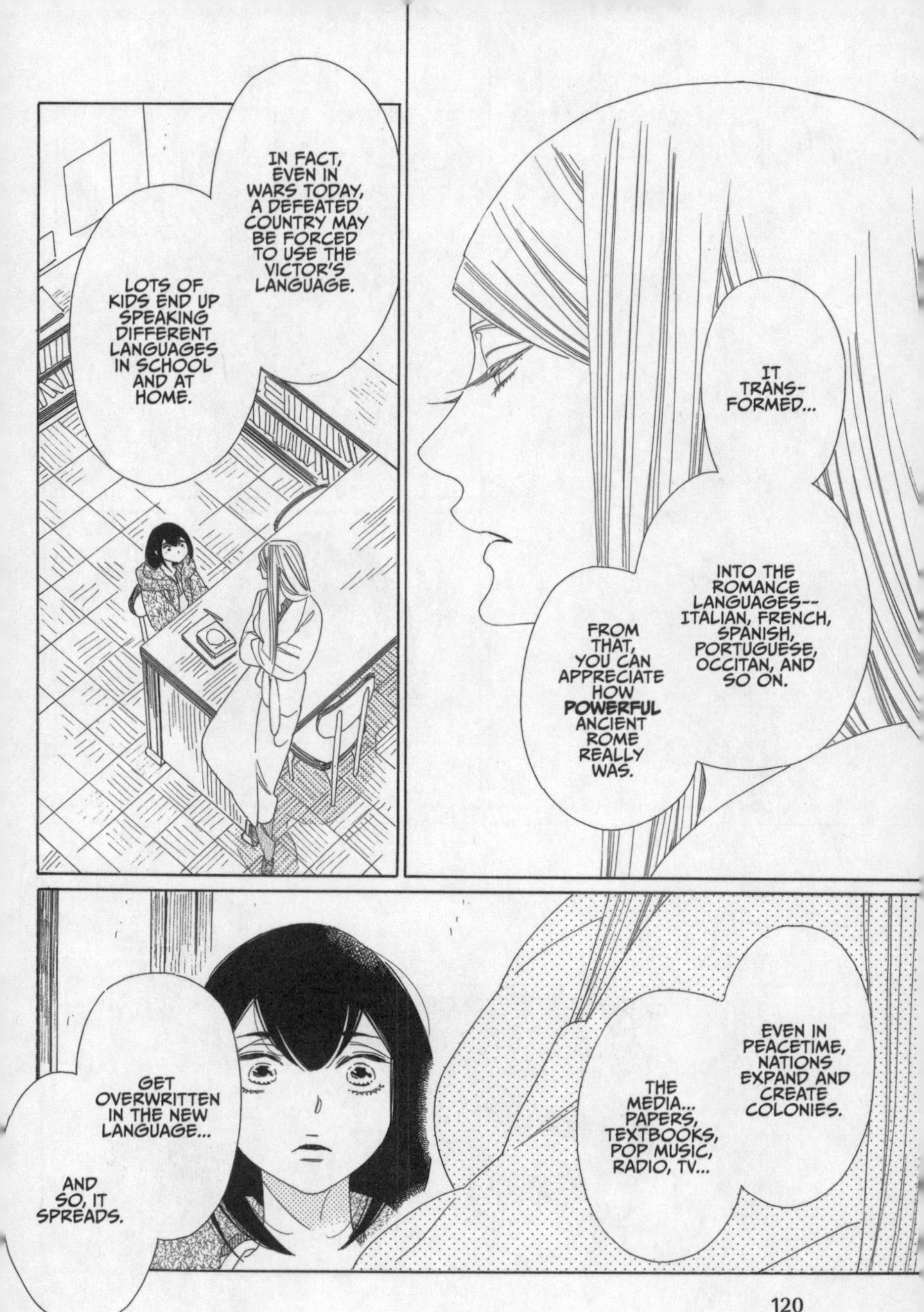
IT TRANS-FORMED...
INTO THE ROMANCE LANGUAGES--ITALIAN, FRENCH, SPANISH, PORTUGUESE, OCCITAN, AND SO ON.
FROM THAT, YOU CAN APPRECIATE HOW **POWERFUL** ANCIENT ROME REALLY WAS.
IN FACT, EVEN IN WARS TODAY, A DEFEATED COUNTRY MAY BE FORCED TO USE THE VICTOR'S LANGUAGE.
LOTS OF KIDS END UP SPEAKING DIFFERENT LANGUAGES IN SCHOOL AND AT HOME.
EVEN IN PEACETIME, NATIONS EXPAND AND CREATE COLONIES.
THE MEDIA... PAPERS, TEXTBOOKS, POP MUSIC, RADIO, TV...
GET OVERWRITTEN IN THE NEW LANGUAGE...
AND SO, IT SPREADS.

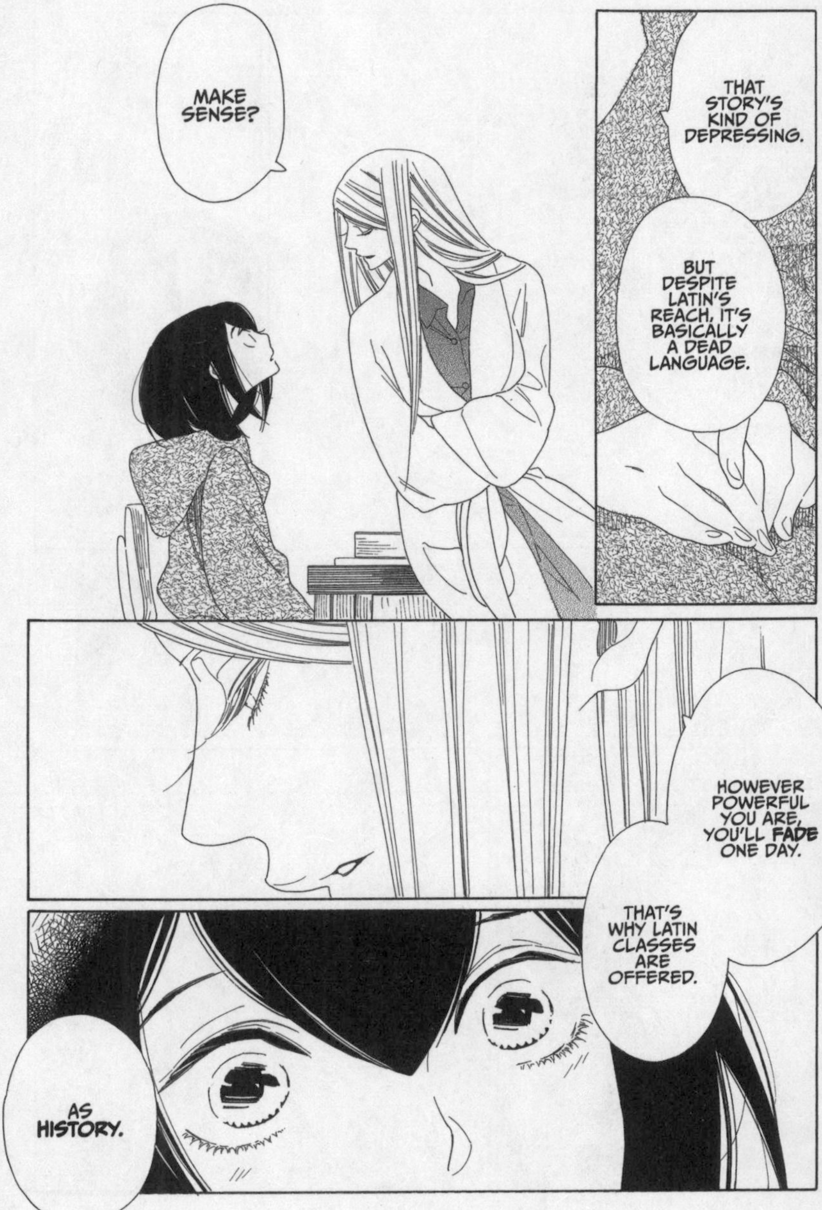
THAT STORY'S KIND OF DEPRESSING.
BUT DESPITE LATIN'S REACH, IT'S BASICALLY A DEAD LANGUAGE.
MAKE SENSE?
HOWEVER POWERFUL YOU ARE, YOU'LL FADE ONE DAY.
THAT'S WHY LATIN CLASSES ARE OFFERED.
AS HISTORY.

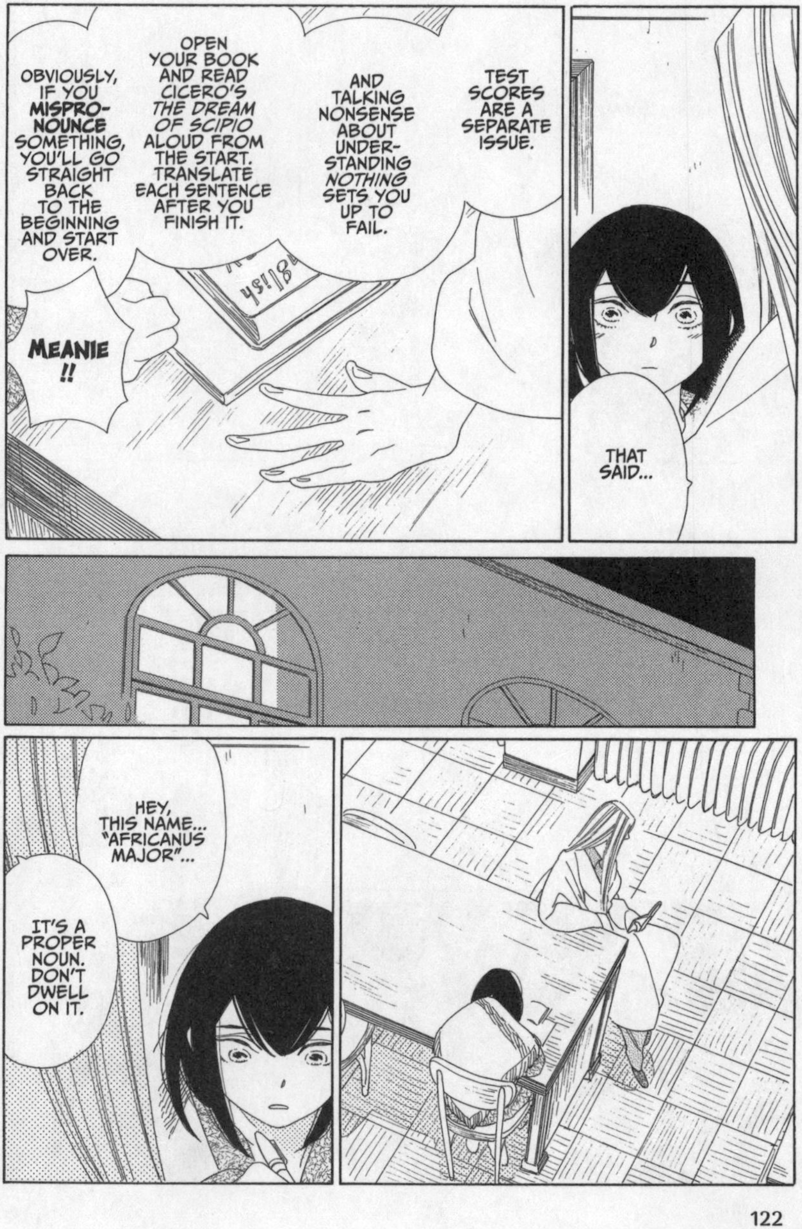
THAT SAID...
TEST SCORES ARE A SEPARATE ISSUE.
AND TALKING NONSENSE ABOUT UNDER-STANDING *NOTHING* SETS YOU UP TO FAIL.
OPEN YOUR BOOK AND READ CICERO'S *THE DREAM OF SCIPIO* ALOUD FROM THE START. TRANSLATE EACH SENTENCE AFTER YOU FINISH IT.
OBVIOUSLY, IF YOU **MISPRO-NOUNCE** SOMETHING, YOU'LL GO STRAIGHT BACK TO THE BEGINNING AND START OVER.
MEANIE!!
HEY, THIS NAME... "AFRICANUS MAJOR"...
IT'S A PROPER NOUN. DON'T DWELL ON IT.

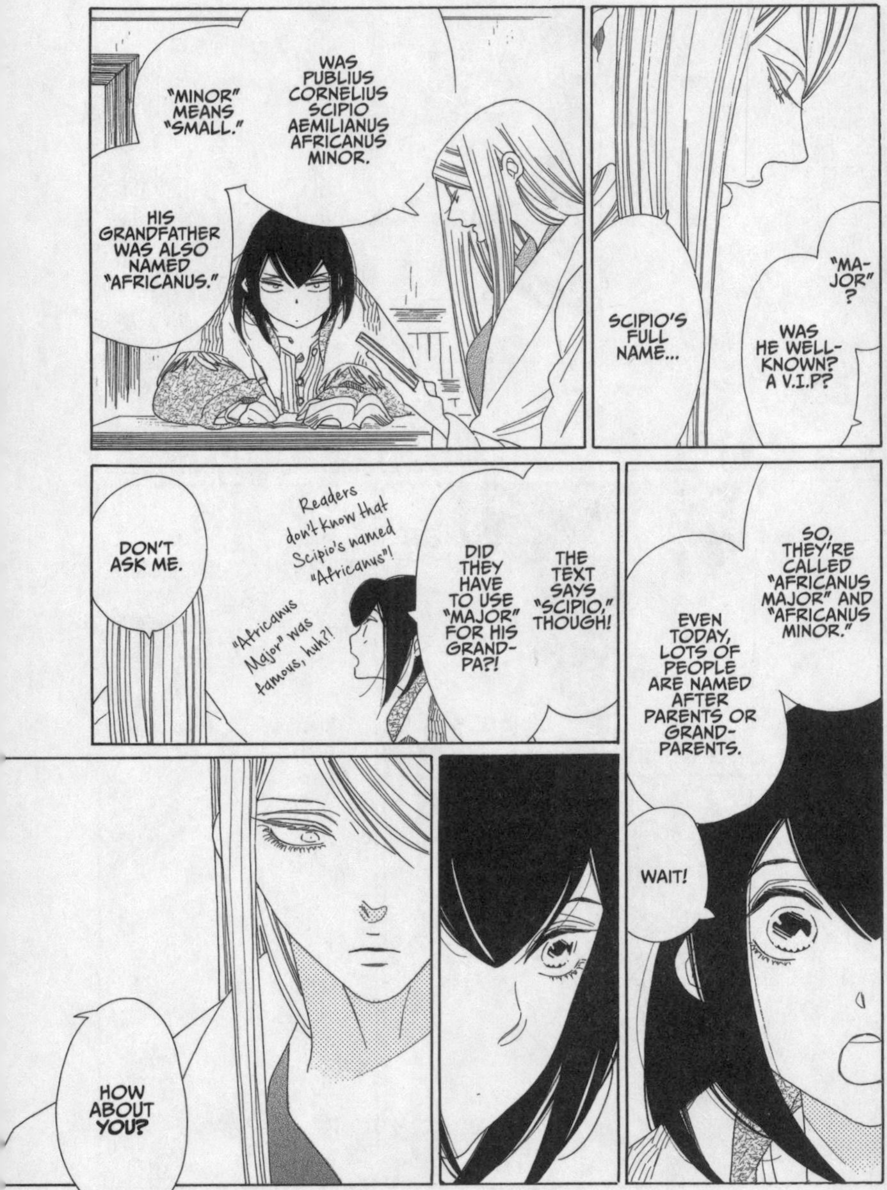
"MAJOR"? WAS HE WELL-KNOWN? A V.I.P?
SCIPIO'S FULL NAME...
WAS PUBLIUS CORNELIUS SCIPIO AEMILIANUS AFRICANUS MINOR.
"MINOR" MEANS "SMALL."
HIS GRANDFATHER WAS ALSO NAMED "AFRICANUS."
SO, THEY'RE CALLED "AFRICANUS MAJOR" AND "AFRICANUS MINOR."
EVEN TODAY, LOTS OF PEOPLE ARE NAMED AFTER PARENTS OR GRAND-PARENTS.
THE TEXT SAYS "SCIPIO," THOUGH!
DID THEY HAVE TO USE "MAJOR" FOR HIS GRAND-PA?!
Readers don't know that Scipio's named "Africanus"!
"Africanus Major" was famous, huh?!
DON'T ASK ME.
WAIT!
HOW ABOUT YOU?

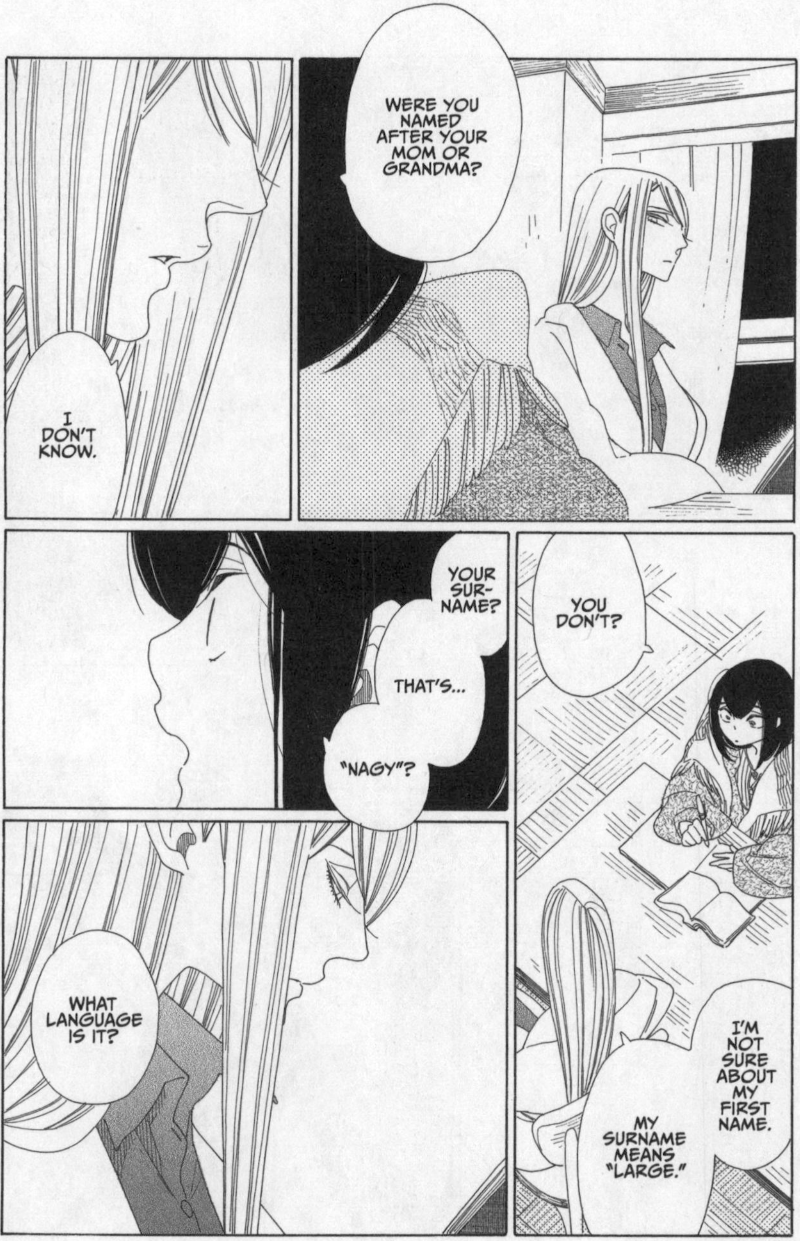
WERE YOU NAMED AFTER YOUR MOM OR GRANDMA?
I DON'T KNOW.
YOU DON'T?
I'M NOT SURE ABOUT MY FIRST NAME.
MY SURNAME MEANS "LARGE."
YOUR SUR-NAME?
THAT'S...
"NAGY"?
WHAT LANGUAGE IS IT?

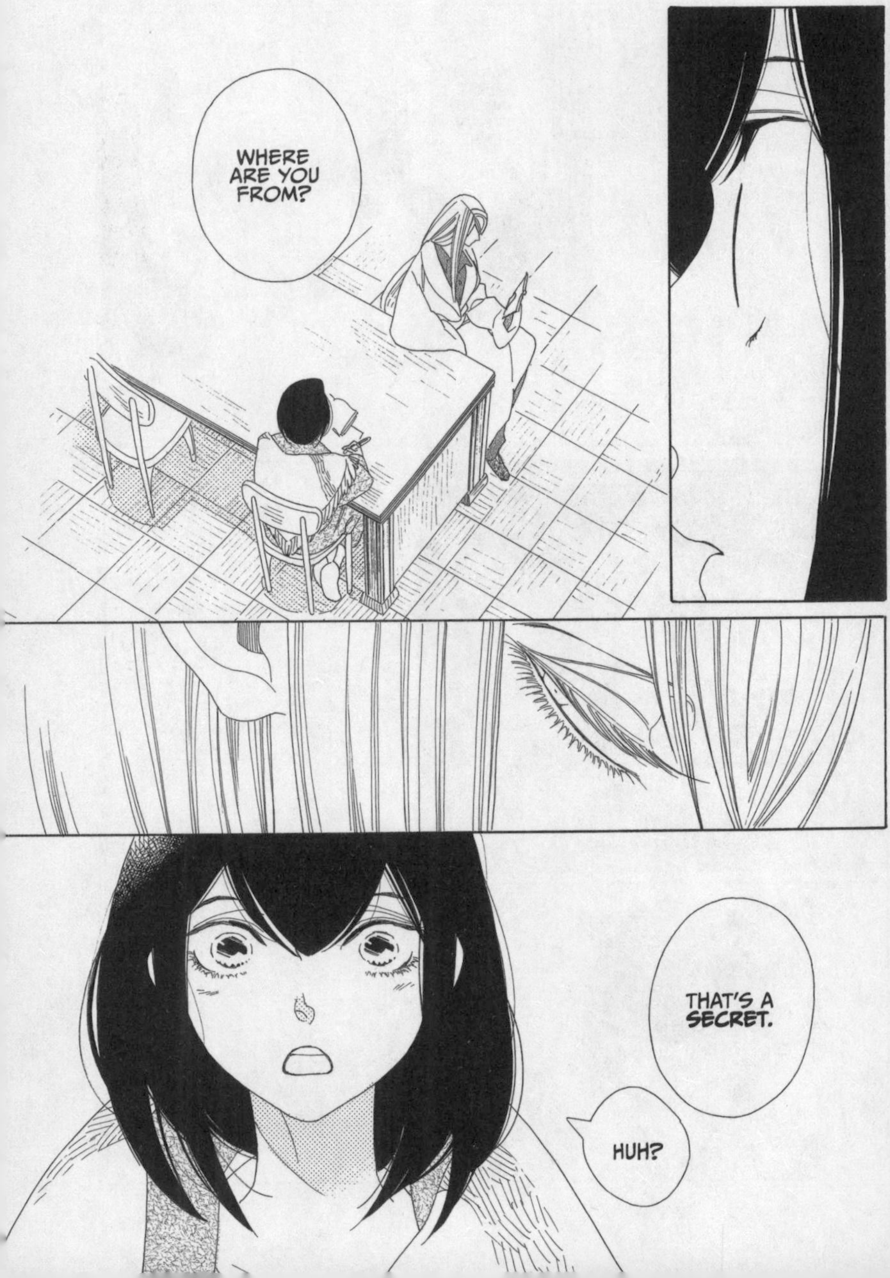
WHERE ARE YOU FROM?
THAT'S A SECRET.
HUH?

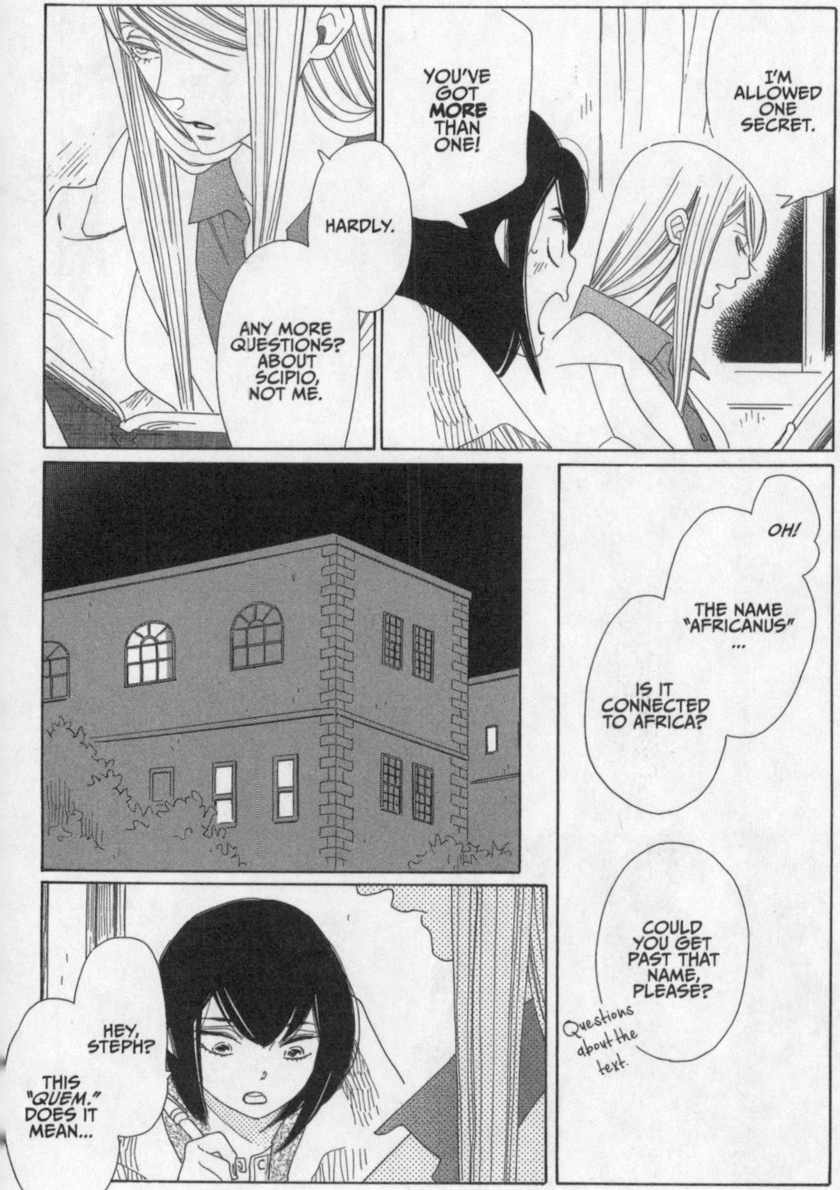
I'M ALLOWED ONE SECRET.
YOU'VE GOT MORE THAN ONE!
HARDLY.
ANY MORE QUESTIONS? ABOUT SCIPIO, NOT ME.
OH!
THE NAME "AFRICANUS" ...
IS IT CONNECTED TO AFRICA?
COULD YOU GET PAST THAT NAME, PLEASE?
Questions about the text.
HEY, STEPH?
THIS "*QUEM.*" DOES IT MEAN...

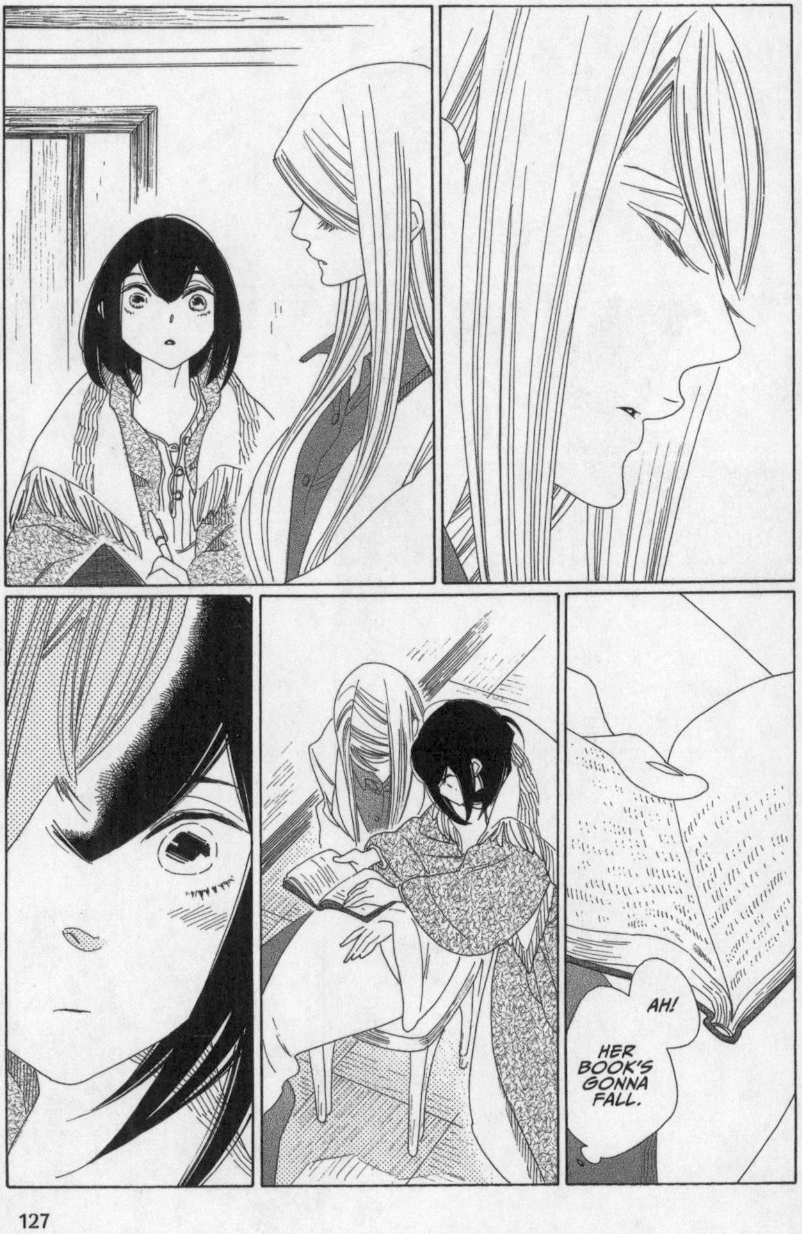
AH!
HER BOOK'S GONNA FALL.

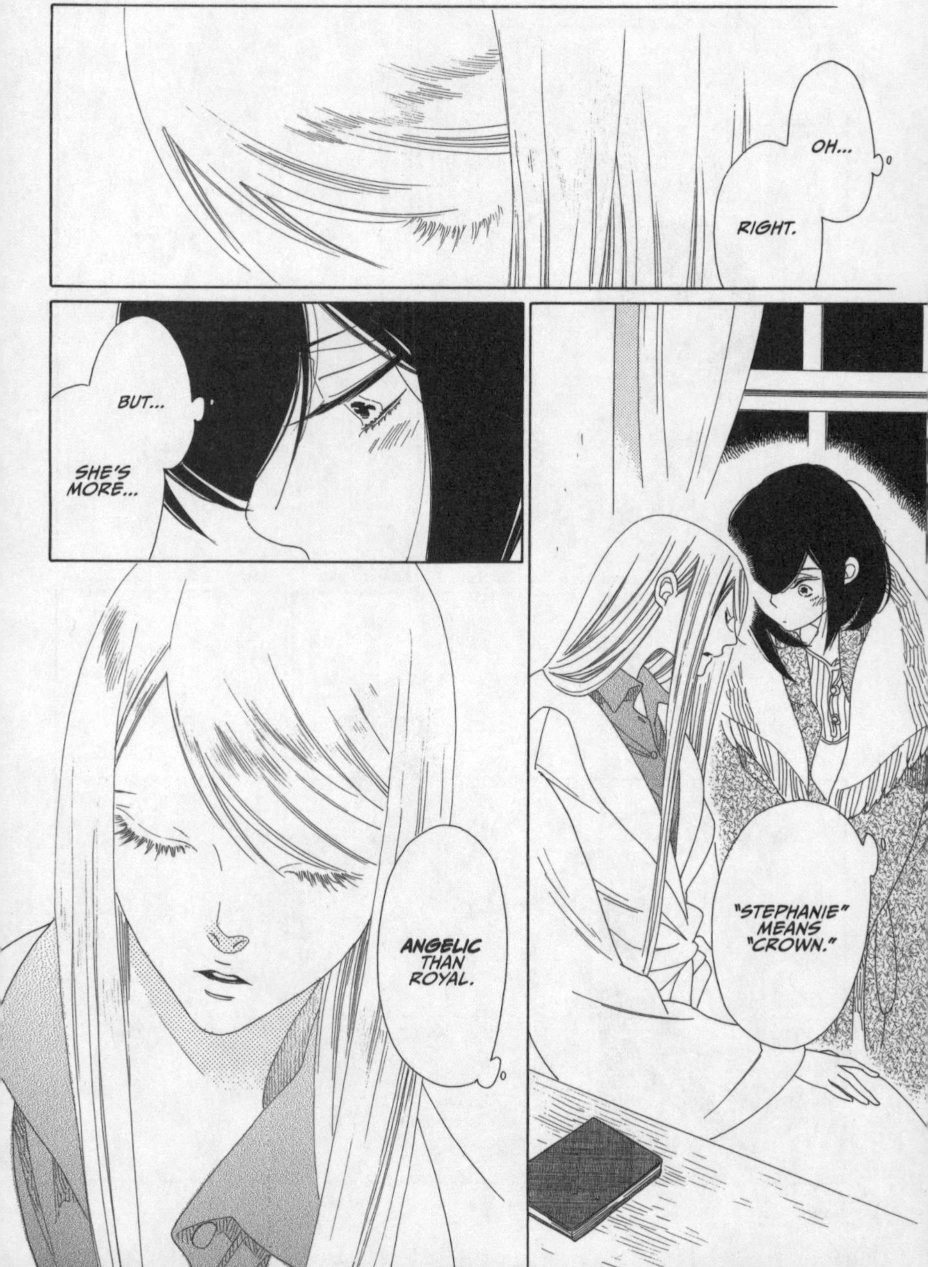
OH... RIGHT.
"STEPHANIE" MEANS "CROWN."
BUT... SHE'S MORE...
ANGELIC THAN ROYAL.

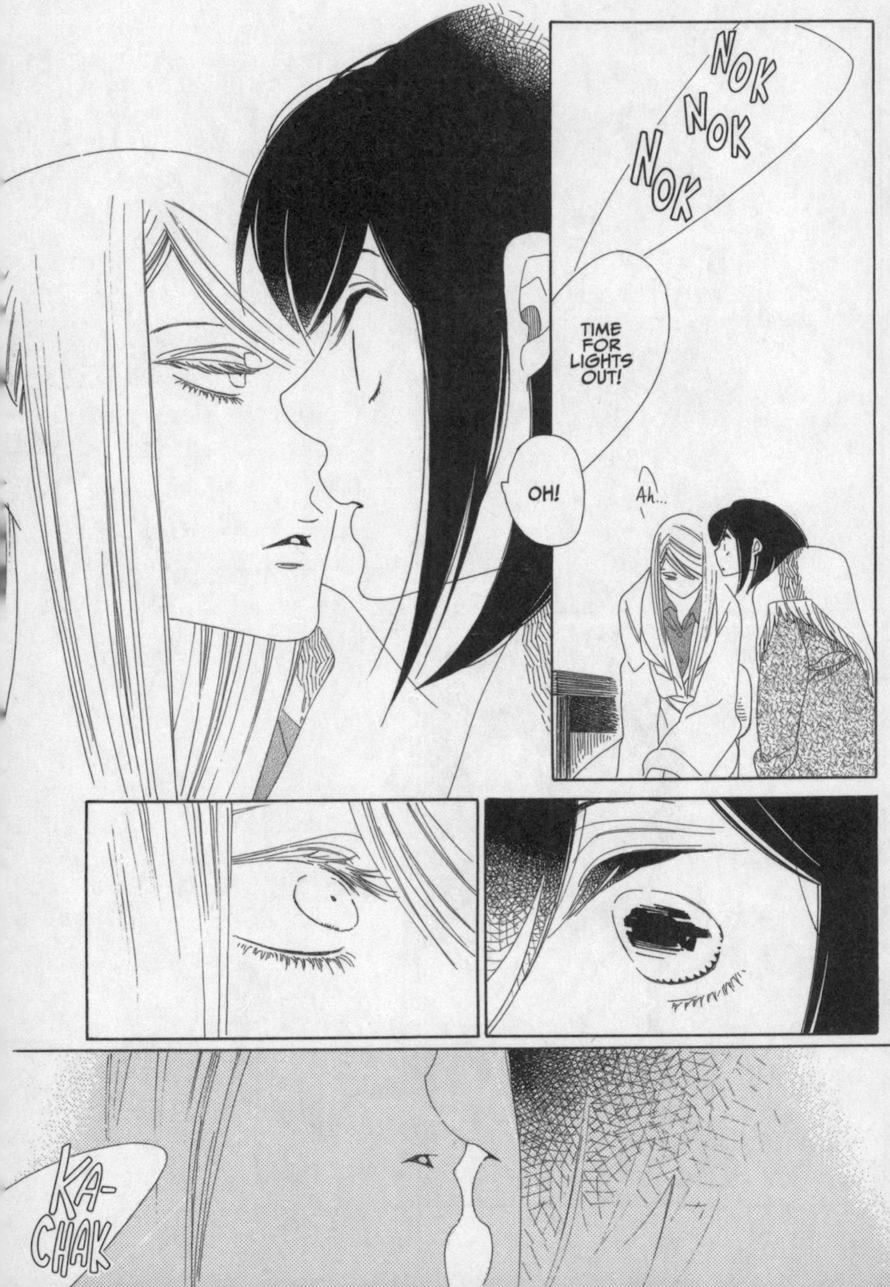
NOK NOK NOK
TIME FOR LIGHTS OUT!
Ah...
OH!
KA-CHAK

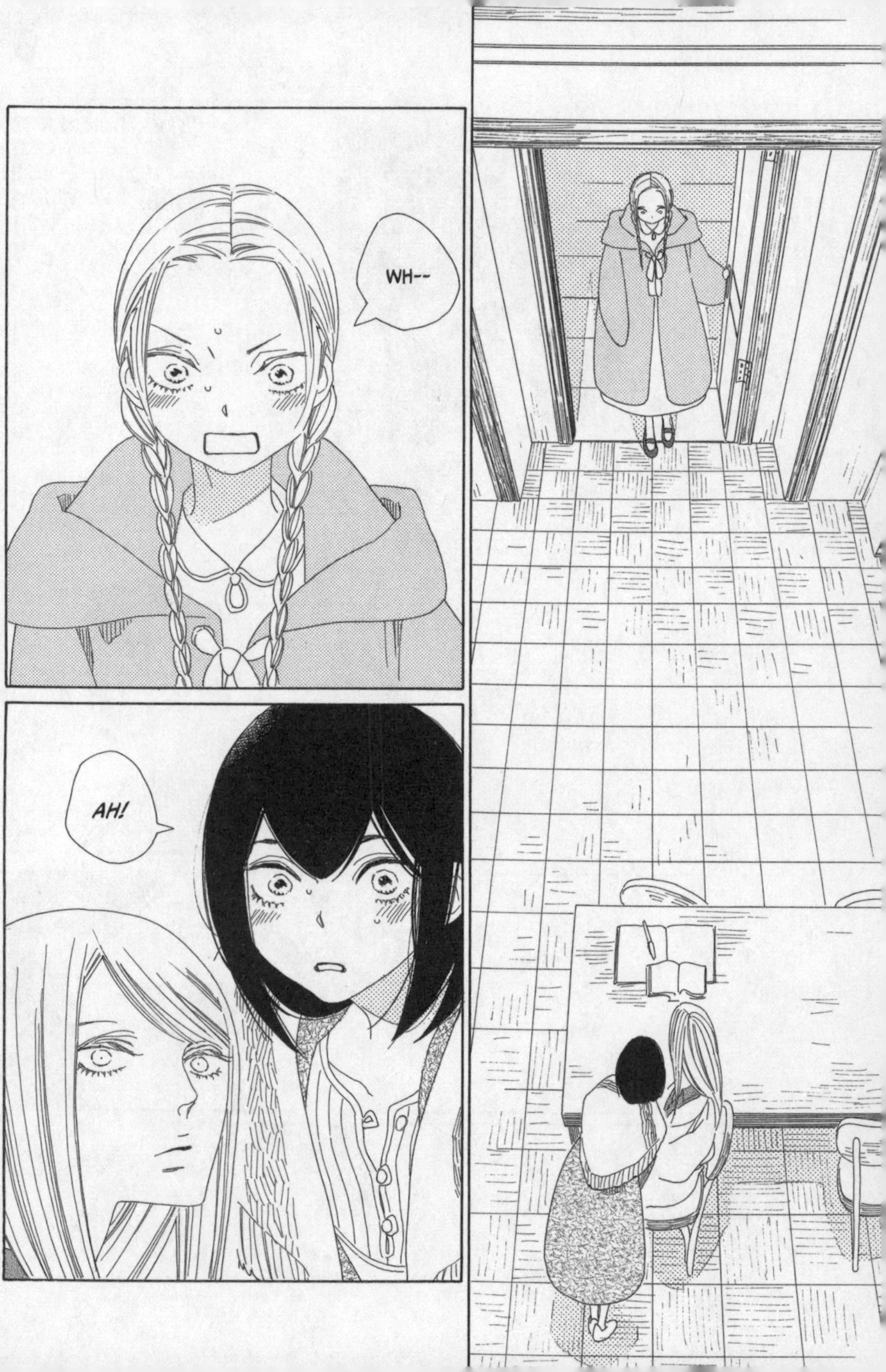
WH--
AH!

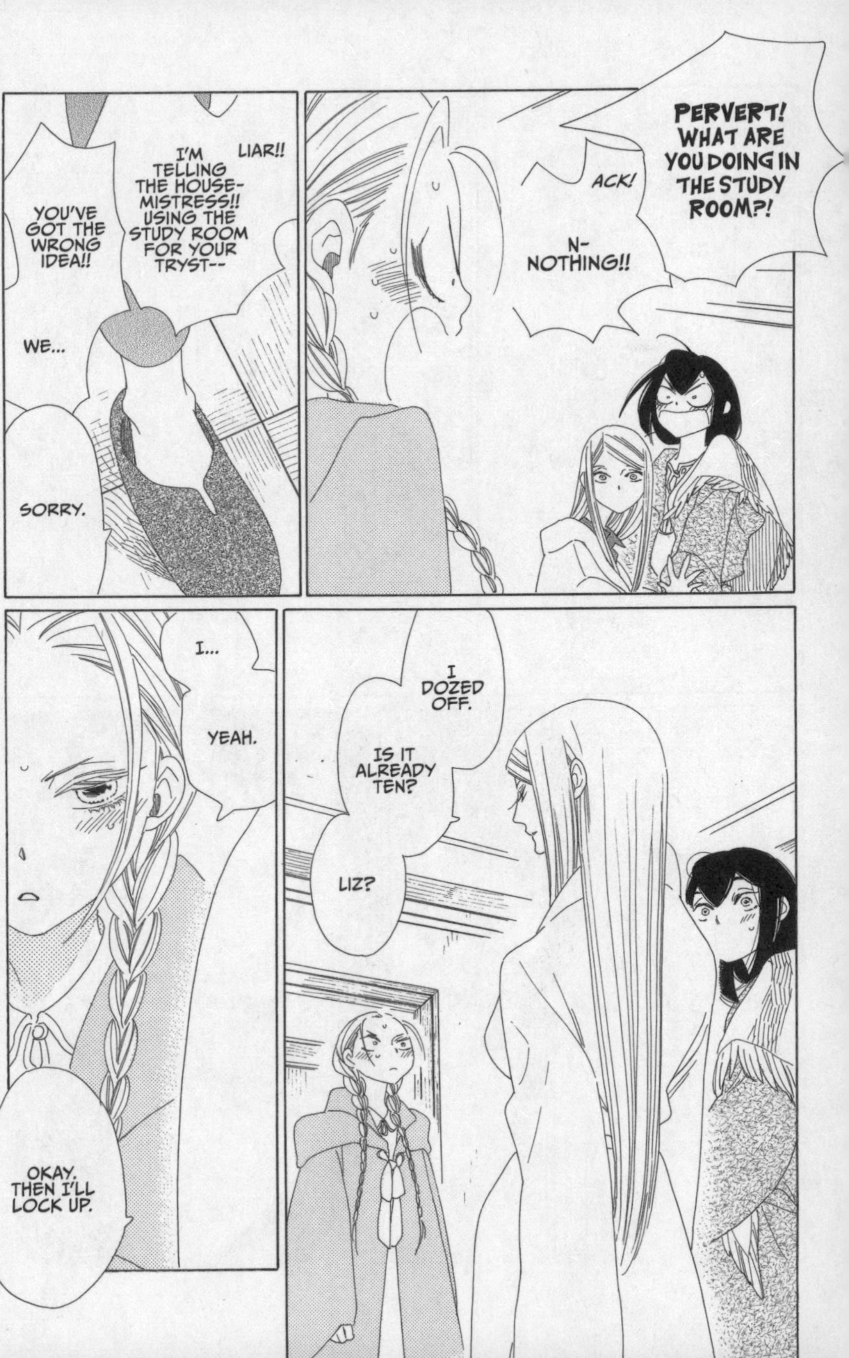
PERVERT! WHAT ARE YOU DOING IN THE STUDY ROOM?!
ACK!
N- NOTHING!!
LIAR!!
I'M TELLING THE HOUSE-MISTRESS!! USING THE STUDY ROOM FOR YOUR TRYST--
YOU'VE GOT THE WRONG IDEA!!
WE...
SORRY.
I DOZED OFF.
IS IT ALREADY TEN?
LIZ?
I...
YEAH.
OKAY. THEN I'LL LOCK UP.

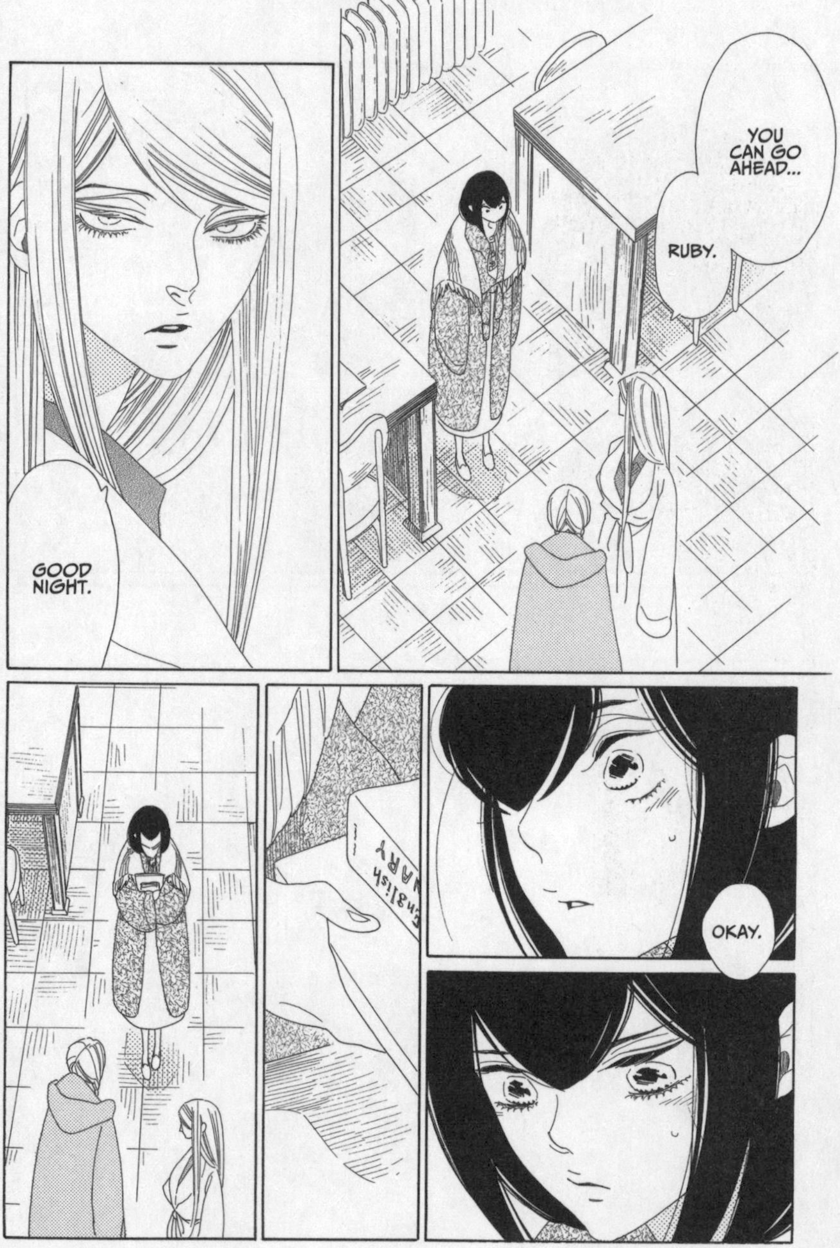
YOU CAN GO AHEAD...
RUBY.
GOOD NIGHT.
OKAY.

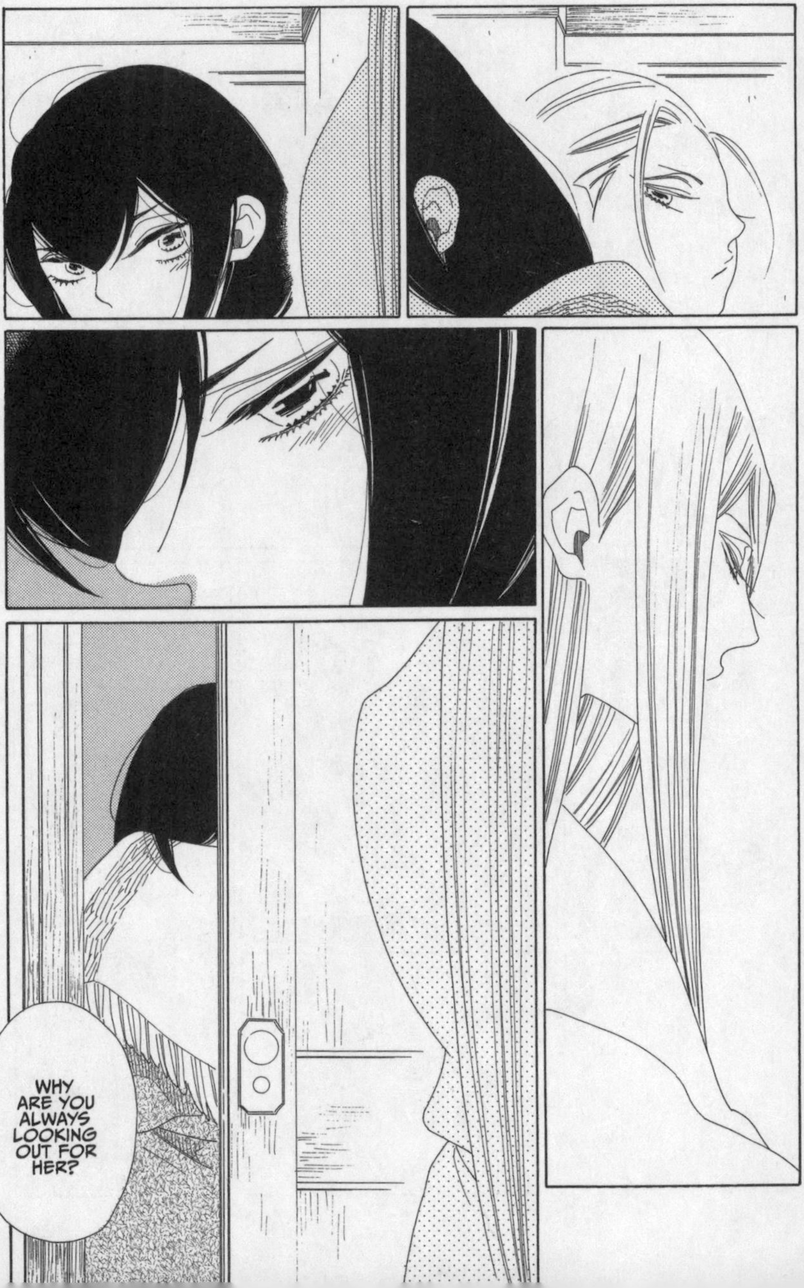
WHY ARE YOU ALWAYS LOOKING OUT FOR HER?

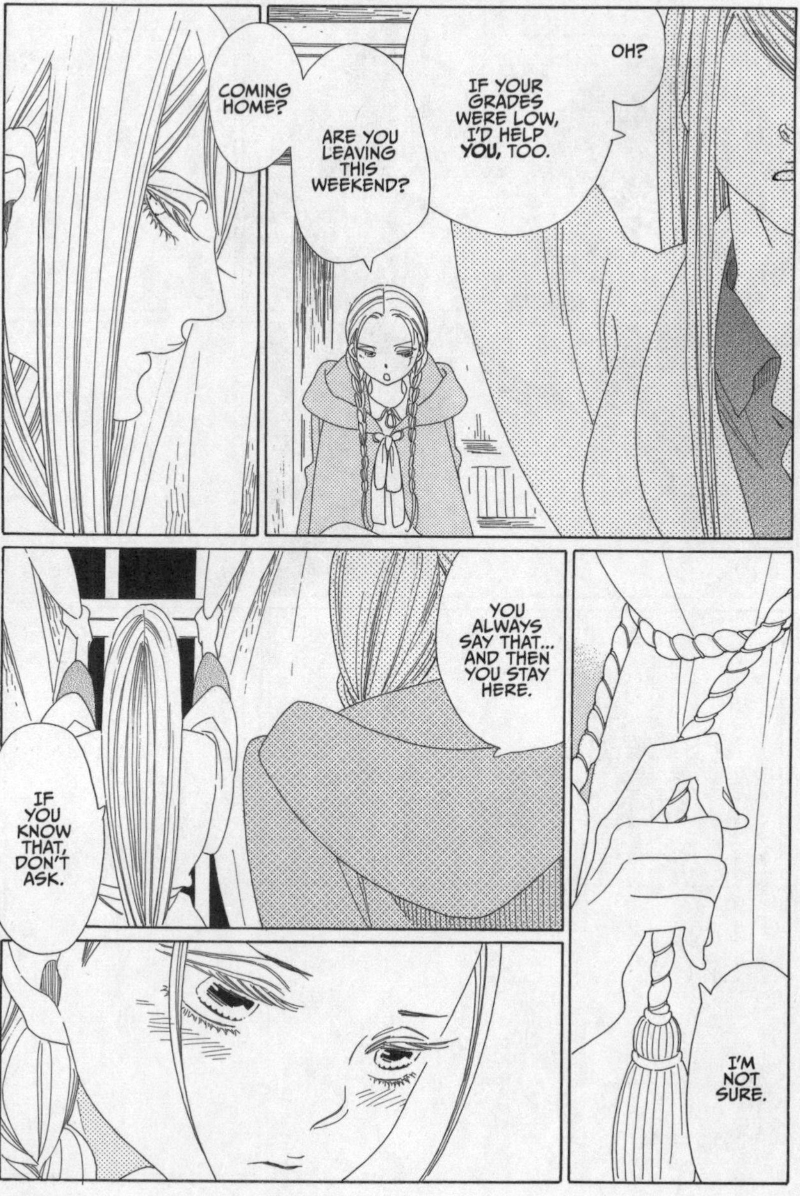
OH?
IF YOUR GRADES WERE LOW, I'D HELP **YOU,** TOO.
ARE YOU LEAVING THIS WEEKEND?
COMING HOME?
I'M NOT SURE.
YOU ALWAYS SAY THAT... AND THEN YOU STAY HERE.
IF YOU KNOW THAT, DON'T ASK.

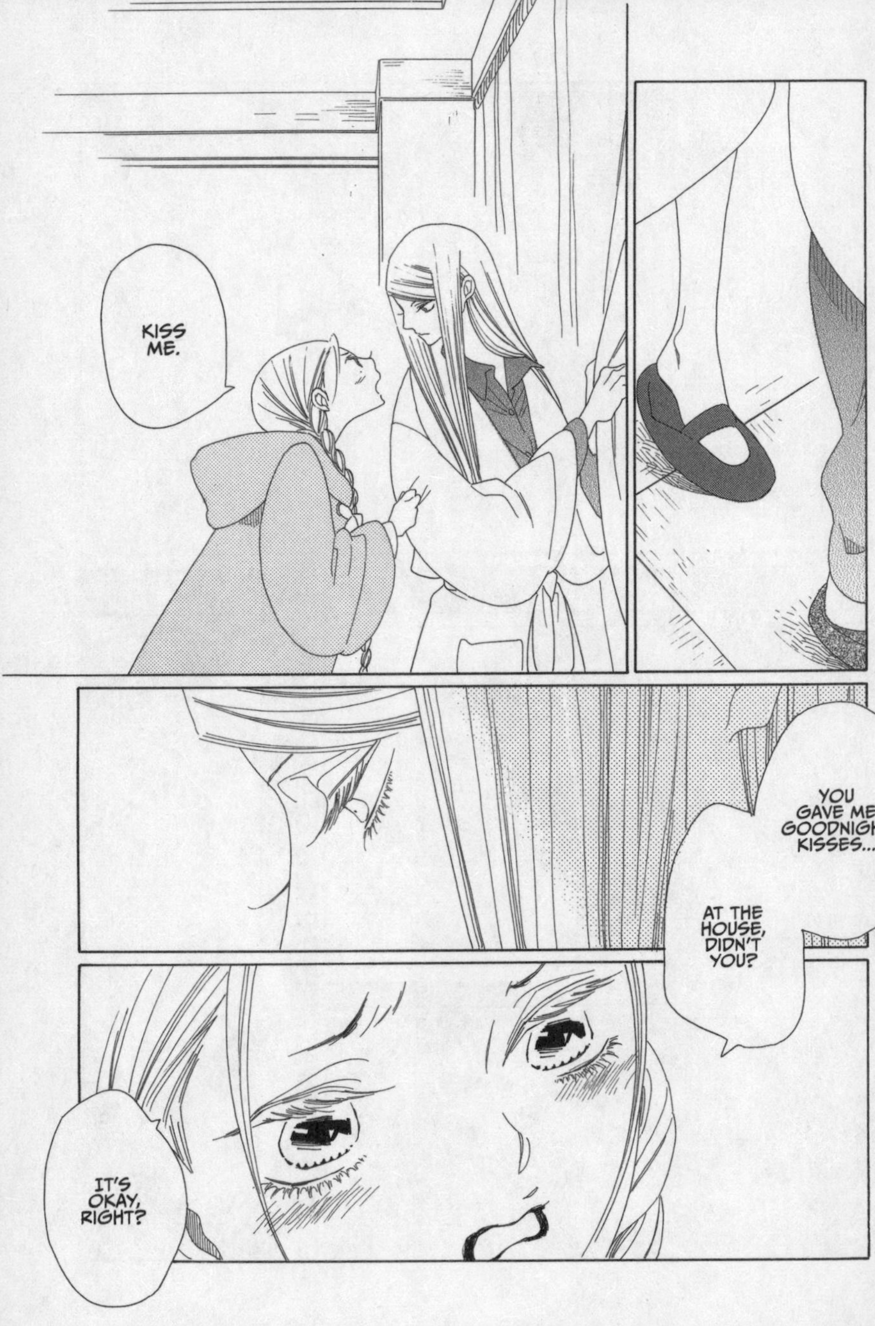
KISS ME.
YOU GAVE ME GOODNIGHT KISSES...
AT THE HOUSE, DIDN'T YOU?
IT'S OKAY, RIGHT?

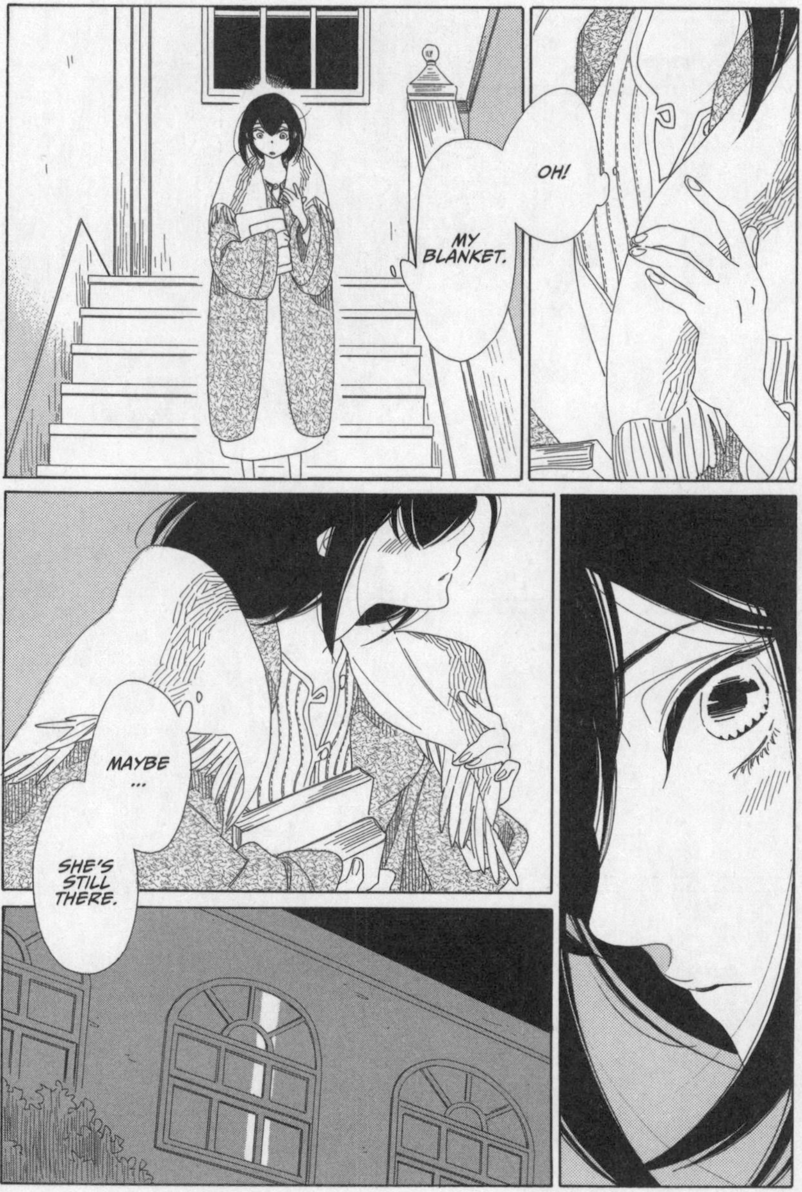
OH!
MY BLANKET.
MAYBE ...
SHE'S STILL THERE.

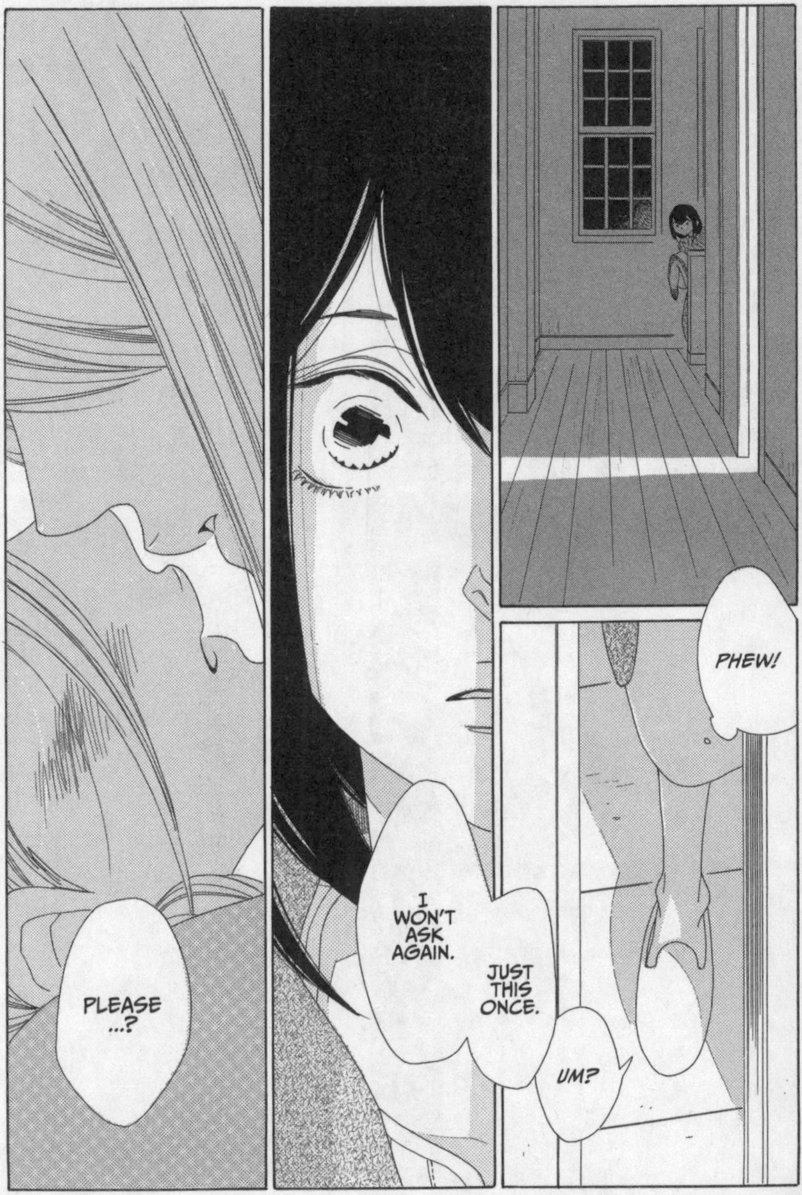
PHEW!
UM?
I WON'T ASK AGAIN.
JUST THIS ONCE.
PLEASE ...?

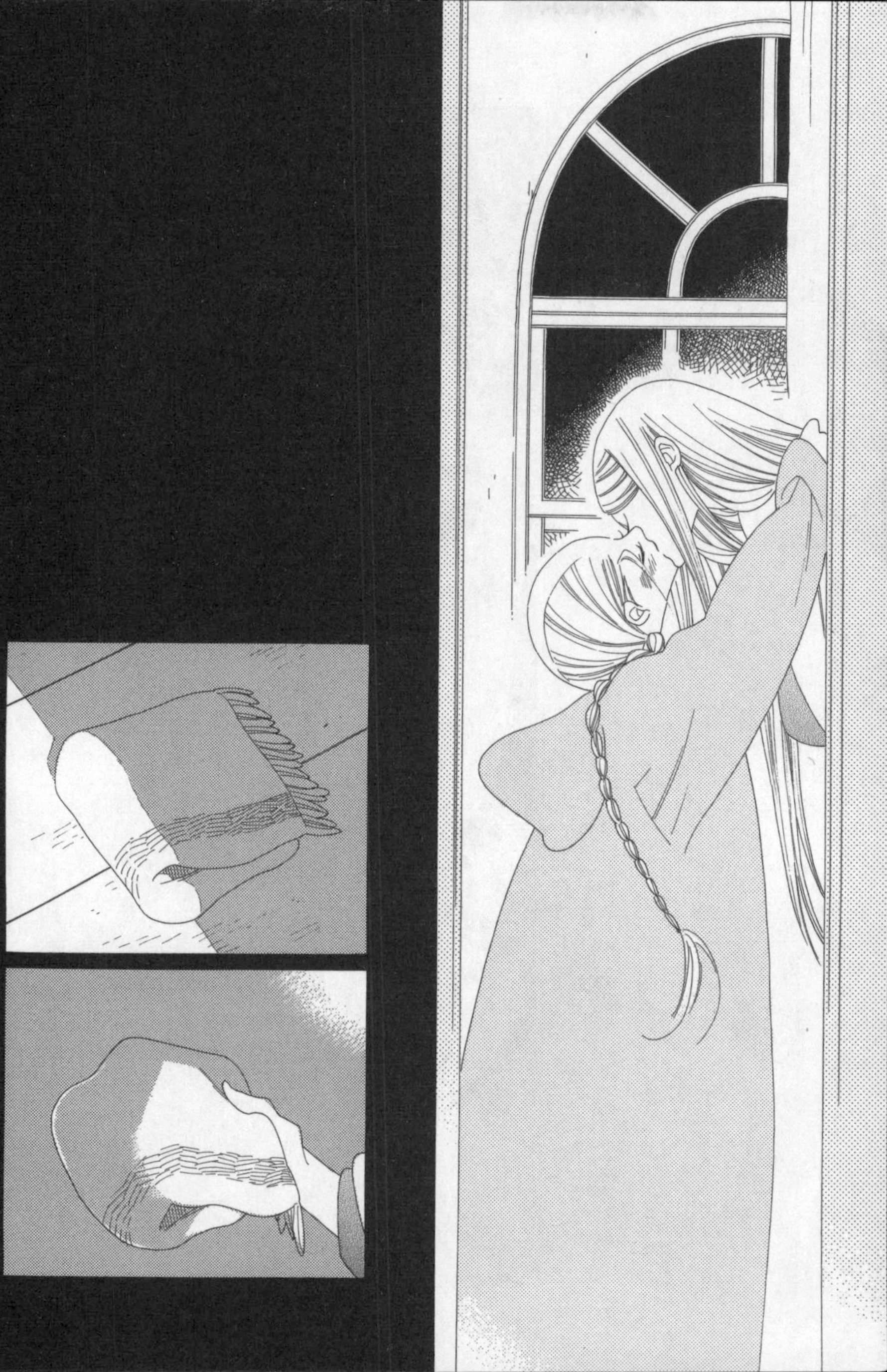

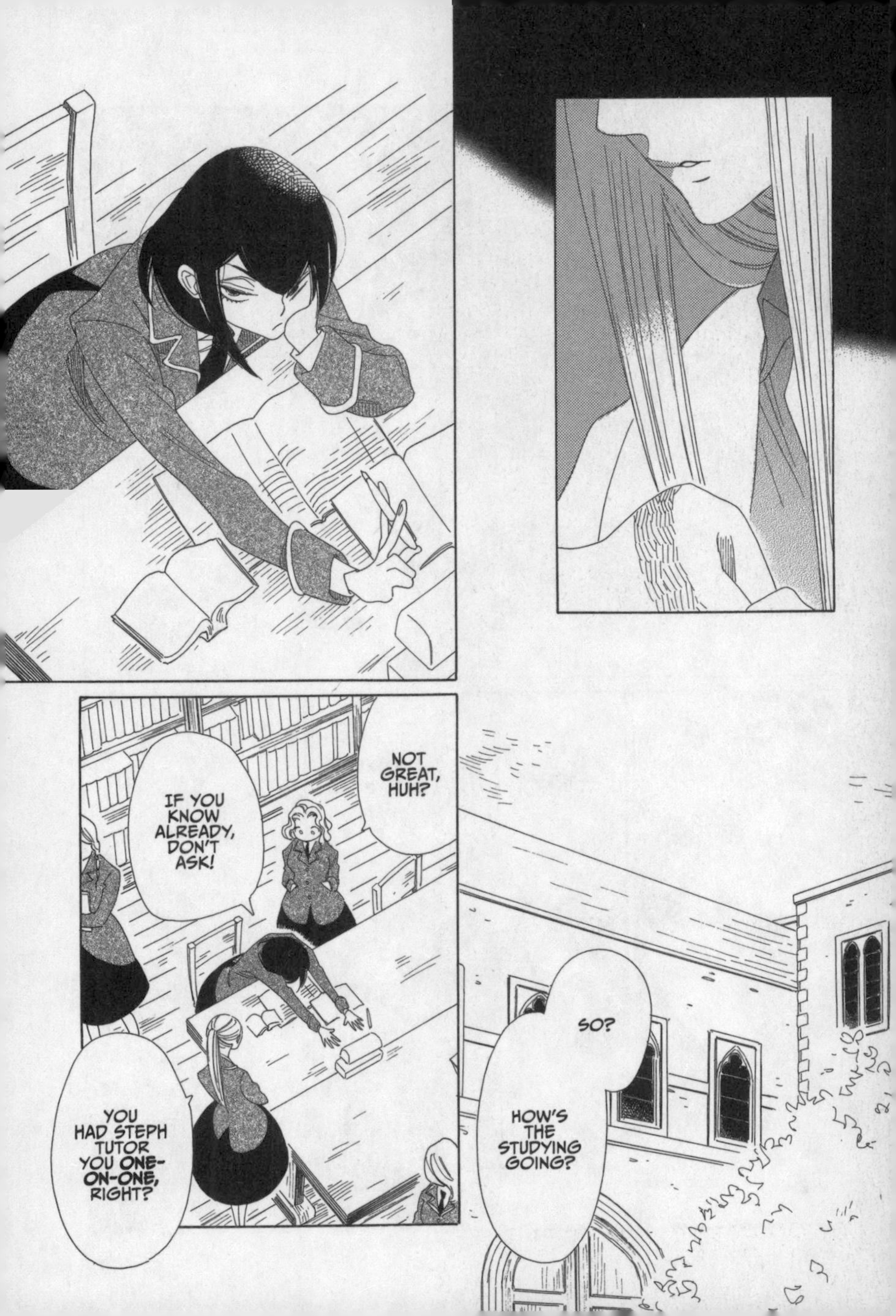
SO?
HOW'S THE STUDYING GOING?
NOT GREAT, HUH?
IF YOU KNOW ALREADY, DON'T ASK!
YOU HAD STEPH TUTOR YOU ONE-ON-ONE, RIGHT?

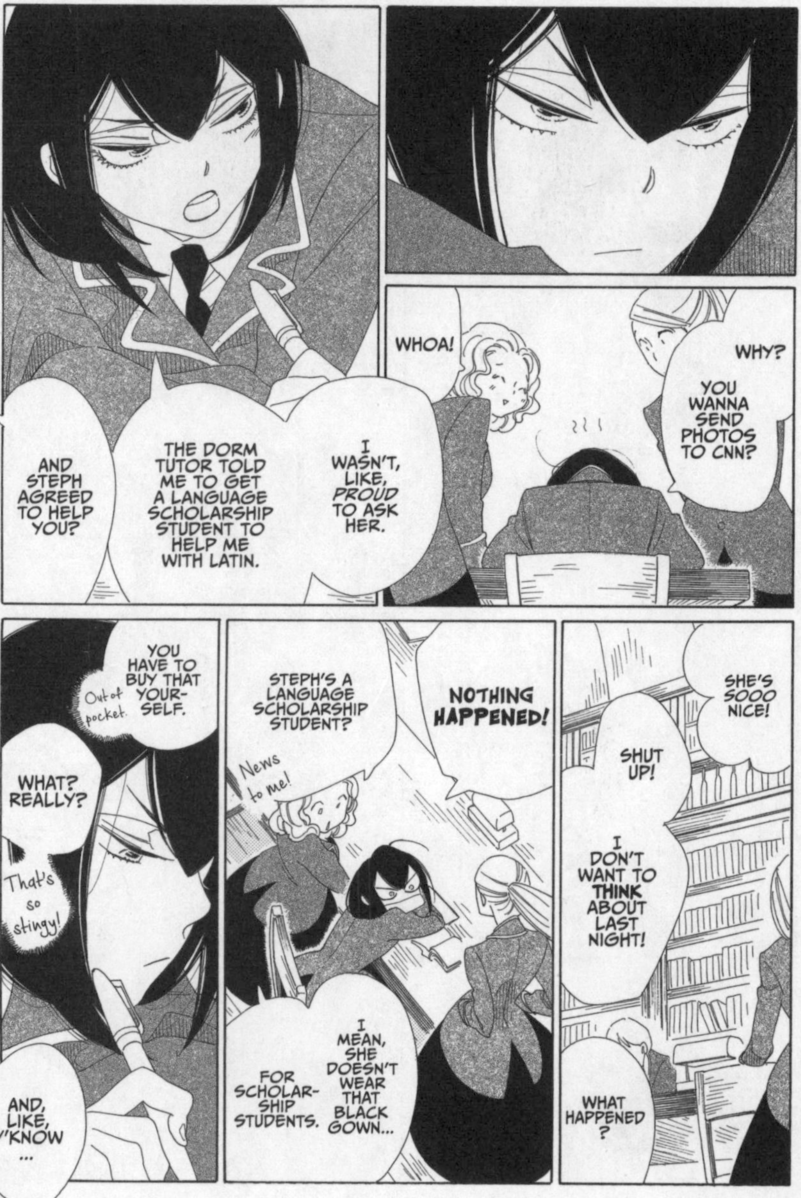
WHY?
YOU WANNA SEND PHOTOS TO CNN?
WHOA!
I WASN'T, LIKE, *PROUD* TO ASK HER.
THE DORM TUTOR TOLD ME TO GET A LANGUAGE SCHOLARSHIP STUDENT TO HELP ME WITH LATIN.
AND STEPH AGREED TO HELP YOU?
SHE'S SOOO NICE!
SHUT UP!
I DON'T WANT TO **THINK** ABOUT LAST NIGHT!
WHAT HAPPENED?
**NOTHING HAPPENED!**
STEPH'S A LANGUAGE SCHOLARSHIP STUDENT?
News to me!
I MEAN, SHE DOESN'T WEAR THAT BLACK GOWN...
FOR SCHOLARSHIP STUDENTS.
YOU HAVE TO BUY THAT YOURSELF.
Out of pocket.
WHAT? REALLY?
That's so stingy!
AND, LIKE, Y'KNOW ...

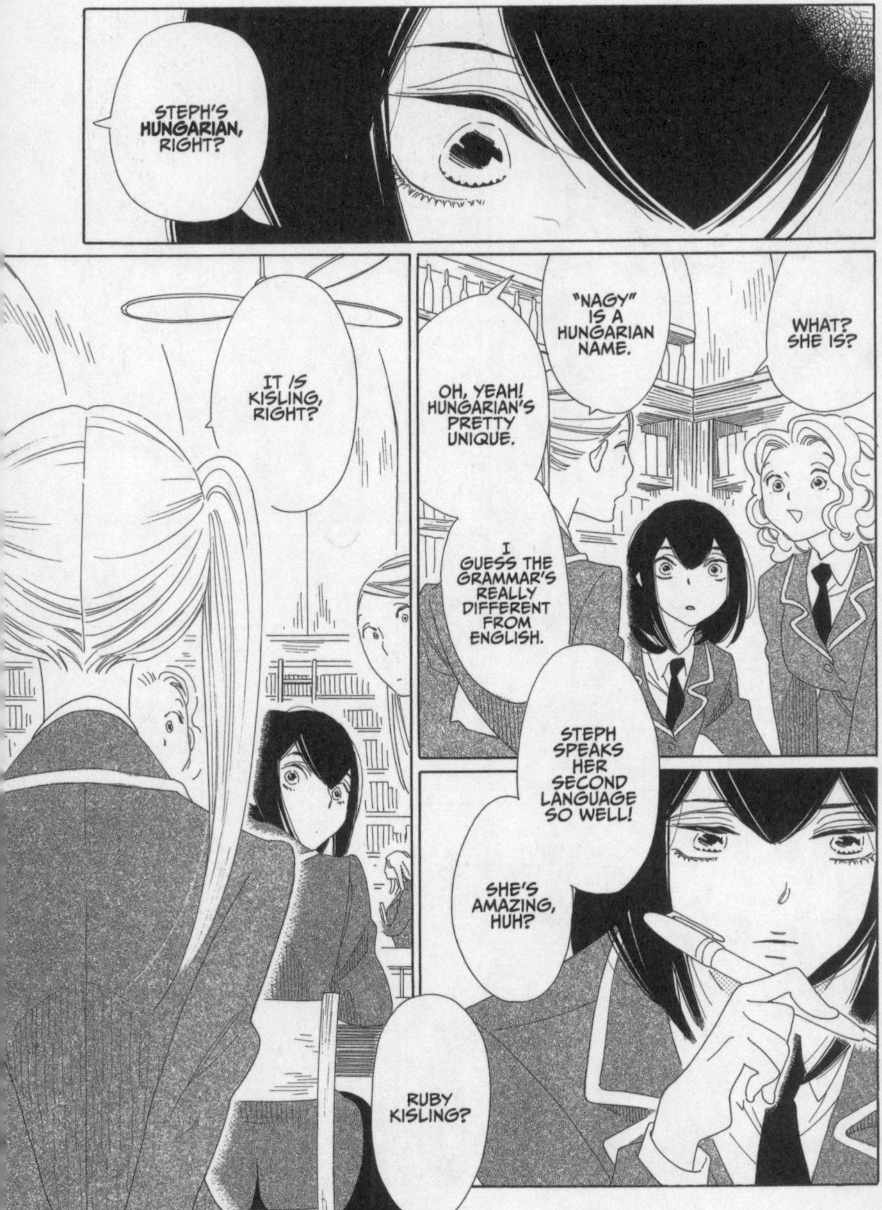
STEPH'S HUNGARIAN, RIGHT?
WHAT? SHE IS?
"NAGY" IS A HUNGARIAN NAME.
OH, YEAH! HUNGARIAN'S PRETTY UNIQUE.
I GUESS THE GRAMMAR'S REALLY DIFFERENT FROM ENGLISH.
STEPH SPEAKS HER SECOND LANGUAGE SO WELL!
SHE'S AMAZING, HUH?
IT IS KISLING, RIGHT?
RUBY KISLING?

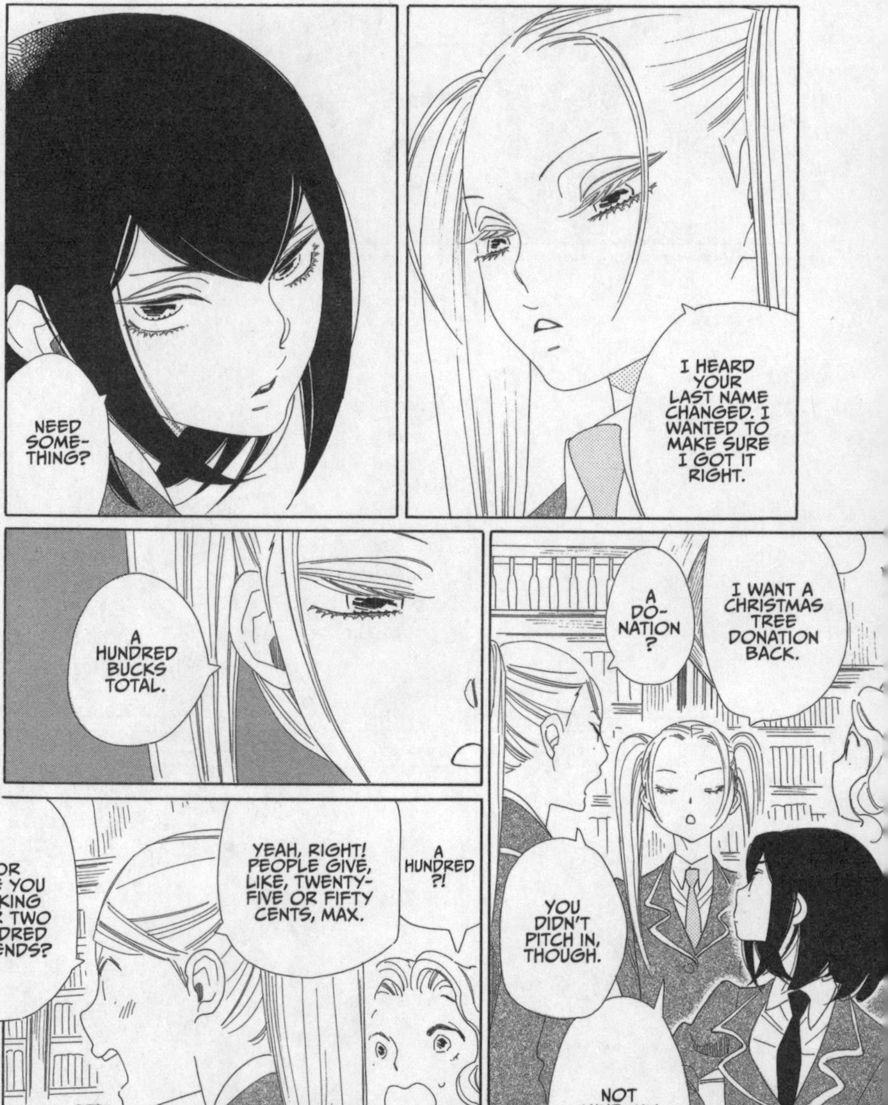
I HEARD YOUR LAST NAME CHANGED. I WANTED TO MAKE SURE I GOT IT RIGHT.
NEED SOME-THING?
I WANT A CHRISTMAS TREE DONATION BACK.
A DO-NATION?
YOU DIDN'T PITCH IN, THOUGH.
NOT MINE. MY FRIENDS'.
A HUNDRED BUCKS TOTAL.
A HUNDRED?!
YEAH, RIGHT! PEOPLE GIVE, LIKE, TWENTY-FIVE OR FIFTY CENTS, MAX.
OR ARE YOU ASKING FOR TWO HUNDRED FRIENDS?

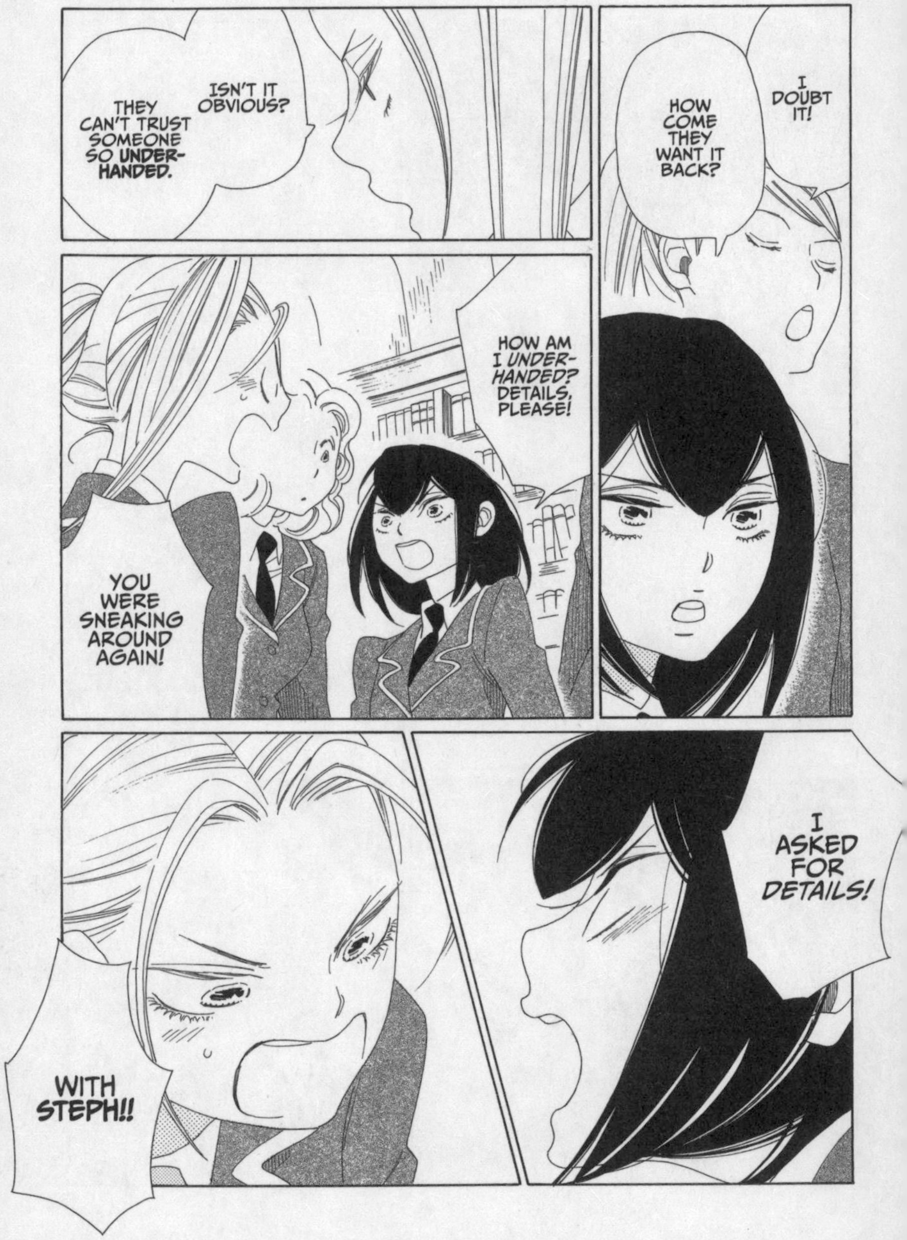
I DOUBT IT!
HOW COME THEY WANT IT BACK?
ISN'T IT OBVIOUS?
THEY CAN'T TRUST SOMEONE SO UNDERHANDED.
HOW AM I *UNDERHANDED*? DETAILS, PLEASE!
YOU WERE SNEAKING AROUND AGAIN!
I ASKED FOR *DETAILS!*
WITH STEPH!!

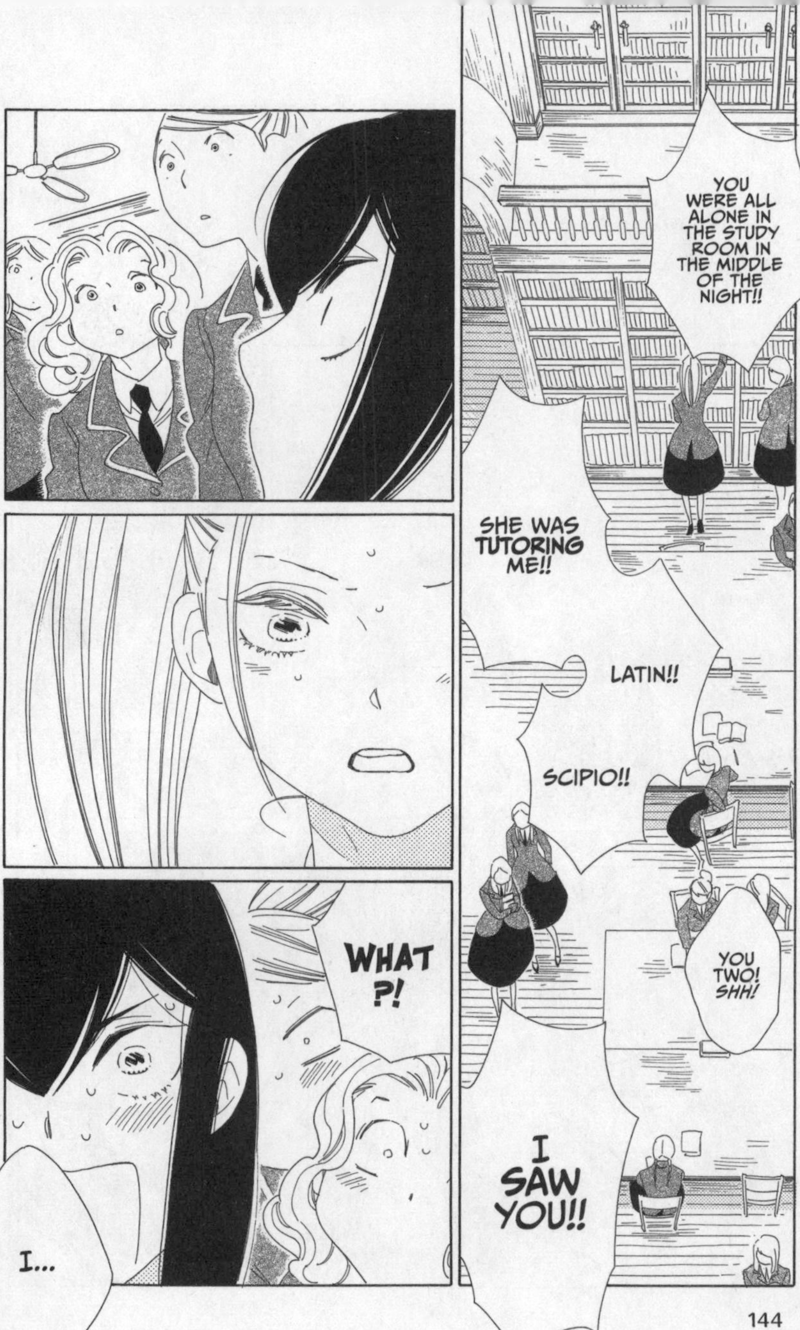
YOU WERE ALL ALONE IN THE STUDY ROOM IN THE MIDDLE OF THE NIGHT!!
SHE WAS TUTORING ME!!
LATIN!!
SCIPIO!!
YOU TWO! SHH!
I SAW YOU!!
WHAT?!
I...

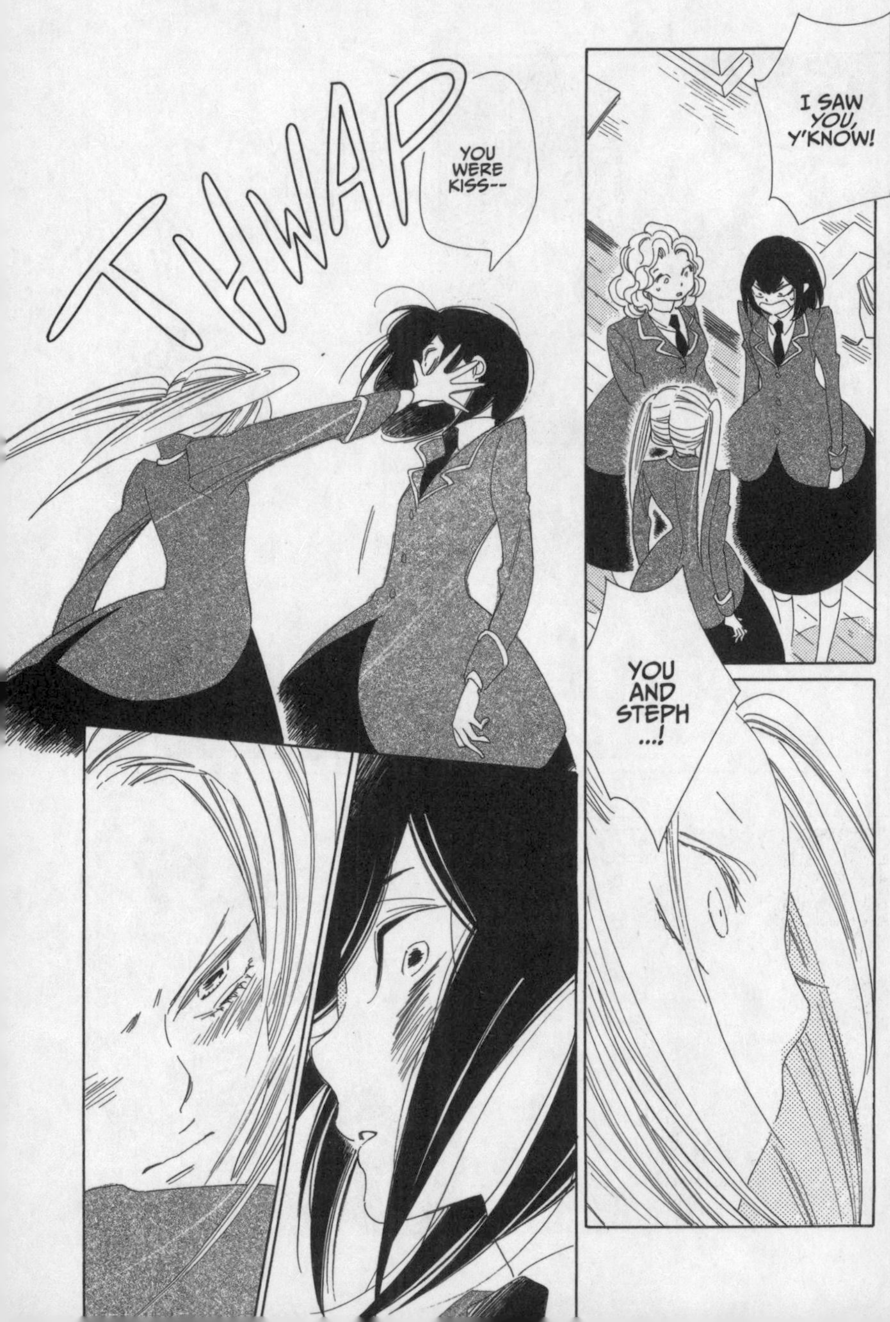

I SAW YOU, Y'KNOW!
YOU AND STEPH ...!
YOU WERE KISS--
THWAP

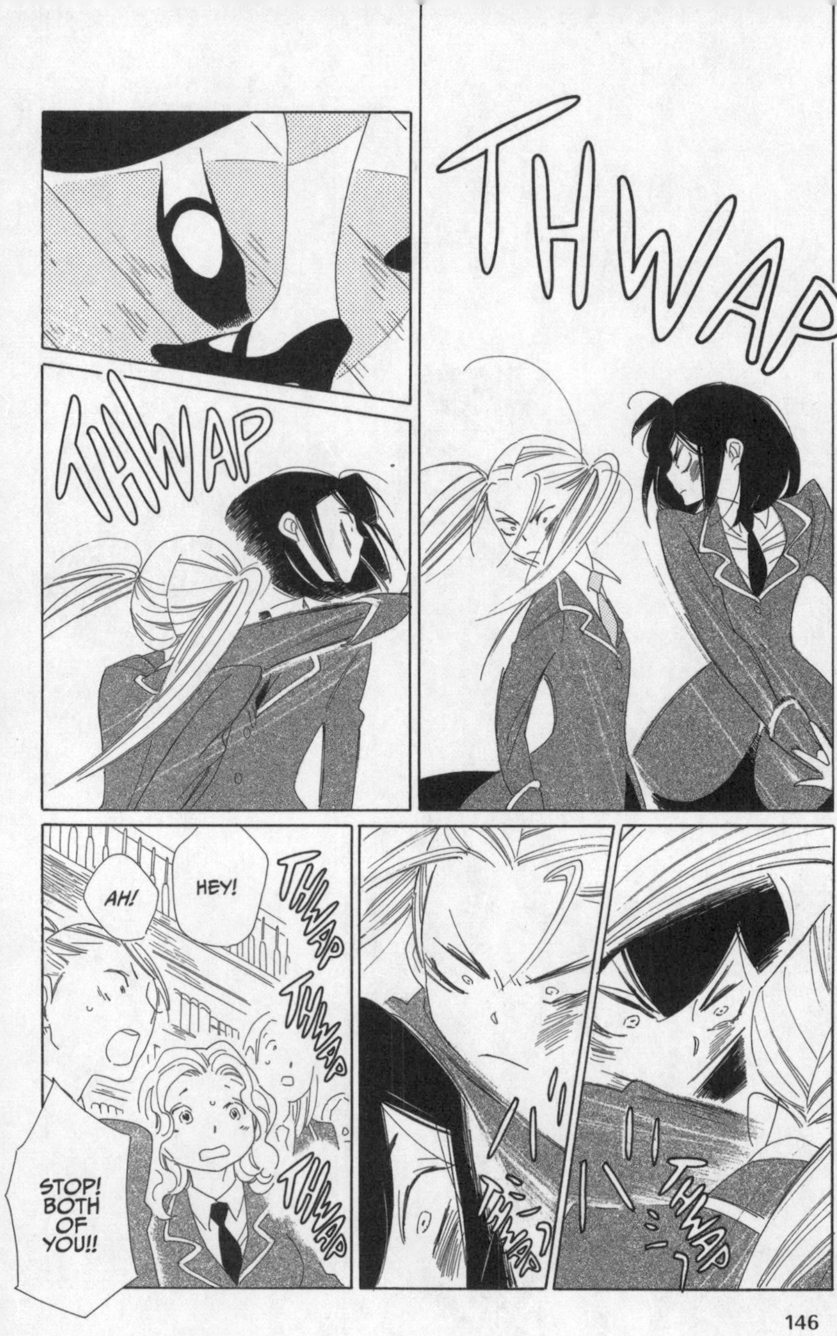
THWAP
THWAP
THWAP
THWAP
HEY!
AH!
THWAP
THWAP
THWAP
STOP! BOTH OF YOU!!

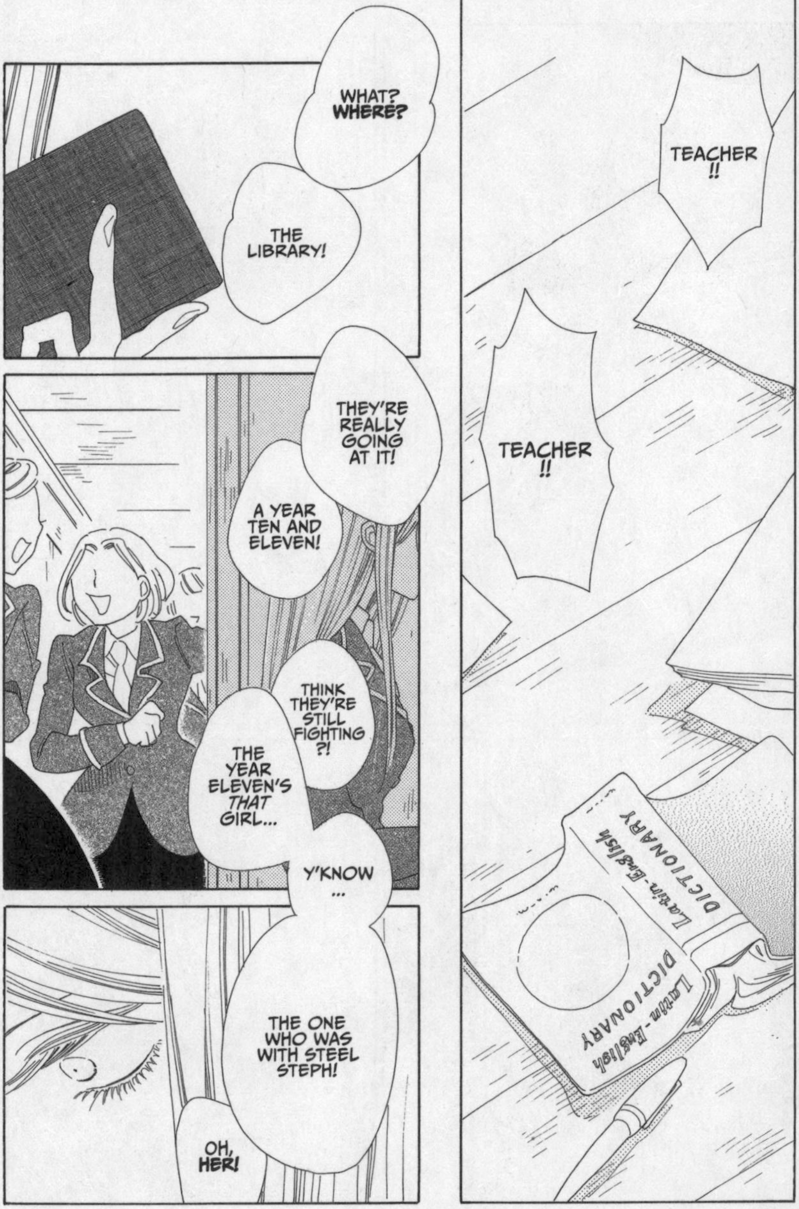
TEACHER!!
TEACHER!!
Latin-English DICTIONARY
Latin-English DICTIONARY
WHAT? **WHERE?**
THE LIBRARY!
THEY'RE REALLY GOING AT IT!
A YEAR TEN AND ELEVEN!
THINK THEY'RE STILL FIGHTING?!
THE YEAR ELEVEN'S *THAT* GIRL...
Y'KNOW...
THE ONE WHO WAS WITH STEEL STEPH!
OH, **HER!**

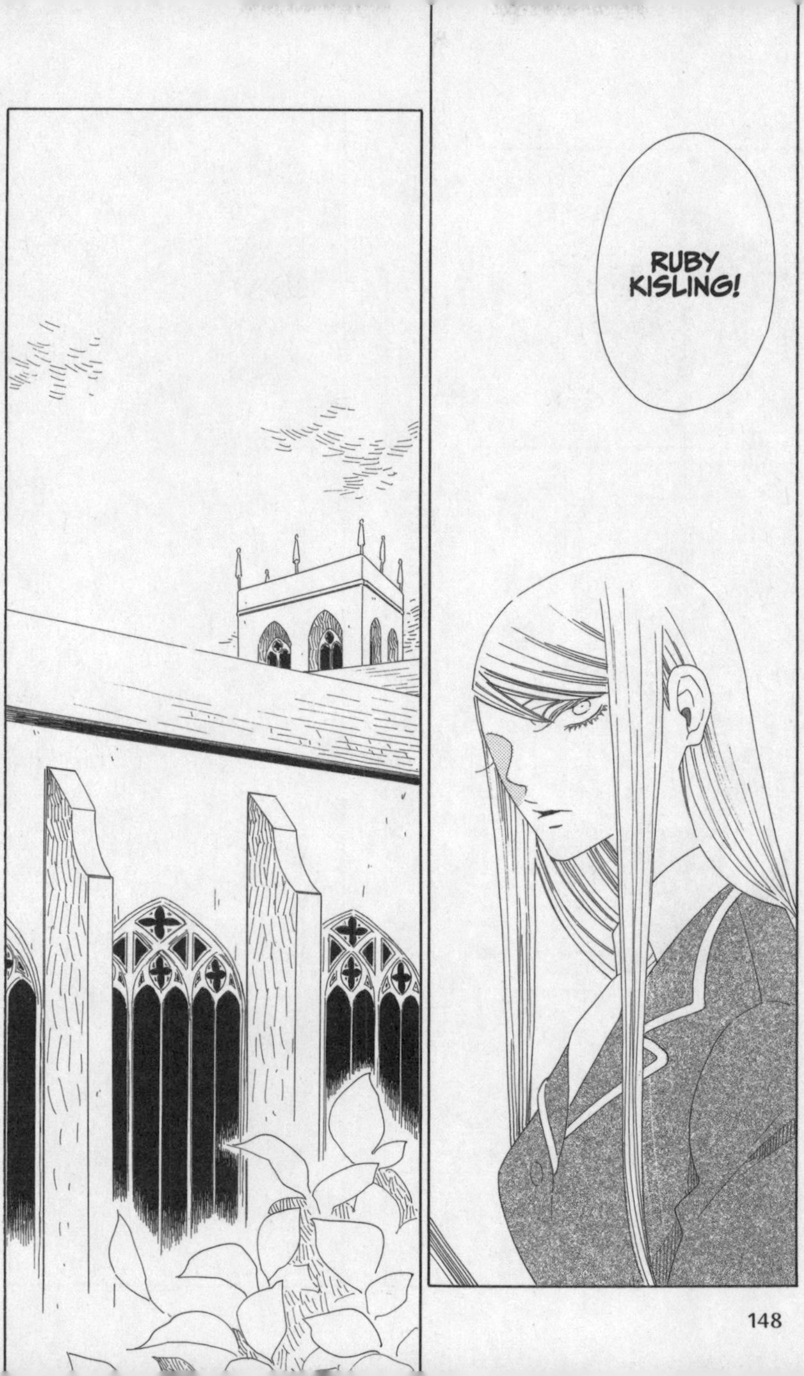
RUBY
KISLING!

メジロバナの咲く

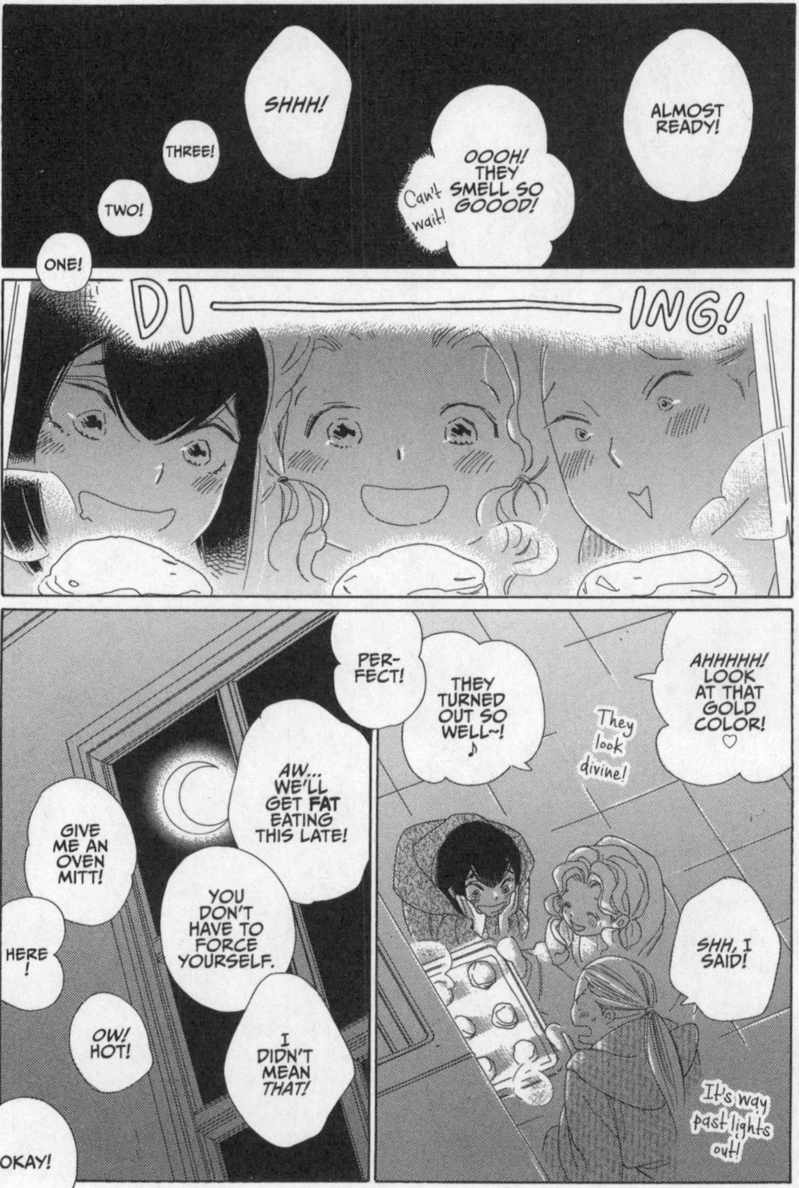
ALMOST READY!
OOOH! THEY SMELL SO GOOOD!
Can't wait!
SHHH!
THREE!
TWO!
ONE!
DI——ING!
AHHHHH! LOOK AT THAT GOLD COLOR! ♡
They look divine!
THEY TURNED OUT SO WELL~! ♪
PER-FECT!
SHH, I SAID!
It's way past lights out!
AW... WE'LL GET FAT EATING THIS LATE!
GIVE ME AN OVEN MITT!
YOU DON'T HAVE TO FORCE YOURSELF.
HERE!
I DIDN'T MEAN THAT!
OW! HOT!
OKAY!

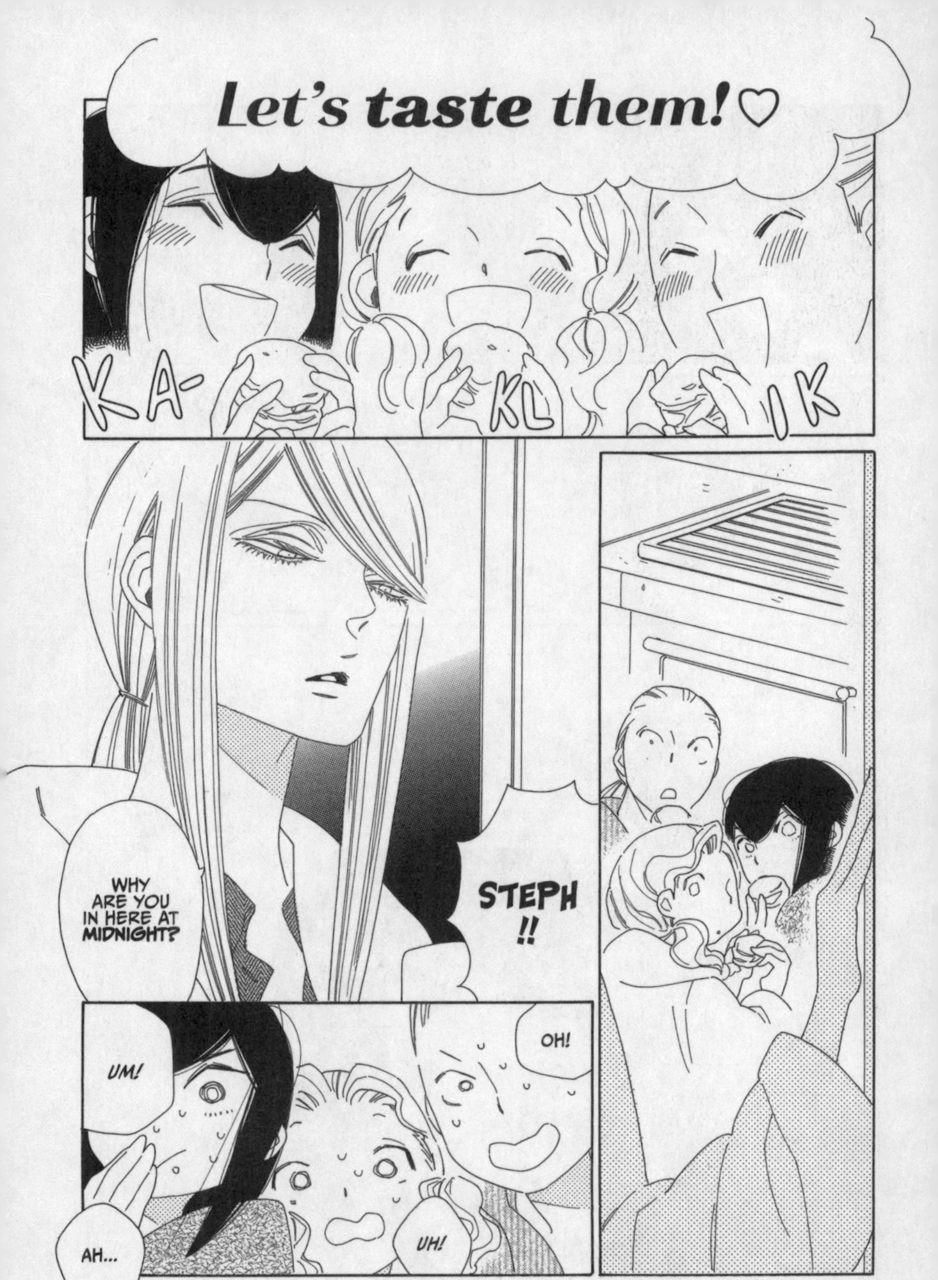
Let's taste them!♡
KA-
KL
IK
STEPH !!
WHY ARE YOU IN HERE AT MIDNIGHT?
OH!
UM!
UH!
AH...

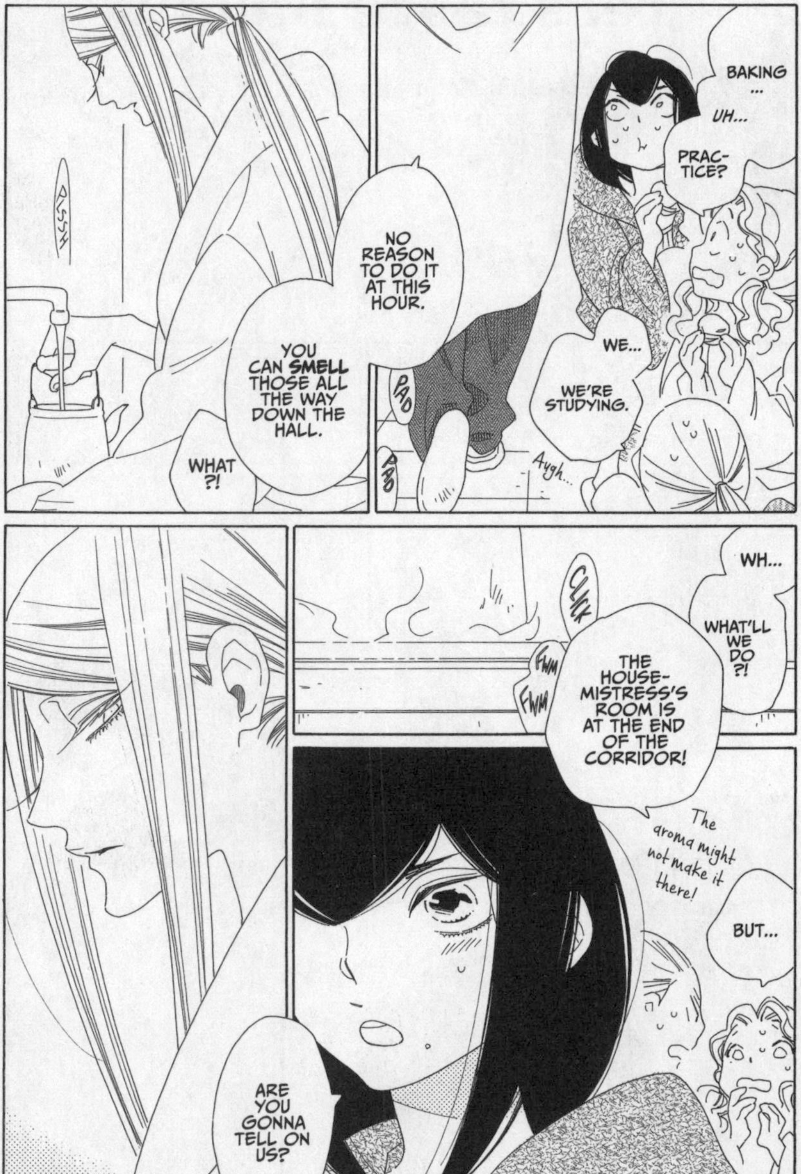
BAKING ...
UH...
PRAC-TICE?
NO REASON TO DO IT AT THIS HOUR.
WE...
WE'RE STUDYING.
PAD
PAD
Aygh...
RUSSH
YOU CAN SMELL THOSE ALL THE WAY DOWN THE HALL.
WHAT ?!
CLICK
WH...
WHAT'LL WE DO ?!
FWM
FWM
THE HOUSE-MISTRESS'S ROOM IS AT THE END OF THE CORRIDOR!
The aroma might not make it there!
BUT...
ARE YOU GONNA TELL ON US?

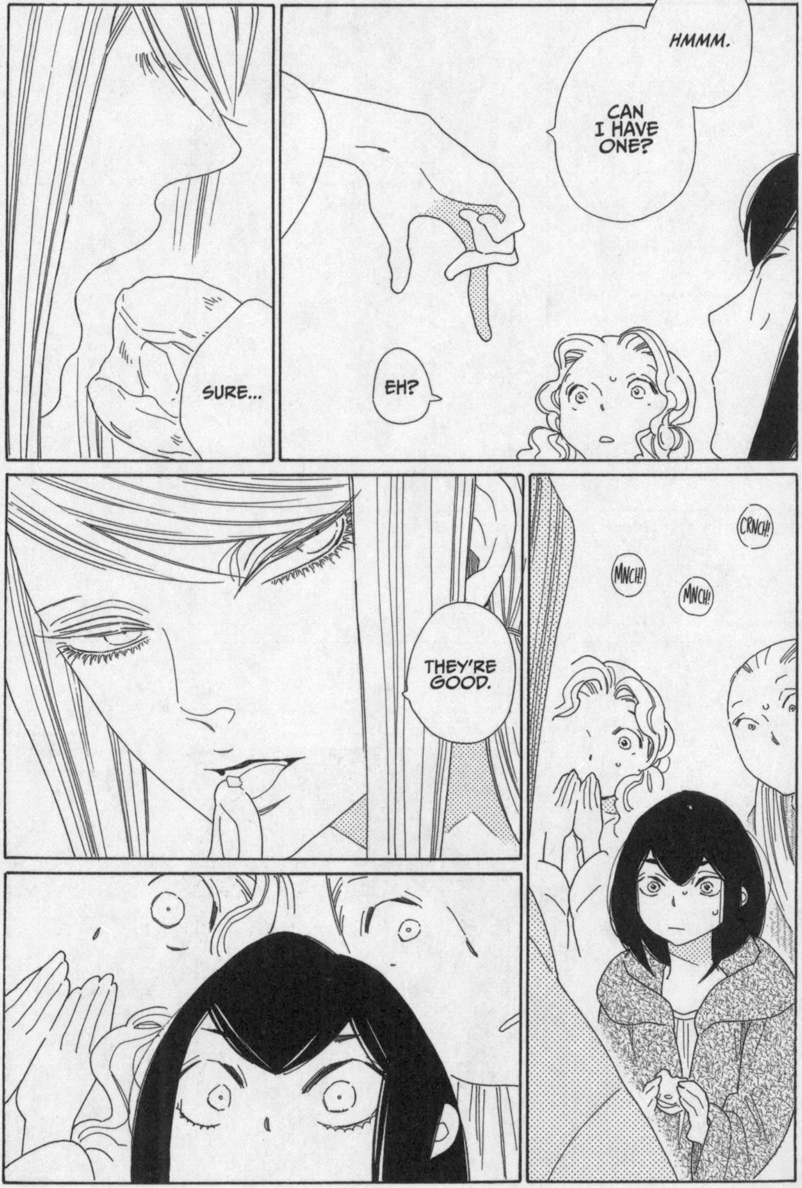
HMMM.
CAN I HAVE ONE?
EH?
SURE...
CRNCH!
MNCH!
MNCH!
THEY'RE GOOD.

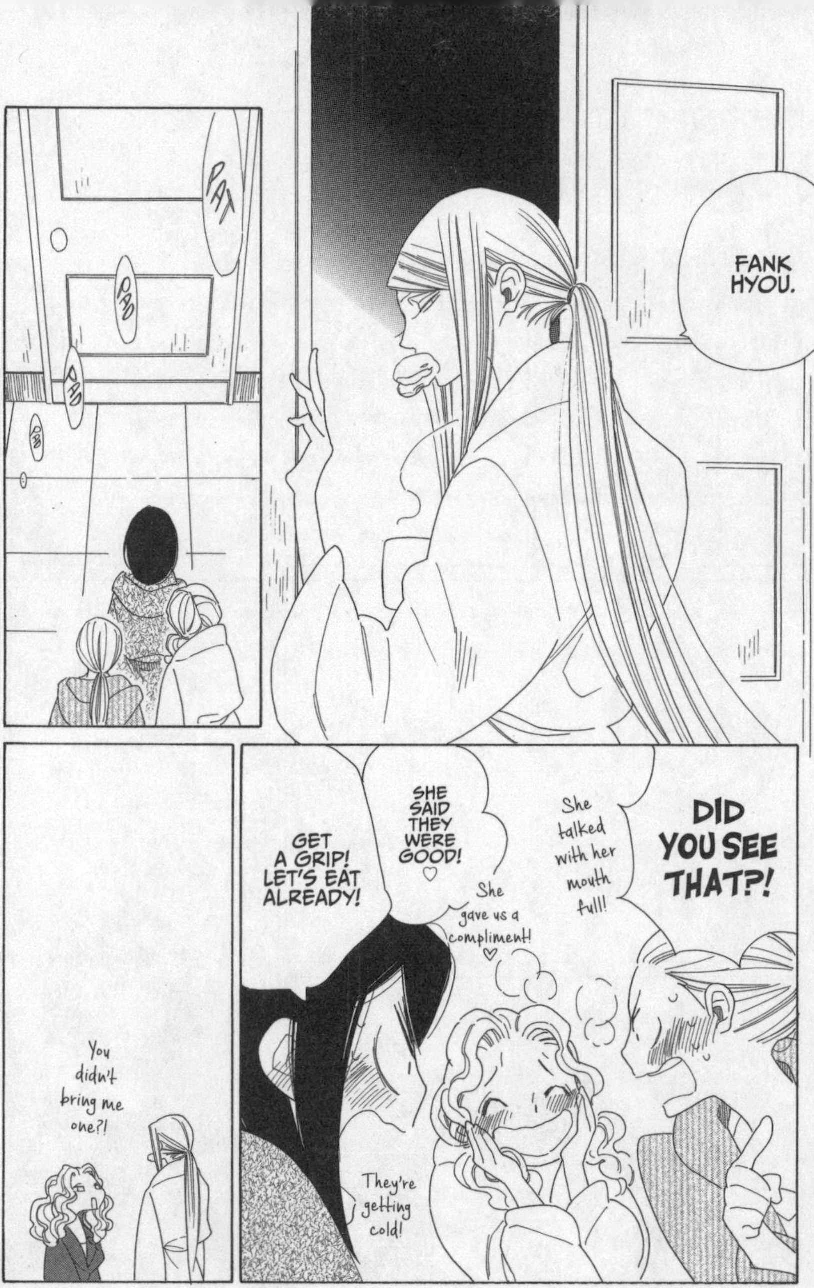
FANK HYOU.
PAT
PAD
PAD
PAD
DID YOU SEE THAT?!
She talked with her mouth full!
SHE SAID THEY WERE GOOD! ♡
She gave us a compliment! ♡
GET A GRIP! LET'S EAT ALREADY!
They're getting cold!
You didn't bring me one?!

The End

# 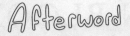Afterword

This is my first long-form girls' love manga! I felt a sense of
déjà vu about this particular world; I had lots of scenes already
in my head. That's thanks to Enid Blyton's *The Twins at St
Clare's*, which I read as a kid. It's not GL, but it's about a girls'
boarding school. The things in that book--the unfamiliar lifestyle,
new desserts and beverages, the secret birthday party, the nice
teacher's nickname, the Christmas card exchanges, the cream
rolls, chocolate bars, sardine sandwiches, peppermint cream, the
canned peach juice with ginger ale--all sparked my imagination.
As we progress bit-by-bit through life at the school and the girls'
crushes, I'd love for you to watch over them.


Once again, so many people helped me with this title. Best wishes
to my editor, I-ta-san. M-guchi-san, who corrected my English.
H-tani-san, the designer. My family and friends. And everyone
kind enough to pick this book up.

Asumiko Nakamura
やすみ 中村 えりこ

### References

- Ishii Rieko, *Utsukushiki Eikoku Paburikku Sukuuru (Beautiful English Public Schools)*,
Ohta Books, 2016.

- Ishii Rieko, *Eikoku Paburikku Sukuuru he Yokoso! (Welcome to English Public School!)*,
Shinkigensha, 2018.

- Arai Megumi, *Paburikku Sukuuru Igirisu-teki Shinshi/Shukujo no Tsurarekata
(How to Make a Gentleman/Lady the English Public School Way)*,
Iwanami Shoten, 2016.

- Kawashima Shiro, *Kihon Kara Manabu Ratengo (Latin from the Basics)*,
Natsumesha, 2016.

- Yamamoto Tarō, *Ratengo wo Yomu Kikero "Sukipio no Yume"
(Read Latin; Cicero's "The Dream of Scipio")*, Beret Publishing, 2017.

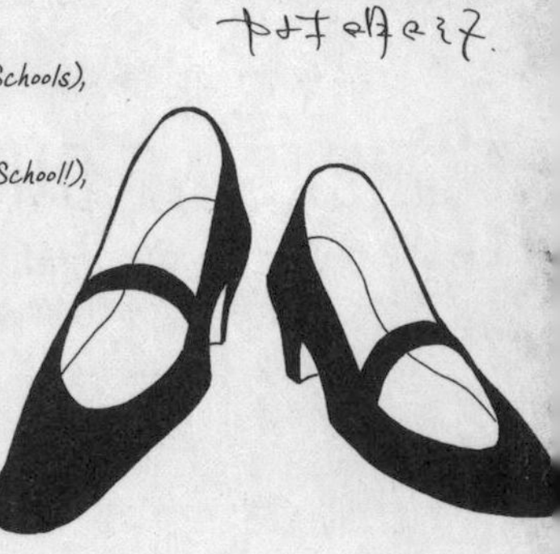

# SEVEN SEAS ENTERTAINM

# A White Rose I

## story and art by ASUMIKO NAKAMURA

VOLUME 1

TRANSLATION
**Jocelyne Allen**

ADAPTATION
**Kat Adler**

LETTERING AND RETOUCH
**Aila Nagamine**

COVER DESIGN
**KC Fabellon**

PROOFREADER
**Dawn Davis**

EDITOR
**Shannon Fay**

PREPRESS TECHNICIAN
**Rhiannon Rasmussen-Silverstein**

PRODUCTION MANAGER
**Lissa Pattillo**

MANAGING EDITOR
**Julie Davis**

ASSOCIATE PUBLISHER
**Adam Arnold**

PUBLISHER
**Jason DeAngelis**

MEJIROBANA NO SAKU by Asumiko Nakamura
© Asumiko Nakamura 2019
First published in Japan in 2019 by HAKUSENSHA, INC., Tokyo.
English language translation rights in U.S.A. arranged with HAKUSENSHA,
INC., Tokyo through TOHAN CORPORATION, Tokyo.

Seven Seas press and purchase enquiries can be sent to Marketing Manager
Lianne Sentar at press@gomanga.com. Information regarding the distribution
and purchase of digital editions is available from Digital Manager CK Russell
at digital@gomanga.com.

Seven Seas and the Seven Seas logo are trademarks of
Seven Seas Entertainment. All rights reserved.

ISBN: 978-1-64505-959-2

Printed in Canada

First Printing: January 2021

10 9 8 7 6 5 4 3 2 1

FOLLOW US ONLINE: *www.sevenseasentertainment.com*

# READING

This book reads from
If this is your first time reading manga, you start
reading from the top right panel on each page and
take it from there. If you get lost, just follow the
numbered diagram here. It may seem backwards at
first, but you'll get the hang of it! Have fun!!

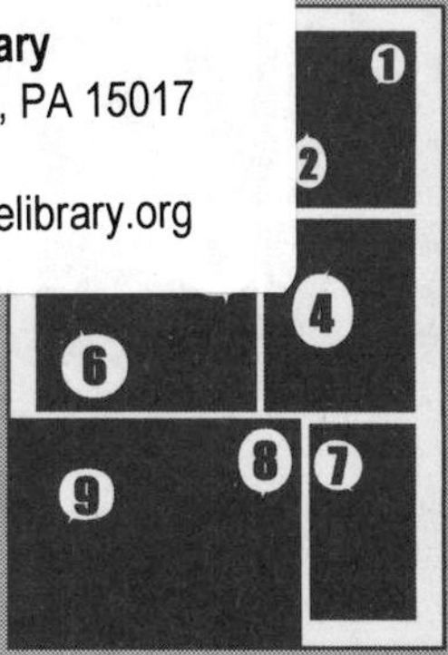